Open for Business

Closed to People

Open for Business

Closed to People

Mike Harris's Ontario

**edited by
Diana S. Ralph,
André Régimbald
and Nérée St-Amand**

Fernwood Publishing • Halifax

Editing: Janet Creery, Mabel Hanson and Donna Davis
Cover photos: Alecia Bock and David Hein
Cover computer imaging: Wendy Snooks
Design and production: Beverley Rach
Printed and bound in Canada by: Hignell Printing Limited

A publication of:
Fernwood Publishing
Box 9409, Station A
Halifax, Nova Scotia
B3K 5S3

Fernwood Publishing Company Limited gratefully acknowledges the financial support of the Ministry of Canadian Heritage and the Nova Scotia Department of Education and Culture.

Canadian Cataloguing in Publication Data

Main entry under title:

Open for Business / Closed to People

    Includes bibliographical references and index.
    ISBN 1-895686-73-3

1. Ontario -- Politics and government -- 1995– * 2. Ontario -- Social policy. 3. Government spending policy -- Ontario. 4. Public welfare -- Ontario. I. Ralph, Diana S. II. Régimbald, André, III. St-Amand, Nérée.

FC3077.2063 1996   971.3'04   96-950169-2   F1058.063 1996

Contents

Acknowledgements

The authors of *Open For Business* all worked hard to complete their chapters and get this book out in under one year. Their enthusiasm, knowledge, and brilliance made our editorial task an unexpected delight. Janet Creery contributed both editorial and copyediting expertise, as well as a wonderfully droll sense of humour which kept us going through rough times. Mabel Hanson did a brilliant job of proofreading accurately and in record time. Sue Brady was amazingly cheerful, fast and efficient in entering the endless drafts of the text. We're grateful to Alecia Bock for allowing us to use on our cover her powerful photograph of riot police "protecting" Harris. Thanks as well to David Hein for the photo of the Toronto Stock Exchange.

Errol Sharpe, our publisher, was consistently flexible, wise and helpful. Thank you as well to the folks at Fernwood Publishing: Donna Davis for her sharp attention to detail when proofreading; Chauna James for typing; Beverley Rach for design and production; and Brenda Conroy for promotion.

Our thanks also to Duncan Cameron for reading this book in several drafts and giving us helpful feedback. Thanks especially to Jean Frances for her unflagging support, encouragement and keen ear for good English.

We also wish to thank Matthew Devine and Allan Moscovitch for transcribing and editing the original tape recorded interview on which chapter seven is based.

The Dean of Social Sciences at the University of Ottawa and the Office of Graduate Studies and Research at Carleton University both provided crucial financial support for this book.

Above all, we want to thank the dedicated union and community activists and socially aware reporters and researchers in Ontario who do the work and take the risks to create a more humane and just society.

Editors
Diana Ralph
André Régimbald
Nérée St-Amand

Preface
Duncan Cameron

With the election of the Conservatives, Ontario is undergoing a social experiment with far-reaching ramifications. The government of Mike Harris is both changing the rules established by successive legislatures and remaking the province over in the image of neo-conservatism. Through its cutbacks in spending on services, it is affecting the daily life of everybody, especially those who rely on wages—including a social wage—for their livelihood.

The Ontario Conservatives have a plan, an ideology, and substantial support for what they are doing. But they also face determined opposition from those most affected by the changes and who see the damage being done. This book is about that opposition. It presents analysis of what is going on in Ontario and how it relates to right-wing politics elsewhere. Authors chronicle the impact so far on citizens, and show how the relationship between governed and government is changing for the worse. They assess opposition politics. What is at stake in the fight for Ontario? How can resistance be best organized? Where does the fight for the future lead?

The electoral success of the Conservatives caught many by surprise. It is important at this stage to undertake a serious examination of what the Conservative social experiment means for people in Ontario, and this book does just that. The authors assess health care, Francophone rights, the climate for workers, social welfare, and conditions for equality-seeking groups. In the practice of social movement politics, independent research and information are key to mobilizing people for change. This book provides activists and all interested citizens with a concrete picture of what awaits us in Ontario. The book deserves the widest possible attention.

Armed by American political consultants with a plan to take power in Ontario, the Harris Conservatives won the battle with the Liberals to replace the NDP government. Tory issues were welfare and taxes: "common sense" decreed that both should be cut. To the surprise of seasoned observers, in the election campaign of 1995 the Conservatives overcame an overwhelming Liberal lead that had stood up for many months.

After 40 years of Conservative governments, in 1985 the Ontario electorate voted in the Liberals under David Peterson. First forming a minority government with support from the NDP, the Liberals won a majority in 1987 but lost to the NDP in 1990. In succession, voters had moved from Conservative, to Liberal, to NDP and then, in 1995, back to Conservative. What political scientists call electoral volatility was clearly at work. It could be explained by factors common to other jurisdictions, particularly the way politicians wear out their welcome quickly in an era where television brings them frequently into our homes. But as well, there were deep-seated changes occurring in Canada that affected Ontario. By the

1990s, economic disappointment was widespread, and growing. And, as political parties jockeyed for advantage under changed economic circumstances, electoral standings changed just as rapidly.

The NDP had the misfortune of being elected in 1990 just after the second recession in a decade had begun. Initiated by tight money policies in Ottawa, and following the introduction of the free trade agreement, the recession caused job losses to mount steadily throughout the first years of the NDP government. Meanwhile, incomes continued to stagnate for all but a privileged few. At first, the government tried to tread water, refusing to cut back on spending in its first budget; indeed it even added a very modest spending package of about $1 billion to slow the downswing.

But the *Toronto Sun*, the *Financial Post*, the Canadian Federation of Independent Business and corporate interests in insurance, banking, mining and manufacturing all lined up to discredit the NDP. Faced with attacks that began on the day it took office, the NDP quickly lost the public relations battle over the recession and gave ground on the economy.

High interest rates meant that the deficit the NDP had inherited from the Liberals grew rapidly. The government went to the market to fund its debt and every bond ratings service and securities dealer had the same message: slash spending. Meanwhile, Ottawa was cutting back on transfers to the provinces, and Ontario was singled out for the biggest cuts. Along with the other "have" provinces, it saw its social assistance transfers capped. But Ontario was hit hard by the recession, and its social spending was not going up any slower because it was wealthy to begin with.

Reluctantly at first, then with the premier taking a spirited lead, the NDP embraced restraint. Rae argued that lower spending would reduce interest rates— the traditional business view of the issue. At the end of the day, the province did not have a central bank, and was unwilling to mount a public campaign to get Ottawa to change monetary policy. Rather it decided to fall into line with the federal minister of finance, the Bank of Canada and the Business Council on National Issues. Ignoring the advice of its own supporters, it decided the recession could not be fought and defeated in Ontario.

Historians will debate the record of the NDP in office. Did they, as their supporters claimed, provide social justice in hard times, adjusting to the new realities of international competition and indebtedness in a responsible fashion? When they accepted the ire of their partisans by legislating a social contract with their own employees rather than initiating massive layoffs, were they making the best of a difficult situation? Or did the NDP sell out social democracy when it suspended collective bargaining, and bought into the politics of austerity, giving up the chance to fight for its electoral programme, the Agenda for People?

However its performance is assessed, from the perspective of the 1995 election one thing stands out. In 1990, the NDP was elected in part, perhaps even mainly, on a campaign for fair taxes, singling out corporations for not paying their share. The NDP did, late in its mandate, bring in a corporate minimum tax. Shortly after taking office it created the Fair Tax Commission. It reported in time for the NDP to build a re-election campaign around the tax issue, but the party chose not to do it. Instead, both the NDP and the Liberals got side-swiped by Mike Harris billing himself as the tax fighter.

The Tories ran a populist style campaign with a twist. The peoples' issue was a pledge to cut taxes. Enough middle-class voters figured they were going to get extra money, proportionately more than people below them on the income scale, to make this attractive. Since people could also expect a reduction in government spending, attacking welfare recipients proved an effective tactic. This lulled middle-class voters into believing that it would cut spending on others, not spending for general services. Harris even pledged he would not cut health care.

Though it is doubtful that the NDP could have done anything to be re-elected—they had simply fallen too far—the Conservatives' plan caught the Liberals off guard. For five years, the main message of business organizations and the corporate media had been the deficit. Then all of a sudden, the Tories talk tax cut and nobody listens when the Liberals say it will worsen the deficit!

It seems that both the Liberals and the NDP failed to understand how business groups viewed deficit politics. In effect, what business organizations wanted was less government and more business. If government spending cuts could create room for businesses to move in on health care provision, transport, electrical power generation or even education—activities traditionally reserved for the public sector—then so be it. If tax cuts reduced the capacity of government to fund public programmes, creating potential for profits through privatization, so much the better.

The NDP deficits made a lot of money for financial houses and the dealers who sold the bonds. Ontario government debt was quickly snapped up because it represented good value, in a safe jurisdiction, with a secure economic base. Indeed, the accumulated NDP deficits were not really a financial issue. What was at stake was the social democratic belief that government spending could create jobs and expand incomes versus the business view that only profits created jobs and incomes. When Harris came out squarely in favour of lower taxes for people, business understood he was supporting an open door for business investment in areas formerly reserved for government.

The social democratic view of the economy was based on wage growth, including rising social wages, fuelling consumption, with business investment following increased consumption. For social democrats, business invested because it expected to make a profit, not because it had profits to invest. The logic of government spending was to support consumption and thus induce business to invest. But what if business did not want to play along? What if Ontario spending was insufficient to restart a stalled economy?

The NDP had concluded that international competition meant that Ontario had to be made more attractive for business investment, and that it could not halt the recession or ignite consumption on its own. Thus it made overtures to business, developed skills programmes to improve the workforce and ultimately backed off business tax reform. It no longer believed that at the margin government could invest new money at a better rate of return for its citizens than business could. Whatever conversion the Ontario NDP went through, it no longer supported the basic social democratic belief that governments spend more wisely than business.

In the 1995 election, even some welfare recipients voted for Harris in the mistaken belief that workfare instead of welfare meant they were going to get a job. But the clear winners were those with the most to gain from less government: corporations and those they retain in law, accounting and advertising. The highest-income earners, those who get tax breaks and can afford private health care or education, came out ahead. The clear losers were those with the least to begin with, those for whom the only possible road to equality was through access to government services in education, health and housing, and who depend on government transfers for their daily bread.

For a generation at least, the conventional wisdom in electoral politics has been that getting the support of great numbers of people was more important than courting the wealthy who had money to spend. Rather than pleasing the well-off, good politics decreed that a party design policies to appeal to the great mass of middle-income voters, not the top 20 percent, but the 60 percent in the middle-income brackets. The bottom 20 percent could be safely ignored, as they could be assumed not to vote. However, their basic needs would be covered, not forgotten or left to charity. The favoured electoral strategy was to unite the middle, build support around programmes with wide appeal, and show how each benefits from programmes available to all. It is this conventional approach that Harris has overthrown, first in his election platform and now in government. He has united upper-income voters around a programme that appeals to the interests of the wealthy, and convinced many middle- and low-income people of the advantages of more business and less government. This combination assures that his government will be a potent force for some time to come.

As the authors of this book show, there is much to distrust about the Harris ideology. While his ideas are straightforward and easy to understand, they are also simpleminded. Right-wing programmes of this nature elsewhere have been disastrous for the poor and marginalized. The majority also see no benefits and many costs.

Yet defeating right-wing governments, whether in New Zealand, Britain or the U.S., has never been easy. The support of the wealthy and of corporations has proven to be a potion for political longevity.

Because the success of the Right comes through carefully managing public opinion, the starting point for defeating the Right is through creating a well-informed public. Therein lies the significance of this book. Rather than dismissing the Harris programme out of hand, it makes a serious assessment of what is going on in Ontario and of what to expect in the future. *Open for Business* gives readers an inside look at the various strategies available to those who want to stop Harris in his tracks. Its publication will fuel the informed debate and discussion that is needed to counter the relentless public relations campaign of the Harris government and its supporters.

Introduction
Diana Ralph

The Common Sense Revolution

On June 8, 1995, Michael Harris led the Tories to a landslide victory in Ontario, taking 82 of 130 seats (but only 44.8 percent of the popular vote). The Conservatives won in part because neither the Liberals nor the NDP offered a real alternative. Both opposition parties campaigned on a watered-down version of the same neo-conservative bandwagon; deficit cutting, getting tough on "welfare fraud," downsizing the public service, and kowtowing to corporate bond raters. Give people a choice between a conservative and a conservative, and they'll pick a conservative every time.

Many also voted for Harris more to oppose the NDP than to support the Tories. Many unions and other social justice groups felt deeply betrayed by the first NDP government in Ontario's history (1990–1995). They felt it had perverted the NDP's social democratic mandate in many ways and especially by imposing on workers a "Social Contract" of wage cuts which overrode collective agreements. As a result, many traditional labour strongholds voted against the NDP, and erstwhile NDP supporters did not put much effort into getting out the vote. Some NDP members may also have voted Liberal to support their female candidate, Lynn McLeod.

But more fundamental than either of these factors was the pervasive sense that something was seriously wrong in Ontario. That something was globalization. Between 1988, when the North American Free Trade Agreement (NAFTA) passed, and 1993, over 20 percent of Ontario's manufacturing jobs—many of them in Ontario—evaporated (Merrett 1996: 91). Maude Barlow and Bruce Campbell estimate that by 1994, over 660,000 fewer jobs existed in Canada than would have been there if pre-1988 trends had persisted (1995: 67). This left industrial cities like Windsor, Oshawa, Hamilton and Cornwall destitute, and many people across Ontario jobless. The resulting unemployment simultaneously reduced the province's tax base and dramatically increased costs for social assistance and other social programs, causing the provincial deficit to balloon. At the federal level, first the Mulroney Conservative and then the Chrétien Liberal governments also had pursued structural adjustment policies—including high interest rates and reduced federal transfer payments. These also contributed to the leap in the Ontario provincial deficit. Bond raters, wary of a "socialist" government, used the deficit as an excuse to downgrade Ontario's credit rating. The corporate media inflamed the resulting insecurity by claiming the NDP government was driving away job-creating investment and leading Ontario into financial ruin.

Capitalizing on popular fear and confusion, Harris's Tories were able to promise a return to the "good old days" of the 45 year reign of Conservatives in

Ontario. Harris's handlers succeeded in marketing him as an ordinary guy with simple, common sense solutions; the candidate who "gathers wisdom at the backyard fence" ("Mike Harris" 1995: A6). Clearly, many Ontario voters bought it.

But Harris's platform was not aimed at returning to a cosy past, but rather at opening Ontario to global business interests. The Tories promised to create a "favourable climate" for investment by wiping out democratic rights, protective regulations, advocacy funding, and social supports. Harris has openly declared himself "as champion of the business community" (Campbell, Mittelstaedt and Rusk 1995: A3).

> "We believe we are the only party that is aggressive in saying, 'Yes, we want the private sector to succeed. Yes, our agenda is for business.'" (Mike Harris quote in Campbell, Mittelstaedt and Rusk 1995: A3)

As a result, the corporate sector rallied to assure Harris his victory. The list of corporations which made the maximum allowable donation to the Ontario Progressive Conservative party reads like the roll call of the Toronto Stock Exchange (Ontario Progressive Conservative Party 1995).

Around the world, these same transnational corporations are promoting similar policies: slashing corporate taxes, environmental standards, labour rights, and social programs (Collier 1995; Marsdon and Warnock 1995; Pollack 1996: D4; Teeple 1995; Tester 1992). Their goal is to create a low-waged, compliant, "flexible" labour force, and an unregulated environment for capitalist accumulation.

Since the Second World War, Canadian people had won protection from extreme exploitation through a complex network of welfare state provisions. Now international capital is revoking Canada's privileged status. It no longer needs to shelter secondary powers like Canada from the gross exploitation that so-called "under-developed" countries have endured for decades (Teeple 1995). The rapacious demands of global capital accumulation require corporations and the federal and provincial governments they control to put profit ahead of any human or environmental considerations. They aim to strip Canadians of the rights and social programs which have protected us from Third World working and living conditions.

Right-wing parties now govern in Alberta, Manitoba, and Ontario. Others are likely to follow. In 1996, British Columbia narrowly avoided electing a Reform-in-Liberal-clothing party. Federally, Liberal Prime Minister Jean Chrétien is outstripping Conservative Mulroney's assaults on Canadian people's rights, and the Reform Party is poised to take over as the official opposition.

In this context, the Tory victory in Ontario, the industrial heartland of Canada, represented a large coup for big business. International bond raters and transnational corporations put heavy pressure on Harris to quickly implement his re-organization of Ontario's government, on pain of losing their support and credit ratings. Immediately after Harris's election, Ian Cunningham, director of policy for the Ontario Chamber of Commerce, publicly threatened reprisals if Harris didn't toe the line:

> [Harris has] made a lot of promises and if he doesn't immediately demonstrate that he's committed to what he's promised, there's going to be a lot of negative reaction. (Narrulla and Bournette 1995: B5)

Frank Mechura, president of Crown Cork and Seal Canada (one of the largest Canadian can makers), also made it clear that his support for Harris was contingent on "whether he walks the talk" (Narulla and Bournette 1995: B5). Both Dominion and Moody's bond rating services welcomed Harris's election but pointedly refused to "review its current ratings on [the Ontario] government debt until after a full budget" (Haliechuk 1995: E1). Walter Schroeder, president of Dominion Bond Rating Service, threatened to slash Ontario's credit rating if Harris fulfilled his campaign promise to cut taxes by 30 percent (Chamberlain 1995: A1).

Although many Canadians don't yet realize it, we are at war; a worldwide class war of capital versus everyone else, a war which the bubble of the Keynesian welfare state temporarily obscured. In this war, the Right has daunting weapons. Over the past 20 years, capital has forged a unified coalition of business, politics, and fundamentalist religion (Barlow and Robertson 1994). It owns most of the national and local media. Through massive campaign donations, it has bought the loyalty of the Liberal, Reform and Tory parties (Campbell 1996), and through threats to withhold credit, it has coerced the reluctant support of the NDP. By its control of over $1.2 trillion in assets (Business Council 1995), members of the Business Council on National Issues can grant or withhold credit and job-creating investment. And through speculative manipulations, they have the power to disrupt the entire Canadian economy (Clarke 1995: 12). As a result, they wield enormous influence over all levels of government and public opinion. The Right speaks with almost one voice (Dobbin 1995a: 1; Neu 1996), and its vision is insinuating itself into the popular consensus:

> The vast propaganda apparatus controlled by the right has convinced most Canadians that reducing the public debt is imperative and unavoidable. To do that, they've been led to believe, our "too generous and unaffordable" social programs must be cut or eliminated, wages must be held down, and interest rates must be kept high. (Finn 1995: 7)

By contrast, the popular sector in Canada is relatively disorganized, reactive, and broke both financially and, in some cases, morally. With the collapse or cooptation of socialist parties and governments worldwide, including the NDP in

Canada, many have lost a clear political direction. The Canadian Left is small, marginalized, and middle-class, disconnected from the masses it claims to represent. Most national labour and advocacy groups are still focused on defending social democratic rights and services. But as Gary Teeple points out, these are no longer realistic options in the world of global corporate rule:

> Social democracy as we have known it has no future, because the conditions that gave rise to it are being transformed and because its policies and programs—the reforms of the nation-state era—were nothing more than what these conditions allowed or even demanded. (Teeple 1995: 146)

Under the onslaught of cuts, local groups find themselves competing for ever-shrinking funds, rather than working for a unified, socialist vision for us all. Unless we can manage to shift this accommodative stance to militant, strategic resistance, the Right will succeed in crushing all Canadians into Third World living standards and authoritarian rule.

Why This Book?

The Harris *blitzkrieg* hit Ontario like a tornado. Every government service, every right, every public sector job, every protection which people had taken for granted is either gone or in jeopardy. Many people in Ontario and elsewhere are unaware of the scope of the attack and confused about its nature. For example, many people on social assistance voted for Harris because they believed his workfare program would give them a real job. (Instead, it will force them to find non-existent jobs. Those who can't find 17 hours a week of unpaid work face losing all their benefits.) In spite of the cascade of cuts, by the end of his first year in office, Harris's popularity rating was still high especially among non-poor Ontarians (Crone 1996: A3).

Two major purposes of this book, therefore, are to unmask the corporate ideological assault underlying the Common Sense Revolution (Part 1) and to spell out the disastrous impacts Harris policies will have on all Ontarians, especially on the most vulnerable (Part 2). Our final purpose (Part 3) is to critically analyze major sites of resistance to the Tories and to propose strategic directions, not only for regaining the rights, jobs, and programs we had in the past, but for a fundamental victory over corporate power.

This book brings together Ontario activists and scholars who are on the cutting edge of analysis and resistance to the Harris agenda. The authors have not attempted to be "objective." Although we have varying analyses, we all agree that the Common Sense Revolution is a bad thing for everyone except the major corporations and the well-to-do.

This book analyzes the first year of the Common Sense Revolution in Ontario (from June 1995 to June 1996). It is too early, of course, to assess the Harris regime from an historian's perspective. But this is not a disinterested history. Harris campaigned on a promise to "re-invent the way [the Ontario government] works" (Ontario Progressive Conservative Party 1995a: 1), and he is well on the way to achieving that. In his first year, Harris has succeeded in wiping out many of the laws, protective regulations, public jobs, and services on which the welfare state was based. As in other new neo-conservative regimes (notably Ralph Klein's Alberta and Roger Douglas's New Zealand), Harris has followed the prescription of "hit 'em hard, hit 'em fast, don't blink." Once these foundations, built over the past fifty years, are lost, it will be difficult to rebuild them.

We cannot wait until the next election to expose the puppet-masters behind Harris and the threats they pose. We hope that this book will encourage readers, before it is too late, to join the movement to oust Harris and the corporate powers he serves.

What's In the Book?

In Part 1, we put the Harris "revolution" into the context of the international corporate war of which it is a part.

Tony Clarke, past co-chair of the Action Canada Network and founder of the Polaris Institute, lays bare the transnational corporate powers backing the Harris government and exposes the threats they pose for Ontario people, and Canadians in general.

Paul Browne and André Régimbald, social policy analysts, describe the parallels between Harris's platform and British Thatcherism on the one hand, and U.S. Reaganism on the other; Browne also shows how the failures of the social democratic governments in Britain and Ontario created the conditions for a conservative victory.

Michelle Weinroth unmasks the ideology of "deficitism" which neo-liberal and neo-conservative governments, have used to justify the assault on their peoples. She shows how the debt hysteria fomented by the federal Tories and then Liberals set the stage for popular acquiescence to the Harris "revolution."

Ian Morrison, director of the Toronto Legal Aid Clinic chair of the Ontario Social Safety Network has been a powerful advocate for the poor and for social justice generally. In this thoughtful chapter, Morrison explains how Harris is wiping out the whole concept of social citizenship and the fundamental obligation of the government to serve and protect its citizens, particularly those who are most vulnerable.

Part 2 of the book spells out the impacts of the Harris policies on those who have been most directly targeted: workers, women and children, the poor, Aboriginal and ethno-cultural communities, and Franco-Ontarians.

Steve Watson, an educator for the Canadian Auto Workers, describes the Harris government's assault on labour rights and the resulting resistance of unions, highlighting the successful strike by Ontario Public Service Employees Union (OPSEU) workers in 1996 and the days of action organized by the Ontario

Federation of Labour (OFL).

Brigitte Kitchen, a social work professor at Ryerson University, specializes in social policy related to family and women. In this chapter, she analyzes the impacts of the Tory cuts on women and their children, especially on those who are poor.

Allan Moscovitch, director of the Carleton University School of Social Work, is one of the most respected experts on Canadian social welfare history and policy. In 1990–1992, Moscovitch chaired the Ontario Advisory Committee on New Social Assistance Legislation, a task force to develop a new social assistance law. All of its recommendations were discarded by the Harris government and replaced by draconian cuts and punitive attacks on the rights of the poor. In his chapter, Moscovitch traces the Harris government's assault on recipients of social assistance, setting it in the context of recent improvements in social welfare rates and rights under the previous Liberal and NDP governments.

Linda Lalonde, a policy analyst with the Social Assistance Recipients Council in Ottawa, draws on her extensive welfare rights advocacy experience to illustrate the devastating implications of social assistance cuts for poor people.

Jean Trickey was one of the courageous Black teenagers who integrated Arkansas' Little Rock High School in 1954. Since then she has devoted her life to challenging racism in all its forms. She has served as director of the National Capital Alliance Against Racism and of Immigrant and Visible Minority Women Against Abuse. In this chapter, Trickey decodes the subtly racist messages behind the apparently neutral rhetoric and policies of the Harris government. She describes the differentially punitive impacts of these policies on Aboriginal and ethno-cultural communities in Ontario.

David Welch, a social work professor at the University of Ottawa, specializes in the history of Franco-Ontarian social services. Welch places the impacts of Harris policies on Franco-Ontarians in the context of two centuries of struggles to establish French language services and rights. Welch demonstrates that the cuts will weaken French programs and further isolate and marginalize Franco-Ontarians.

Part 3 describes a broad range of resistance approaches developing in Ontario, and spells out principles for long term strategies to win.

Michèle Kérisit and Nérée St-Amand, professors at the University of Ottawa School of Social Work, studied over seventy alternative community resources in Ontario. These groups, they demonstrate, create the basis of family and community on which resistance depends. Egalitarian and empowering, they offer a striking contrast to Harris's emphasis on paternalistic charity. Kérisit and St-Amand argue that, without state aid, these precious resources will be crippled, and they suggest that this may be part of Harris's motivation for slashing their funding.

John Clarke, founder and leader of the Ontario Coalition Against Poverty (OCAP), spells out the strategic principles and creative tactics that its member group, the Toronto Direct Action Coalition (TDAC) has used to mobilize large masses of people to oppose Harris and to expose the corporate beneficiaries of his government's cuts.

Jim Turk was one of the principle organizers for the "days of action"—massive one-day strikes and demonstrations rotating through Ontario cities. Drawing from his own experience, Turk describes the evolving tensions and unity within the labour movement and between it and community groups. Turk critically analyzes both the strengths and limitations of the days of action as a tactic and proposes directions for further mobilizing.

Diana Ralph, a professor at the Carleton University School of Social Work, has organized in the anti-poverty and other social justice movements for over thirty years. Arguing that the resistance movement needs to shift the focus of its criticism from the government to its corporate backers, she lays out strategic directions that will win over the long haul, long after Mike Harris is defeated.

Harris's First Year: Attacks and Resistance
Bill Dare

Just a little over a year after the launch of the Common Sense Revolution platform on May 3, 1994, the Ontario Progressive Conservative Party won power. The platform includes: a 20 percent cut in non-priority government spending without touching the health care budget; a 30 percent cut in provincial income tax rates; the elimination of bureaucratic barriers to jobs, growth and investment; doing better for less; a balanced budget within the first mandate; slashed welfare benefits and implementation of workfare; and the creation of 725,000 new jobs in the next five years.

This chapter lists key actions of the Progressive Conservative Party of Ontario in its first year. These actions have been felt throughout Ontario society as legislation, policy and fiscal decisions have been implemented. The effects are myriad. This listing also includes some of the major acts of resistance to the Common Sense Revolution, though it doesn't report on the many widespread local actions.[1] (The following list of events appears in chronological order. Where possible, specific dates are provided.)

June 1995
- June 8th, 1995. The Progressive Conservative Party of Ontario, with a Common Sense Revolution platform, wins a majority government in Ontario.

	Conservative	Liberal	NDP	Independent
Seats won:	82	30	17	1
Percentage of vote:	44.8%	31.3%	20.6%	

- June 29th, 1995. Harris announces his support for Liberal-initiated cuts to federal transfer payments to health, post-secondary education and social assistance.

July 1995
- July 21st, 1995. Ernie Eves (Ontario minister of finance) announces $2 billion dollars in cuts.
- Ontario Ministry of Health ends the MultiService Agencies program which had been centralizing long term care services.

August 1995
- Workplace Health and Safety Agency is disbanded and taken over by Workers' Compensation Board, removing worker input; Occupational

Disease Panel, accident prevention program is ended: mandatory inquests when workers are killed are abolished.

- Wage Protection Fund, which guarantees wages, benefits, severance and termination pay to laid-off workers, is chopped back to wages and benefits only and the maximum is cut from $5000 to $2000. Termination of the program is scheduled.
- August 21st, 1995. Harris says the province is bankrupt and warns municipalities of 20 percent cuts. The next day Eugene Williams, a financial analyst with the Canadian Bond Rating Service, says that Ontario is not "insolvent."
- August 29th, 1995. Harris meets Federal Reform Party leader, Preston Manning, to explore forming an alliance.

September 1995

- September 12th, 1995. Anthony Dudley George, an Aboriginal activist, is killed when protesters concerned about land claims clash with the Ontario Provincial Police at a Chippewa burial ground in Ipperwash provincial park. Later in the month, Harris refuses to have an inquiry into the conduct of the police and the political processes involved with the incident.
- September 12th, 1995. Minister of Education John Snobelen apologizes for urging education bureaucrats to invent a crisis in education.
- September 15th, 1995. Minister of Social and Community Services David Tsubouchi suggests that people who can't cope with welfare cuts buy food in bulk and shop for dented cans. In the ensuing weeks he issues a welfare diet of $90 a month ($3 a day), on which he claims people on welfare can realistically live.
- Spouse-in-the-house rule is reinstated to cut single moms off family benefits if it is alleged they are living with a man; a three month wait for welfare is imposed as a penalty for quitting a job or being fired; youth welfare is restricted; a provincial fraud line is set up.
- The out-of-country Ontario Health Insurance Plan (OHIP) rate (to $400 from $100 per day) is restored.
- September 27th, 1995. Ontario legislature opens amid demonstrations and protests.

October 1995

- Ontario Training and Adjustment Board 1995–96 budget is cut by $20 million.
- October 1st, 1995. Welfare rates are cut by 21.6 percent; thousands of people with disabilities are included and eligibility is "tightened."
- Local protests mount as Harris travels through Ontario.
- Cancellation of 390 co-op and non-profit housing projects (many already

under construction); the dismantling of rent control is identified as a goal for the Ministry of Housing.

- Harris cancels jobsOntario, a short term incentive to employers to hire low-income earners, which the previous NDP government had initiated.
- Twenty-five halfway houses which help offenders to re-enter the community are closed with Solicitor General Bob Runciman stating that the Ministry was not in the housing business.
- Alabama-style chain gangs of prisoners forced to do road work in Eastern Ontario is being planned by the government. Prisoners would wear electronic ankle bracelets rather than chains. Harris claims this will give them work experience.
- October 31st, 1995. Bill 7, Labour Relations Employment Statutes Law Amendment Act 1995 is passed. It dismantles NDP labour law reforms, allowing replacement workers (strike breakers) to be used during strikes and during certification votes to start new unions. Employers are allowed to mount an anti-union campaign and initiate de-certification votes with already established unions.
- Successor rights for employees in crown corporations (collective agreement and bargaining rights) are stripped if the corporation is privatized.
- Ministry of Labour is cut in half with the loss of 457 ministry staff, one-third of the employment standards inspectors are laid off and the support for health and safety inspectors is essentially eliminated.

November 1995

- The bi-partite board of directors for the Workers' Compensation Board with equal labour and management membership is fired, to be replaced with an employer-dominated board; there are plans for the privatization of income loss insurance for the first four to six weeks of injury and contracting out of vocational rehabilitation, medical services and claims management.
- November 29th, 1995. Ontario Government Fiscal and Economic Statement is presented to the legislature; $3.5 billion is cut from government current spending ($5.5 billion in cutbacks to end of fiscal year 1995–96).
- The Ministry of Health budget is cut by $1.5 billion, with 18 percent of hospital budgets cut over the next three years: $365 million in 1996–97, $435 million in 1997–98 and $507 million in 1998–99.
- Grants to school boards are cut by $1 billion dollars over a full year; 15 percent cut in community colleges ($120 million) and universities ($280 million) with university fees rising 10–20 percent and college 15 percent. A new student aid program utilizing an income contingent loan system is promised.
- Junior kindergarten is made optional for school boards.

- Child care subsidies are eliminated and a voucher system for child care is being studied. This threatens the sustainability of licensed daycare centres.
- The costs of licensing teachers, through the newly established College of Teachers, will be passed on to teachers.
- Provincial grants to municipal governments are reduced by 48 percent over the next two years; transit grants cut 21 percent over two years; libraries are cut $12 million over two years; recycling (blue box) funding is eliminated; conservation authorities are cut 70 percent over two years; rural communities are asked to pay $220 per household as a special tax for Ontario Provincial Police service.
- In the arts communities, 28 percent ($220 million) is cut from galleries, museums, public and non-profit broadcasters and regulatory boards.
- Bill 26, Savings and Restructuring Act (Omnibus Bill) is introduced on the day of the Fiscal and Economic Statement. It amends forty four statutes, creates three acts and repeals two others under it.
- The health minister is given authority to eliminate hospital boards and take over hospitals directly to shut down, run, merge and decide on what services will be provided; drug prices are deregulated and user fees and deductibles are applied to seniors; Ontario Medical Association loses collective bargaining rights and minister has power over location of practice; minister given unprecedented authority for access to and distribution of individual health records.
- Pay equity in the public sector is rolled back by ending proxy method.
- Minister for municipal affairs given power to abolish local government and create mergers and amalgamations; allows new forms of local taxation, new user fees, gasoline and head tax (poll tax); checks and balances for democratic control such as the municipal referendum and accountability to the legislature are removed (privatization is allowed with no need for a referendum).
- Arbitration for certain public sector workers (such as police, firefighters, teachers and hospital workers) is significantly reduced.
- Environmental laws concerning abandoned mines and forest protection are scrapped.
- Freedom of information laws are changed to make it more difficult to gain access to government information.
- One-day walkout by daycare workers. Many families who have children in daycare support the walkout with a demonstration at the Ontario legislature.
- Strict Discipline Task Force of community members and MPPs is formed

23

to develop a pilot facility for young offenders.

- Grants for business, such as the Economic Development Fund, are canceled.

December 1995

- December 6th, 1995. Liberal and NDP opposition MPPs disrupt legislature to ensure public consultation on the Omnibus Bill; Liberal MPP Alvin Curling has an all-night sit-in at the legislature.
- From the 1995 base, the government announced its commitment to $8.2 billion in budget cuts. The cuts are still short of the over $10 billion needed to balance the budget and provide the 30 percent tax cut promised in the campaign.
- December 11th, 1995. London, Ontario shut down on a Day of Action called by the labour movement.
- December 13th, 1995. Bill 8, Job Quotas Repeal Act 1995 passed. The former NDP government Employment Equity Act is repealed "to remove business-inhibiting employment legislation in Ontario." This also eliminates pay equity.

January 1996

- Harris goes to the World Economic Forum in Davos, Switzerland, then Tokyo and Hong Kong.
- Interfaith Social Assistance Reform Coalition decries Bill 26 (Omnibus Bill).

February 1996

- Students protesting the cuts in higher education disrupt the legislature.
- February 24th, 1996. Hamilton Day of Action (with 100,000 protesters) occurs at the same time as an Ontario Progressive Conservative Party convention is protected by a strong police presence.
- Hong Kong businesses praise Harris on return to conservatism in Ontario.
- Government seeks bids from private companies for homecare.
- February 9th, 1996. A court challenge to welfare cuts by recipients is defeated by Ontario judges. They rule it does not exceed government's power.
- February 26th, 1996. Over 50,000 Ontario Public Service Employee Union (OPSEU) workers go on strike to protect job security.
- Power Workers, Liquor Control Board of Ontario, teachers unions and public service unions launch advertising campaigns describing impacts of cuts and privatization of crown corporations for Ontario.

March 1996

- March 18th, 1996. OPP riot squad is let loose on union protesters who were blocking MPPs access to the legislature. Harris is forced to form an all party inquiry into the incident.

- March 29th, 1996. OPSEU strike ends with a new respect for the ability of the union to effectively challenge the agenda of the Ontario government and maintain solidarity. The strike ensured that:
  - union members receive stronger protection if their positions are privatized; this includes the government ensuring comparable terms and conditions of employment;
  - seniority respected during layoffs;
  - workers receive their automatic 2 percent increase when the NDP social contract ends and some will receive a 3 percent merit increase;
  - all laid-off workers receive the normal six months notice and severance of two weeks per year of service;
  - guarantees from the government that there will be no legislative changes to the pension plan and any changes must be negotiated; the union retains the right to bargain wage rates for current and future job classifications. As well, wage rates will not be reduced.

April 1996

- April 1st, 1996. Federal government eliminates the Canada Assistance Plan (CAP) and launches the Canada Health and Social Transfer (CHST) on a single block of funding that includes: health, post-secondary and social welfare funding. Overall funding for these areas is reduced and the eventual elimination of cash transfers over the next 10–15 years is anticipated.
- April 10th, 1996. Salaries of MPPs are increased to $78,007 a year but pensions are reduced.
- April 19th, 1996. Waterloo Day of Action.
- The newly initiated "business plans" for each ministry are announced with 10,600 public sector layoffs as first instalments of the plans.

May 1996

- May 1st, 1996. Women's March for Bread and Roses, involving communities across Canada, is launched in Vancouver at Canadian Labour Congress (CLC) convention. It arrives in Ottawa on June 14th, 1996.
- May 7th, 1996. 1996–97 budget announced with the tax break as the key job strategy for Ontario and confirmation of the $8.2 billion in cutbacks.
- May 13th, 1996. Provincial Labour Minister Elizabeth Witmer says unions will be allowed to negotiate lower standards for working conditions.

June 1996

- Launch of workfare program (Ontario Works) with pilot communities being selected to start putting to work an eventual 50,000 social service recipients with organizations such as the Kiwanis and Rotary clubs.

Ottawa and Kingston pass resolutions against the initiative being applied to their communities.

- June 7th, 1996. Report on restructuring Ontario Hydro, recommends privatizing most of it except for Niagara Falls and nuclear power stations.
- June 24th, 1996. Peterborough Day of Action.

Note

1. This document draws substantially from the Ontario Federation of Labour's fact sheet, *The Common Sense Revolution: 11 Months of Destruction.*

Part One

Putting the Harris Government in Context

Chapter I

The Transnational Corporate Agenda Behind the Harris Regime

Tony Clarke

The media have been fond of quoting Mike Harris's claim that the so-called Common Sense Revolution was the product of consultation with Main Street Ontario. Throughout the 1995 election campaign, the Harris team repeatedly declared that their platform priorities and proposals came from Ontarians demanding radical changes in the role of government. These reminders, in turn, were followed after the election with feature stories showing how the market-based ideology of the new regime at Queens Park was made possible by rapidly shifting values and priorities in Ontario's political culture.

While there is undoubtedly some truth to all this, it by no means tells the full story of what lies behind the Common Sense Revolution. The Harris platform was primarily crafted to serve the interests of transnational investors and the bond rating agencies on Wall Street. The focal point of its accountability is Bay Street, not Main Street. Yet, once in the hands of the Tory spin doctors, the Common Sense Revolution was cleverly bound and sold as a manifesto arising from the people of Ontario.

To understand these developments, we need to take a look at how Mike Harris's agenda for Ontario relates to the rise of corporate power and the takeover of public policy making on both global and national levels.

New Global Economy

Beginning with his election night victory speech, Mike Harris has never lost sight of his mission to proclaim to the rest of the world that Ontario is finally "open for business." When he joined Prime Minister Jean Chrétien and 130 chief executive officers (CEOs) of Canadian corporations for the Team Canada II trade mission to India and other Southeast Asian countries in January of 1996, Harris's sales pitch was well tuned to attract foreign investment to Ontario. But it was his appearance two weeks later at the World Economic Forum in Davos, Switzerland that demonstrated the top priority which the Harris government puts on courting transnational investors.

The World Economic Forum in Davos, Switzerland has become the annual meeting place for many of the world's leading corporate executives and heads of state. During the first week of February 1996, 1000 CEOs along with 40 heads of state and 200 senior government officials met to share the latest information on global economic trends. But the main attraction of this prestigious event is what *Globe and Mail* reporter Madelaine Drohan described as "the eager horde of political leaders seeking to persuade giant corporations to invest in their countries" (Drohan February 5, 1996: A10). Political leaders and officials from all over the world descended on this quaint Swiss village to sell the virtues of their country as havens for profitable transnational investment to the CEO of corporations such as Ford Motor, Microsoft, Procter and Gamble, Daimler–Benz, Toyota Motor and Coca-Cola (to name but a few). Mike Harris, as it turned out, was the top ranking Canadian politician at the event.

The World Economic Forum simply illustrates the powerful role that transnational corporations now play in the new global economy (Barnet and Cavanagh 1994). After all, 50 of the 100 top economies in the world today are transnational enterprises. In the past decade and a half, the number of transnational corporations (TNCs) has skyrocketed from 7000 to almost 40,000. Over 70 percent of current global trade in goods and services is controlled by a mere 500 of these corporations. Some 350 of these, in turn, own half the total stock of direct foreign investment throughout the entire world. Moreover, since the collapse of the Berlin Wall, transnational corporations have expanded their pools of investment capital to meet the demands of new markets worldwide. In 1996 alone, according to the recent United Nations world investment report, transnational corporations will generate some $5 trillion (U.S.) of wealth through operations outside their home countries (United Nations 1995).

In this new global economy, a massive transfer of power has been taking place—out of the hands of nation states and into the hands of transnational corporations (Korten 1995). To compete for transnational investment, nation states and governments (including Canada) have surrendered some of their key sovereign powers and strategic policy tools required to improve the economic, social and environmental living conditions of their own citizens. This power grab has been carried out through a series of "structural adjustment programs" promoted by big business, including: the deregulation of foreign investment and national economies; the privatization of crown corporations and public utilities and services; the negotiation and implementation of free trade regimes; the reduction of public deficits through massive social spending cuts; the erosion of national controls over monetary policy; and the reduction of public revenues through lower corporate taxes and higher interest rates.

Through the application of these structural adjustment programs, the role and powers of governments and citizens in a liberal democracy have been altered radically. It is no longer the prime role of governments to intervene in the marketplace on behalf of the public interest in order, for example, to stimulate job creation, redistribute wealth through social programs, or ensure that industrial production meets environmental standards. Instead, the prime role of governments is to serve the interests of big business by providing a favourable climate for transnational investment through lower corporate taxes, lower wages, lower social spending, and lower environmental standards. As a result, the basic democratic rights of citizens—to adequate food, clothing, and shelter, or education, employment, and health care, or a safe environment, social equality, and decent public services—are either being hijacked or rapidly eroded.

Even though these basic citizen rights are enshrined in United Nations covenants,[1] they are superseded today by the rights of corporations in the new global economy. The recently established free trade regimes (i.e. North American Free Trade Agreement—NAFTA; General Agreement on Trade and Tariffs—GATT) constitute a bill of rights for TNCs (Barlow and Campbell 1993). Functioning as the constitutions of the new global economy, the new free trade rules guarantee protection for the rights and freedoms of transnational corporations. The "national treatment" clauses in NAFTA and GATT, for example, guarantee that foreign investors have the same rights and freedoms as domestic firms. The "investment codes" further ensure that certain regulatory measures introduced by national or provincial governments such as foreign investment requirements, export quotas, local procurement, job content, or technology specifications shall be considered unlawful legislation and must be removed.

The growing power of transnational corporations over democratically elected governments is further fortified by a network of global institutions. The World Bank and the International Monetary Fund (IMF) are directly linked to transnational banks through their borrowing and lending operations. Loan agreements affecting the lives of peoples in various countries are routinely negotiated in secret between banking and government officials without any public accountability. Moreover, the newly established World Trade Organization (WTO) is primarily designed to be a global governing body for transnational corporate interests. Armed with legislative as well as judicial powers, the WTO has a mandate to eventually eliminate all barriers to international investment and competition. What this means is that a global parliament composed of unelected officials will have the power to override economic, social and environmental measures which have been developed and implemented by democratically elected legislatures in countries around the world (Wallach 1994).

The next major step is expected to be the creation of an international investment treaty under the auspices of the WTO. The proposed treaty would guarantee "free entry and establishment for foreign investors, full national treatment for established investors and high standards for investment protection" in all countries (Brittain 1992; *Agreement* 1995). Foreign investors would be granted legal rights to operate in all sectors of a country's economy without discrimination or restriction. The treaty is also expected to include a "standstill commitment" not to include new restrictions and a "roll-back" commitment to gradually eliminate regulatory measures that run counter to trade liberalization along with a commitment to open up any previously closed sectors of the country's economy. The proposed investment treaty is scheduled to be a major topic on the agenda of the first full meeting of the WTO trade ministers in Singapore, December 1996. If an investment treaty along these lines is adopted, the WTO will be in a strategic position to almost exclusively coordinate (along with the IMF and the World Bank) global economic and social policy making.

Creeping Corporate Rule

Mike Harris is not only aware of this transnational corporate agenda but is anxious to ensure that Ontario accommodates to the new economic and political order. Indeed, this may have been what the architects of the Common Sense Revolution really had in mind when they drafted their platform for Ontario's future. After all, the main theme behind the Common Sense Revolution is the call to re-invent the role and responsibility of government in Ontario. While the idea of a "limited" and "downsized" government, along with a 30 percent slice in personal income tax, was sold to Ontario voters during the election, there was a lot more to the Harris agenda for "re-inventing" government. Simply put, the government was getting out of the business of ensuring that the basic rights of Ontario citizens were met regarding employment, housing, education, health care, environmental safeguards, and social equality. Instead, the government's prime responsibility is to secure the kind of economic and social conditions required to make Ontario an attractive place for profitable transnational investment.

Under the Common Sense Revolution, therefore, the role of government is being re-invented and re-engineered to serve the interests of transnational capital. There have always been, of course, linkages between governments and corporate interests. From the historical role of the Hudsons Bay Company and the Bank of Montreal to the family empires of the Bronfmans, Reichmans, Thompsons, Irvings, Black and Desmarais, as well as the CEOs of Canada's leading corporations on Bay Street, big business has had a powerful influence in the corridors of Queens Park and the House of Commons. But, in the past, labour unions and other social organizations often formed a counterweight to the influence of big business, and the process was largely ad hoc and informal. Today, a much more formal corporate–government structure has emerged in which big business exercises almost exclusive influence over public policy making.

The origins of these new corporate–government regimes date back to the mid–1970s. During that period, the world's leading business and government elites began gathering on a more regular basis through what became known as the Trilateral Commission. Composed of some 325 leaders in business, government and civil society, the Commission became *the* forum for mapping out global agendas and strategies for public policy making. Commission members included the presidents and prime ministers from all the industrialized countries of Western Europe, North America and Japan plus the CEOs of five of the world's six largest banks, four of the five largest transnational corporations and the major media conglomerates in all three regions. It was here that policy platforms and strategies for dealing with deregulation, privatization, inflation, free trade, social policy reform, corporate taxation measures and monetary policy options were often formulated and vigorously promoted.

At the same time, the CEOs of the largest corporations were forming their own big business coalitions in most of the industrialized countries. In the United States, the Business Round Table, composed of CEOs from 200 leading corporations, was set up in 1974 (Korten 1995: 144–145). Its membership includes the heads of forty two of the fifty largest corporations, seven of the eight largest U.S. commercial banks, seven of the ten largest insurance companies, five of the seven largest retail chains, seven of the eight largest transportation companies, and nine of the eleven largest utility corporations. Armed with extensive resources for policy research, congressional lobbying and political advertising, the Business Round Table has played a strategic role over the past two decades in shaping the direction of U.S. economic and social policy. Their influence on new policy directions ranging from domestic platforms like the Contract with America to the passage of NAFTA and the GATT has been immeasurable.

In Europe, a similar corporate–governmental regime has been operating on a continent-wide basis. The European Round Table of Industrialists (ERT) is composed of forty men, all CEOs of major transnational corporations mainly based in the European Union (Doherty and Hoedeman 1994). ERT membership includes eleven of the top twenty European companies—British Petroleum, Daimler–Benz, Fiat, Siemens, Unilever, Nestlé, Philips, Hoechst, Total, Thyssen and ICI—all of which are listed among the world's top fifty companies. Formed in 1983, the ERT has become the *eminence grise* behind the economic integration of the twelve countries that comprise the European Union. In 1984, the ERT launched a campaign for the creation of a single European market through a five-year plan that called for the elimination of trade barriers, the harmonization of regulations and the abolition of fiscal restrictions. With direct access to the top decision makers in government at both the European Commission and its member countries, the ERT has been highly effective in influencing, if not directing, policy changes on a broad range of fronts including competition, transportation, education, employment, environment, and social reforms.

Here, in Canada, we have seen the emergence of a corporate–government regime through the operations of the Business Council on National Issues (BCNI) (Langille 1987). Established in 1978, the BCNI was modelled after the Business Round Table in the U.S. It is composed of 160 member corporations with combined assets of over $1.2 trillion (Clarke 1995). The BCNI's membership includes the five big banks (Royal, CIBC, Montreal, Scotia, and Toronto Dominion), plus the leading corporations involved in the other key sectors of Canada's economy: manufacturing (e.g. General Motors, General Electric); resources (e.g. Brascan, Noranda Mines); insurance (e.g. Manulife, Sunlife); retail (e.g. T. Eaton, Sears), telecommunications (e.g. Northern Telecom, IBM Canada, Rogers Communications); agriculture (e.g. Cargill, Quaker Oats); energy (e.g. Imperial Oil, Shell Canada); and transportation (e.g. Air Canada, Canadian Pacific, Bombardier)—to name but a few.

For the past two decades, the BCNI's operations have been a prime example of creeping corporate rule in Canada. As political scientist David Langille points out, the BCNI functions "as a virtual shadow cabinet" behind the federal cabinet in Ottawa (Langille 1987:55). Its thirty six member council establishes task forces around the major economic and social policies of the day. Chaired by CEOs, these task forces are decidedly pro-active, designing public policy agendas and strategies to be pursued by the federal government. Fortified by corporate "think tanks" like the C.D. Howe and Fraser Institutes and citizen front groups like the National Citizens' Coalition and the Canadian Taxpayers Association, the BCNI and its member corporations have been singularly effective in their campaigns to bring about major policy changes in Ottawa—on deregulation, privatization, inflation, competition, energy, tax reform, free trade, the deficit and social spending. As a result, the framework of economic and social policy making in this country has been radically altered. At the same time, the role and powers of federal and provincial governments have been re-engineered to privilege the interests of transnational capital, rather than the broader public interest.

Ontario's Corporate Regime

Mike Harris' Common Sense Revolution was designed primarily to remake government in the image of big business. Like his predecessors—Bob Rae, David Peterson, Bill Davis—Harris is well aware that the CEOs on Bay Street have a powerful influence at Queens Park. Moreover, the BCNI has its own direct connections. Unlike the other provincial capitals where the BCNI generally works through business associations like the Conseil du patronat in Quebec or the British Columbia Employers Association, the channels of communication, consultation and decision making between the BCNI or its members and the Ontario government are much more direct. After all, this makes perfect sense, given the fact that most of the member corporations of the BCNI are headquartered in Toronto, largely on Bay Street. What the Harris team did, in effect, was to forge a political platform which they knew would be ideologically in keeping with their existing and potential allies on Bay Street.

It comes as no surprise, therefore, that the Common Sense Revolution won ringing endorsements from big business. During the '95 election campaign, Harris himself released a list of 100 CEOs and corporations that had endorsed his platform (Mittelstaedt May 27, 1995: A5). The list included numerous members of the BCNI such as John Eaton of the T. Eaton Co. and Trevor Eyton of Brascan. When Harris and his finance minister Ernie Eves initially outlined their budget plans in July 1995, the headlines in the business section of one newspaper read: "Bay Street Cheers Tory Chainsaw" (Valpy July 25, 1995: A11). Commenting on the Harris regime's plans to fight the deficit through massive cuts in government program spending, one of the big five banks (Scotia) emphasized in its report that "a positive signal has been sent to financial markets." The Harris cuts, the bank pronounced, "are an important first step towards regaining control of Ontario's finances." In contrast to the deep cuts proposed for social spending by the budget announcement, the bank's report went on to comment favourably on the fact that "business subsidies were frozen—not eliminated" (Valpy July 25, 1995: A11).

Indeed, the Harris government's budget strategy is primarily designed to respond to the demands of Wall Street. The world's two leading bond rating agencies, Moody's and Standard and Poor on Wall Street in New York, had already issued a stiff warning to the Rae government by lowering Ontario's cherished credit rating. In the new global economy, these agencies operate as private sector police forces over government finances (Wamsley 1996: 19–20). If Ontario wanted to attract foreign investment, it had better get its financial house in order by slashing the government's deficit. By announcing its plans to slice a whopping $8 billion out of Ontario program spending over a three year period, the Harris government sent a clear signal to Wall Street that deficit cutting would be the top priority. This set the stage to regain the stamp of approval that Harris needed from the bond raters to attract foreign investment. But the Harris team may have taken one step too many. The promise of a 30 percent tax cut, which lured many Ontarians to vote for the Tories in the '95 election, was promptly rejected by Standard and Poor and the Dominion Bond Rating Service (who warned that an early tax cut would explode the deficit) (Chamberlain 1995: A1; Wamsley 1996: 19–20).

Yet, the cornerstone of the Common Sense Revolution, namely, the model of corporate government which Mike Harris has in store for Ontario, was largely unveiled through the infamous Omnibus Bill. Introduced as the Savings and Restructuring Bill, it called for amendments to some forty three separate pieces of legislation on the Ontario statute books. As *Toronto Star* columnist Thomas Walkom observed, the Harris government's Omnibus Bill served to centralize power in the hands of the cabinet to an unprecedented degree while, at the same time, transferring power into the hands of corporations through extensive forms of deregulation and privatization (Walkom December 2, 1995: C1). In other words, the Harris agenda is not to eliminate government, as many of its critics initially charged, but to re-engineer government to serve the interests of transnational capital. As Walkom describes it:

> Harris is getting government out of the business of helping the poor. He is getting government out of the business of environmental and business regulation. But where Harris figures state action is needed to promote private enterprise, government power is being strengthened." (Walkom December 2, 1995: C1)

Take the manufacturing sector's opposition to the labour laws adopted under the previous NDP government. Labelled as the NDP's anti-scab legislation for its ban on the use of replacement workers during a strike, the law also included the right to organize and picket on third party property such as shopping malls, rules making it easier to consolidate bargaining units, provisions ensuring that union contracts would be continued if a business was sold, and mandatory arbitration for first contracts in newly organized workplaces. Bay Street industrialists waged a relentless campaign against this new labour law, insisting it would become a major block to investment in the province and demanding that the legislation be scrapped. During the election campaign, the Harris team promised to repeal the new labour legislation. Yet, once in power, the Harris government not only moved quickly to introduce legislation repealing the NDP labour relations code, but also added its own measures such as the introduction of workplace productivity goals, reform of the Workers' Compensation Board, elimination of the Employers Health Tax for small to medium sized businesses, removal of the Workplace Health and Safety Agency plus a freeze on the minimum wage and review of all regulations affecting corporations.

The Harris government has also eliminated a series of environmental restrictions on the operations of resource companies. When a mining corporation, for example, shuts down a mine in Ontario, it no longer has to satisfy the government, and thereby the surrounding community, that it has a plan to clean up the toxic waste it has produced. It only needs to tell the government of its plans to meet provincial standards. Meanwhile, the new law will replace comprehensive inspection procedures of tailing sites with random spot checks. Forest companies will also face fewer restrictions when it comes to building access roads across public lands. Companies planning to construct dams on Ontario river systems will have an easier time getting past environmental restrictions in the future (Walkom December 2, 1995: C1). On top of all this, Ontario's conservation boards, which protect wildlife areas, are being shut down across the province.

One of the Harris government's key planks in its platform to promote transnational investment in Ontario are measures taken to open the door to U.S. health care corporations. In addition to giving the minister of health sweeping powers to unilaterally shut down hospitals and cut or increase medical fees paid to doctors, the new laws quietly drop the preferential treatment granted to Canadians to set up non-profit, independent health facilities (Walker December 2, 1995: A3; Wright 1995: A3). In effect, this opens the door of Ontario's health care system for American for-profit corporations to establish facilities for a wide range of services from cataract surgery to abortions to kidney dialysis (Wright 1995: A3). Moreover, transnational drug companies will finally get their wish to have prescription drug prices deregulated. As a result, drug prices in the non-governmental market (where 60 percent of pharmaceuticals in Ontario are sold) are expected to shoot up dramatically along with the profit margins of the transnationals (Walkom December 2, 1995: C1).

In the final analysis, it appears that the organizing principle of the Harris experiment in corporate–government is investment security. Indeed, as a government run ad in the *Globe and Mail* put it: "Ontario is not just open for business: Ontario is Business" (June 9, 1996). The name of the game is to *secure* a favourable climate in Ontario for profitable transnational investment and competition. The broad spectrum of public policy making—fiscal, economic, social, environmental, cultural and political—must be subordinated to this principle. To effectively carry out this kind of agenda requires an increasingly authoritarian regime. That is why the original omnibus legislation was drafted with "military style secrecy" where only senior bureaucrats were kept informed and then only on a "need-to-know basis" (Walkom December 2, 1995: C1). That is why certain ministers have been granted sweeping powers such as the authority to merge cities and towns, thereby altering community boundaries, regardless of whether local councils agree or not. That is why, in several cases, the requirements to hold citizen referenda have been suspended and why major economic and social legislation is being rammed through Queens Park with precious little public consultation or input.

In effect, we have entered a new age of corporate rule in Ontario. The Common Sense Revolution has to do with a lot more than "slash and burn" economics. Above all, the Harris agenda is to build a new and permanent model of corporate government for Ontario that can respond to the demands of transnational investment in the new global economy. Mike Harris himself is quoted as saying: "We must never lose sight of the fact that this is an exercise in bringing permanent change to the public sector" (Winsor November 28, 1995: A3). In turn, this calls for new strategies for democratic social change. To simply replace the Harris Tories in the next provincial election with the New Democrats, let alone the Liberals, will accomplish little. The challenge that lies ahead is to develop a new politics aimed at both unmasking and dismantling the systems of corporate rule that are operative in Ontario and Canada. To move in this direction, both social movements and political parties will need to be re-tooled and transformed.[2]

Notes
1. See, for example, the *Universal Declaration of Human Rights*, the *Covenant on Economic, Social, and Cultural Rights*, the *Covenant on Civil and Political Rights* and the *Earth Charter* from the Rio Summit on the Environment and Sustainable Development—all of which are published by and available from the United Nations in New York.
2. For a further development of this point see Tony Clarke (1996).

Chapter 2

Déjà Vu: Thatcherism in Ontario

Paul Leduc Browne

Déjà Vu

The idea of a revolution suggests something overwhelming, all-encompassing and new. Much of the rhetoric surrounding the current right-wing transformation of Canada implies that the Right is innovative and creative, while the Centre is stagnant and the Left lost in nostalgia for the past. Hence the title of the much-hyped get-together for right-wingers recently organized by David Frum: "The Winds of Change." Hence also the title of Newt Gingrich's book, "To *Renew* America" (emphasis added).

The Conservative "revolution" in Ontario has presented itself in a paradoxical guise. It is the "Common Sense" Revolution. Common sense, as everyone knows, is as old as the hills, the compendium of experience, tradition and prejudice. It is inherently bound to the way things are or appear to be in the light of popular wisdom or everyday forms of reasoning.

To assess Mike Harris's Common Sense Revolution, it is instructive to compare it to examples of conservative ideology and government in the countries to which Ontario is most closely affiliated in term of history, trade and cultural influence, namely the United States and Great Britain. In the light of this comparison, it will be seen that the Common Sense Revolution is neither revolutionary, in the sense of involving radical innovation, nor commonsensical—rather, it echoes the ideas and policies of Anglo–American conservatives over the past twenty years.

Mike Harris's first year in government is highly reminiscent of the early Thatcher years in Great Britain. The Harris Tories have espoused a Thatcherite philosophy, a potent neo-conservative brew of neo-liberal economics and "authoritarian populist" social policy. They have the same fundamental objective, the redistribution of income from the "worse-off" to the "better-off" sections of society.

Thatcherism is most closely tied to Margaret Thatcher's eleven-year tenure as prime minister of Great Britain from 1979 to 1990. It brought about deep and decisive changes in British society in the 1980s and 1990s: the end of the social-democratic consensus around the welfare state under the onslaught of neo-liberal individualism; the subordination of every aspect of social life to market forces protected by a strong central government; the long term weakening of trade unionism and marginalizing of progressive politics.

Components of Thatcherite Ideology: The Social Market Doctrine

Throughout most of the twentieth century, the British Conservative Party had eschewed being too closely identified with the free market ideology. It had instead projected the image of "the party of the national economy and the state, the party of the community rather than the market, the party of protection, imperialism, paternalism, and intervention, not the party of free trade, cosmopolitanism, self-help, and laissez-faire" (Gamble 1983: 119). In Ontario, the Conservatives under Bill Davis stretched their party's stay in power to forty two years (1943–1985) by monopolizing the middle ground of politics and ruling by consensus.

The disintegration of the British Empire and the historic decline of the British economy after the Second World War, and especially the failures of Edward Heath's government in the early 1970s, led to a major realignment of the Conservative Party. With Margaret Thatcher's rise to power, the Conservative Party became the vehicle of a radical *neo-conservative* attack on the welfare state that shattered the post-war social-democratic consensus. Thatcherite neo-conservatism can be characterized as a combination of social market ideology (neo-liberalism) and authoritarian populism (class resentment, nationalism, racism, imperialist nostalgia)—what Joan Smith calls "class war conservatism" (Smith 1995: 188; Gough 1983: 154; Gamble 1983). Both components of class war conservatism—neo-liberalism and authoritarian populism—target the welfare state, because it is seen by the first as interfering with the proper functioning of a market economy, and by the second as encouraging immoral, deviant and criminal behaviour that undermines the central social institutions of work, family and state (Gough 1983: 154–155).

The social market ideology holds that a strictly capitalist society provides greater individual freedom than any other form of social order: it frees individuals from the tyranny of the state and dependence on others, subjects them all equally to the forces of the market, and allows them to succeed or fail on the basis of their own abilities, initiative, risk-taking and hard work. In this scenario there needs to be a strong state to ensure that the rules of the marketplace and the sanctity of private property are respected by all. Beyond this, however, the state must not interfere with the workings of the market. All forms of government regulation of the economy, whether of financial markets through regulations on banks or of labour markets through minimum wage legislation, laws guaranteeing trade union rights, unemployment insurance, etc. are regarded by neo-conservatives with considerable reservations, if not outright suspicion.

While most believers in the social market doctrine would accept the need for some support for the destitute, the sick and the elderly, this is to be kept to a minimum so as to interfere as little as possible with market outcomes. Anything else would be inefficient and even immoral (Seldon 1995). In their eyes, "social justice resides not in what individuals get, but in the rules governing how they get it. In return for economic liberty, individuals must reconcile themselves to great and often arbitrary inequalities" (Gamble 1983: 114). It follows from these principles that the welfare state with its large public sector must be unproductive and parasitical, leeching wealth away from those sectors of society that create it (i.e. business) and giving it to those that do not (i.e. the poor, public servants). Thatcherism has these ideas in common with Mike Harris's Tories and the American Right.

In the name of its social market philosophy, the Thatcher government proceeded to dismantle many alternatives to the market; to privatize and commercialize public services, such as water and electric power utilities, nationalized industries, the health service, post-secondary education and so on; to abolish or hobble local government; to attack national minimum standards for services; to eliminate universal social programs, in particular to replace social insurance principles with means testing; to shift responsibility for support and care from the state to the family; to replace unemployment benefits with a "job seeker's allowance" (substituting a market-oriented policy for one more oriented to income support); to replace social housing with private home ownership; to curtail trade union rights drastically; to use unemployment to discipline labour; to increase bureaucratic control over welfare recipients; to replace property- and income-based taxes with flat taxes (such as the infamous poll tax).

Broadly speaking, this is the same agenda that the Harris government has announced and begun to implement: the large income tax cuts spelled out in the 1996 provincial budget, which are to be compensated for by the introduction of various flat taxes, such as user fees; a massive attack on trade union rights and employment standards (Bill 7); huge cuts to social assistance benefits; workfare; a freeze on the construction of new social housing and the privatization of existing public housing; the privatization and commercialization of public services and institutions (e.g. Ontario Hydro, TV Ontario); the centralization of bureaucratic and political control over the public sector and broader public sector by way of the abolition of consultative bodies and local authorities (Bill 26, the "Omnibus Bill").

Components of Thatcherite Ideology: Authoritarian Populism
British society in the 1970s was in many ways characterized by the persistence of diverging class cultures, made manifest in differing linguistic idioms and accents, table manners, ways of dressing, preferred forms of entertainment, and so on. The resulting stratification to some extent hindered social and economic mobility and, together with the enduring feudal institutions of the British state (monarchy, House of Lords, etc.) bred corporatist mentalities in the working class as much as in the aristocracy or the middle class. Such corporatism, mixed with the culture of trade unionism, served as a powerful defensive rampart against social and economic change.

The Thatcher government could not have implemented its neo-conservative agenda in such a context without translating it into a "populist idiom," without "hard-faced economics" being converted "into the language of compulsive moralism" by what Stuart Hall dubbed "authoritarian populism." Entrenched feelings of class identity had to be broken and replaced with an individualistic, consumerist mentality oriented towards personal gain and private family life. Arthur Seldon, who was an important ideological influence on Margaret Thatcher's Tories through the Institute of Economic Affairs, describes radical conservatism as:

> the philosophy that sees the prime mover of social and economic vitality and advance in the individual and his family. This is not to erect self-interest, or selfishness, as the mainspring of human conduct. It is to recognize that, except in short bursts of war or emergency, men can work only for the people and the purposes they know, and understand, and love: their families, their friends, their personal, local, causes, clubs, churches, hospitals, schools (Seldon 1995: 347).

At the same time, an alternative sense of collective identity had to be fostered. Two ideological strategies stand out in particular, patriotism and the emphasis on "values":

> "Being British" became once again identified with the restoration of competition and profitability; with tight money and sound finance...—the national economy debated on the model of the household budget. The essence of the British people was identified with self-reliance and personal responsibility, as against the image of the over-taxed individual, enervated by welfare state "coddling," his or her moral fibre irrevocably sapped by "state handouts." This assault, not just on welfare over-spending, but on the very principle and essence of collective social welfare...was mounted... through the emotive image of the "scrounger": the new folk-devil (Hall 1983: 28–29).

The "folk devils" were both inside and outside of Britain. In pushing renewed patriotism, the Thatcher government could rely on the popular memory of the Second World War when Britons had learned to endure great hardship uncomplainingly, pulling together against a common foe. And of course, the Conservatives were saved by their daring but successful gamble of going to war with Argentina, after the latter had seized the Malvinas (Falkland Islands) in the South Atlantic. Argentinian generals and Irish terrorists were useful figures against whom to rally the British people.

But inside the country, the poor and unemployed could be vilified as "not pulling their weight," by exploiting traditional middle- and working-class notions of self-reliance. Gays and lesbians could be demonized in a climate of moral panic around the spread of AIDS. The sale of public housing to individual tenants could draw on deeply-held values of privacy ("an Englishman's home is his castle").

In attacking the poor, the Chrétien and Harris governments have been hunting down similar folk devils and pursuing their own forms of nationalism in their rhetoric about the country's debt crisis (see Weinroth, Chapter 4). Of course, Ontario society displays much less overt and entrenched class cultures than Britain did. The social resistance to the neo-conservative cultural onslaught is consequently of a different nature. A highly individualistic ideology already prevails in Ontario. And although there is strong support for some universal social programs, such as medicare, it has been extremely easy for the Ontario Conservatives to establish workfare, tax cuts, and rolling back government as the main foundation of their popularity.

The official statements by Mike Harris's Conservatives all emphasize the idea that people do not look beyond the bounds of their families and ought not to do so. The 1995 Throne Speech celebrates this individualism: "Ms. Mason and the Harts already have plans for the dollars the tax cut will return to them. For Ms. Mason, it's home improvements; for the Harts, it's replacing an appliance, or new clothes for their children" (Throne Speech 1995: 2).

Similarly, the Harris government's attack on affirmative action policies exploits the populist belief that individuals are solely responsible for their own fate and that none should therefore be given any special consideration. It also banks on less openly voiced fears among men and the majority white, English-speaking population, that women and minorities might overcome their hitherto subordinate position in society and threaten the dominance of those who have enjoyed all the privileges.

The Essence of Thatcherism: Class-War Conservatism
The Harris and Thatcher governments' hostility to the welfare state finds its voice in the social-market doctrine and its concepts of individualism and market freedom. But in seeking to understand what drives these governments, it would be naive to take their self-justifications at face value. They may claim to act in order to maximize individual liberty. Yet their policies further the interests of some individuals and undermine the interests of others.

The welfare state in Western societies developed very much as a compromise between capital and labour (Esping-Andersen 1989; Pierson 1991; Struthers 1995; Banting 1986; Cloward and Piven 1993; Massé 1995; Offe 1984; Teeple 1995). It brought about a significant redistribution of wealth, vastly increasing access to affordable housing, health care, education and social services for most people. This "social democratic settlement" satisfied the most pressing demands of the working class, while meeting the interests of business by fostering social peace and making possible the consumer society.

The welfare state may help or hinder long term economic growth. The redistribution of wealth puts more money into the pockets of more people. The resulting increase in consumption stimulates the economy. On the other hand, the greater power and higher standard of living of the working class exacerbates the conflict between capital and labour. State policies to redistribute wealth and guarantee everyone protection from the risk of ill health, homelessness or unemployment "remove part of the real living standards of the working class from the wage system, and allocate this part according to some criteria of social need and citizenship. Citizenship rights are counterposed [sic] to property rights" (Gough 1983: 160). Employers' power within the workplace and the market in general is somewhat curtailed.

The decisive issue, as Ian Gough argues, is how a welfare state may either subvert or complement market mechanisms—and in his view, the pre-Thatcherite British welfare state was not able to adapt to accomplish the latter. The British trade union movement was able, from the 1950s to the 1970s, to increase and then maintain its members' share of the national wealth quite successfully. At the same time, Britain's social policies were not linked, as in Sweden or West Germany, to economic policies designed to boost the competitiveness, productivity and profitability of private enterprise. As the crisis of Britain's post-imperial economy deepened in the 1970s, the trade union movement had the defensive strength to thwart any moves to restrict its power or restructure the economy. The key example of British trade union power is the strike by the powerful National Union of Mineworkers that effectively toppled the Conservative government of Ted Heath in the early 1970s. The central concern of the Thatcher government was to destroy this power of organized labour, and to make the interests of private enterprise absolutely paramount within the British state.

Since the labour movement had the power to bring down a Tory government in 1974, how was Margaret Thatcher able to rout it in the early 1980s? The explanation lies in the nature of trade union power and its political expression in the Labour Party.

Despite its considerable success in influencing the distribution of wealth, the trade union movement did not in any way question the capitalist system or attempt to secure for itself any far-reaching control over the production of wealth. In the context of a long term decline in rates of profit, combined with a post-imperial economy's weakness with respect to its major competitors, the trade union movement profited from the welfare state. Yet it was neither dominant in society, nor able to put forward a viable and practical political alternative to the right.

Between 1974 and 1979, the left-wing Labour Party, a party intimately connected to the trade union movement, was in power. Following on the miners' defeat of the Heath government, this seemed to open the way to fundamental realignments and changes in British society. Yet Labour's five years in power rather paved the way for the longest running and most right-wing Conservative government of the 20th century.

Social democratic parties such as the Labour Party display a fundamental contradiction (Hall 1983): in order to win power, they must position themselves as the representatives of the working class, as the agents capable of mastering

42

social and political crises and defending workers' interests. While social democratic parties are in opposition, a strong class-to-party relationship develops, mediated by extensive corporatist bargaining between the party and unions. This link between unions and party is what gave Labour its claim to be the natural governing party in Britain's political and economic crisis of the 1970s.

Once in power, however, social democrats see their mission as managing the economy within the parameters of capitalism. They must therefore win the consent and support of significant elements in the world of business. But, as Stuart Hall puts it, "this requires that the indissoluble link between party and class be used not to advance but to discipline the class and the organizations it represents" (Hall 1983: 27). Typically, social democratic parties shed or transform the class-to-party relationship, replacing it with a discourse about their special relationship as a government to the whole nation (Hall 1983: 27), a claim frequently heard from Bob Rae's 1990–1995 NDP government in Ontario with respect to the whole electorate (Walkom 1994).

Thus, while the 1974–1979 Labour government pursued a corporatist strategy of consultation with the trade union leadership through its so-called "social contract," its strategies for managing the economy included the implementation of neo-liberal economic policies and the "disciplining" of labour, culminating in the 1978–1979 wave of strikes by the most poorly paid sectors of the organized labour movement, the so-called "winter of discontent" that heralded Thatcher's coming to power.

In Ontario, similarly, the Rae government did an about-face on many of its election promises, such as public automobile insurance. On the key issue of the deficit, it capitulated to the Right's insistence that the province's fiscal crisis had to override all other concerns and could only be dealt with by restraints on public spending. The logical consequence was the Ontario version of the social contract, which scrapped public service collective agreements and rolled back public servants' wages and benefits. The resulting breach between the NDP and the public sector unions, as well as deepening divisions within the labour movement itself, sealed the NDP's doom in the 1995 general election.

Ontario Conservatives, then, like their British counterparts under Margaret Thatcher, came to power on the ruins of a social-democratic government (the NDP in Ontario, Labour in Britain) that had already abandoned many of its own principles and embraced neo-liberal economic doctrines.

In order to raise profits at the expense of workers' incomes, the Thatcher government had to break the resistance of organized labour. It adopted economic policies that accelerated the trends intrinsic to the recession of the early 1980s. By keeping tight control over the money supply and very high interest rates, the government sucked money out of domestic industry as well as from abroad into the banking sector, pushing up exchange rates, hampering exports and depressing industrial investment. The outcome was a huge wave of plant closures, deindustrializing whole regions of Great Britain. The resulting unemployment exerted strong downward pressure on wages and seriously weakened trade unions. At the same time, public sector layoffs and cutbacks in social programs made workers more desperate and willing to accept lower pay and inferior working conditions. As Britain emerged from the recession, the profit rates of surviving industries were to increase (Jessop, Bonnett and Bromley 1990; Livingstone 1983: 69).

In Canada, many of the corresponding economic policies were introduced at the federal level in the 1980s by the Mulroney government. The downturn in the business cycle at the end of the 1980s was made much deeper and long-lasting by the Bank of Canada's "anti-inflationary" policy of keeping real interest rates (and consequently the value of the dollar) at a record high. The cost of borrowing became exorbitant and investment in manufacturing much less attractive than investment in financial markets. Many businesses went under; government debt soared. The high dollar made Canadian business less competitive just at the time the Free Trade Agreement with the United States made it more vulnerable. Ontario, as the industrial heartland of Canada, suffered economic devastation as plants closed and unemployment soared.

The increase in the number of unemployed workers and therefore in the supply of labour could only exert a downward pressure on wages, all the more so as the federal government made cuts to unemployment insurance and reduced its contribution to social assistance costs under the Canada Assistance Plan. To its credit, the Rae government did not slash welfare benefits or reduce eligibility; on the contrary, it raised benefits, despite receiving less money from Ottawa. This shielded workers somewhat from the impact on wages of rising unemployment. It is scarcely surprising that the Harris government's first actions should have been to reduce social assistance benefits and greatly weaken the protection afforded workers by the labour laws brought in by the NDP. In carrying out these actions, the Ontario Conservatives were only following through on the assault on workers initiated by their federal counterparts.

To conclude, the objectives of Thatcherism, as of Mike Harris's Ontario Conservatives, were to tilt the balance of wealth and power further towards the private sector and business, and away from the public sector and workers. However, Thatcherism was also about the cultural and ideological transformation of British society, from a corporatist welfare state stratified by region and class culture to an individualistic consumer society stratified by income and property. Finally, Thatcherism came to power, survived and prospered, because of the failings of the Labour Party and the trade union movement. The Left could not provide the people with a credible alternative project for society, let alone translate such a project into a political platform around which a united mass movement could organize and mobilize. Any progressive resistance to Harris's Tories will have to learn to recognize and combat the economic and cultural dimensions of their conservatism, and especially to create a genuine alternative and rally the people of Ontario around it.

Chapter 3

The Ontario Branch
of American Conservatism[1]
André Régimbald

The right-wing policies Ontario is weathering today are based on precepts and dogmas that are far from new to North America. The ideological outpourings of Ontario conservatism flow not only from the fount of Thatcherism, but also from the New Right that sprang forth in the United States during the 1970s and 1980s. Long before Mike Harris's "Common Sense Revolution," conservative American intellectuals like Daniel Bell, Irving Kristol, Charles Murray and George Gilder were speaking out against the welfare state and its social security system. Like Newt Gingrich today, groups such as the American Coalition for Traditional Values sought to recover the "moral purity" of the American nation. Some were even attracted by the right-wing religious fundamentalism of Jerry Falwell's Moral Majority, just as they are today by Ralph Reed's Christian Coalition.

In the area of economic thought, the 1970s and 1980s were dominated by monetarism, supply-side economics, and rational-choice theory which are all characterized by methodological individualism. Although they diverge in their approaches to economic problems, these various schools of thought all aim "to restore the market and free enterprise and to abolish Keynesianism as a legitimate policy option" (Chorney, Hansen and Mendell 1987: 106).

During the 1970s and 1980s, intellectuals, government officials and politicians in the United States, Britain, and even France,[2] were engaged in assessing the outcome of thirty years of Keynesian policies. In Canada, the Macdonald Commission on Canada's economic union and development prospects (1985) inaugurated the conservative and neo-liberal redefinition of the Canadian state. The Commission's report stated that governments should generally work to enhance the functioning of market mechanisms, rather than seek to intervene more in the economy (Guest 1993: 335). Criticism of the welfare state was very much a feature of the intellectual climate of the 1980s.

An Economic Critique of the Welfare State
The Chicago School played an important part in criticizing the welfare state. Influenced by the work of the pro-free-market economist and anti-socialist philosopher Friedrich von Hayek, the Chicago School became dominant in the 1970s and 1980s. Under the leadership of Milton Friedman, it became the focal point of a virulent critique of state interventionism and equity-seeking social policies.

Besides their emphasis on the role of the money supply in the economy, monetarists spread the view that government intervention destabilizes the economy. In their view, capitalist economies tend toward equilibrium by virtue of market laws. Government intrusion into the economy disrupts the economy more than it stabilizes it. State intervention is therefore deleterious. Monetarists thus reject workplace health and safety standards, minimum-wage policies, regulations affecting the prices of goods and services, and the existence of state monopolies (post office, power utilities, nationalized industries) (Élie 1982: 168). The best states are those that withdraw from economic activity and abolish all regulations.

Whatever school of thought American conservative intellectuals draw inspiration from, they all base their criticism of the social state and welfare policies on the ideology of individualism. Their fundamental belief is that individuals are solely responsible for their respective successes and failures. The only thing that counts for conservatives is the "ethic of individual responsibility" (Gingrich 1995: 33).

Characteristically, conservatives accept and legitimize the inequality of individual conditions and fortunes. Conservatives of all stripes see inequality not only as the natural outcome of free market activity, but as economically productive. Echoing John Locke and Jeremy Bentham, they believe that "the rich man is the poor man's bank, the latter benefiting from the former's industry and rationality; consequently...'society' owes thanks to the owners of capital, who invest, take risks, take chances" (Saunders 1988: 86). It goes without saying that the income redistribution policies that have typified the welfare state for the past fifty years conflict with such beliefs.

The conservative approach led directly to the macroeconomic monetarist and supply-side theories that governed economic policy under the Reagan administration. The tax cuts awarded wealthy Americans—like the tax cuts introduced by the Harris government—were inspired by the supply-side approach expounded by Arthur Laffer and Jan P. Seymour in their book, *The Economics of the Tax Revolt* (1979). Laffer was the mind behind the tax revolt that swept California in 1978 when Ronald Reagan was state governor, leading to the notorious Proposition 13. Laffer and Seymour spelled out the future creed of "Reaganomics": "taxes on high incomes and profits discourage initiative, savings and productive endeavour" (Beaud and Dostaler 1993: 157). Laffer and his followers blamed excessive taxation for the major problems of modern economies. "Tax rates must be lowered and income taxes made less progressive in order to stimulate supply and kick-start production" (Beaud and Dostaler 1993: 396).

This view of taxation was linked to "trickle-down" economics, according to which the further enrichment of the rich eventually benefits the poor. Cutting taxes for the wealthy was supposed to lead to an investment and employment boom. The Reagan administration used Laffer's theories to justify the $749 billion tax cut it awarded high-income earners and corporations over a four-year period. In his first report on the economy, Ronald Reagan declared that instead of using the tax system to redistribute income, his policy had been to restructure it significantly in order to encourage people to work, save and invest more[3] (Beaud and Dostaler 1993: 164). Chorney, Hansen and Mendell point out that adepts of monetarism and supply-side economics, like Norman Ture and Beryl Sprinkle, had a decisive influence on the Reagan administration's economic policies (Chorney, Hansen and Mendell 1987: 106). That is not even to mention the direct influence of Milton Friedman, who was an advisor to Presidents Nixon and Reagan (the latter appointed him to the Economic Policy Advisory Board).

Reaganism and Ontario Conservatism:
Ideological Foundations and Political Objectives
In the early 1980s, the recurring themes of the American Right seduced a population attempting to deal with the de-industrialization of the United States, the rise in unemployment, the economic insecurity of the middle class, and a decline in American imperial power in comparison with the economic success of the Asian bloc.

In Ontario, similar economic conditions caused the electorate to find in Mike Harris's Conservative Party an answer to the crisis afflicting the province since 1990. The de-industrialization and industrial restructuring of Ontario has combined with the rise in unemployment and the increase in the number of people on social assistance to bring back those who, as in the United States, have been able to present the resurrection of the past as a promise for the future (Wills 1987). Today, the Conservative Party in Ontario espouses a "fundamentalist" outlook which closely resembles the "conservative verities" summed up by Robert Nisbet:

> a minimal state, a strong but unobtrusive government, *laissez-faire* in most matters, family, neighbourhood, local community, church and other mediating groups to meet most crises, decentralization, localism, and a preference for tradition and experience over rationalist planning, and withal an unconquerable prejudice against redistributionist measures (Nisbet 1986: 95).

In this anti-collectivist and anti-state outlook, the belief in freedom and responsibility for self blends with the traditional conservative themes expressed by Edmund Burke: obeying authority, respecting tradition, preserving social stability (Saunders 1988: 76).

The ideological postulates of Reaganism are a clever mixture of the conservative values of the past described by Nisbet, and the economic dogmas of a hard-line liberalism converted to supply-side economics and monetarism. With the exception of the religious element that traditionally links conservatism and Christian fundamentalism in the United States, American and Ontario conservatives share the same ideological postulates.

What is happening in Ontario is quite reminiscent of the Reagan administration's economic and social program. During its two mandates (1981-1988), the Reagan administration implemented the following program:

- Taxes on high incomes were cut by $749 billion; taxes on gifts and inheritances were massively reduced.
- Social spending was cut by $112 billion, especially in the area of social assistance.
- In 1981, Congress passed a bill establishing compulsory workfare for the heads of single-parent families on AFDC (Aid to Families with Dependent Children), as well as reducing AFDC by $1.2 billion. This excluded 500,000 families from the program. In 1987, the Reagan administration cut a further $5.25 billion from the program.
- Housing subsidies were drastically reduced and the construction of low-income housing was halted.
- Rents for public housing went from 25 percent to 30 percent of tenants' incomes.
- Legal aid for the poor was reduced by a third.
- A review of federal social programs was accompanied by intensive reassessment of each recipient's file.
- The in-depth investigation of each program was justified in the name of presumed generalized fraud and abuse, the campaign against alleged dishonesty and laziness constituting a useful strategy to mobilize public support.
- Most community groups that help the underprivileged, women, and immigrants were stricken from federal funding lists.
- Medicaid (health care for the poorest members of the population) was cut by $1.1 billion in 1981 and more than $4 billion between 1982 and 1985.
- The minimum wage was frozen in 1981.
- As a result of federal government withdrawal from aid to the poor, volunteers and charities were expected to bring relief to the unfortunate. As with the Harris government today, voluntary agencies were charged with making up for the insufficiency of state funding without however being given the means to do so (Lesemann 1988).

In the United States, as in Ontario, the aim was clearly to pull the carpet out from under the popular organizations that might have fought back against the conservative agenda.

The May 1996 budget speech, following on *The Common Sense Revolution* and the Throne Speech, promised Ontario the "volunteer revolution" so dear to the American conservative Right since it goes hand in hand with its critique of the welfare state and its bureaucracy: "Promoting and encouraging both the spirit and the commitment of volunteers is a high priority for our government. We all understand that Ontarians working together can do much more for their communities than government can do alone" (Eves 1996: 13). It is thus scarcely surprising to find that the treasurer of Ontario intends "to improve regulation and provide a higher yield to charities" (Eves 1996: 13). The rationale for such measures finds a lyrical expression in Newt Gingrich's nostalgic remarks: "the last part of the nineteenth century and the years before World War I were the golden age of volunteerism." It was the era when "people turned first not to government, but to themselves and their neighbours when they sought to solve problems" (Gingrich 1995: 104).

The overriding goal of the conservative revolution is to weaken the idea and efficiency of the welfare state; state intervention that benefits the working and middle classes is to cease, leaving the business elite in full control. Income security and redistribution policies are rejected because they do not correspond to hard-line liberal values. According to the ideals of the Republican Party in the United States, such policies are at odds with the spiritual and moral dimensions of what Newt Gingrich calls "American civilization." This "civilization" has always, in his view, emphasized "personal responsibility as much as individual rights." But today, there is a situation of great urgency: "our civilization is at risk" (Gingrich 1995: 7). Newt Gingrich and other U.S. conservatives of the recent and more distant past identify American values with the values of a capitalism purged of all government intervention. To them, therefore, the welfare state is a real threat.

Of course, Ontario conservatives refrain from evoking "a threat to civilization." However, they too consider government economic and social intervention to have been a failure. In their eyes, the state is an obstacle to overthrow: "We live in a province whose potential is unlimited. We have skilled and hard-working people, abundant resources, and innovative entrepreneurs. We have every reason to expect a future that is better than today—with better jobs, greater prosperity, a better life for ourselves, and real hope for our children. But we can't get there with the size of government that has been built up over the years. Government is bigger and more costly than it needs to be" (Eves 1996: 2). The goal is clearly to do away with what Gingrich calls "the modern infatuation with big government" (Gingrich 1995: 101).

Dismantling the Welfare State

Conservatives past and present blame the welfare state for all economic woes. It is accused of sapping the spirit of free enterprise, of fostering an attitude of dependency in the population as a whole but especially among workers, and of having burdened future generations with excessive debt in order to pay for its extravagant programs. "We run a deficit because we have become a huge welfare state with massive transfer payments and a big centralized bureaucracy" (Gingrich 1995: 89).

Republicans in the south and Conservatives in the north blame income security policies, such as unemployment insurance and social assistance, for weakening the work ethic or at least the incentive to work. In their view, such policies strip individuals of their responsibility for themselves. No other unintended outcome of social programs is as damaging to the work ethic of the poor as the creation of dependency (the so-called "welfare trap"). This was a key message of George Gilder's *Wealth and Poverty* (1981), considered the bible of the Reagan revolution. Criticizing President Johnson's 1964 War on Poverty, Gilder, like his Republican contemporaries, complained that "in the time since the war on poverty was launched, the moral blight of dependency has been compounded and extended to future generations by a virtual plague of family dissolution" (Gilder 1981: 12). This is echoed today by Newt Gingrich:

> The Welfare State reduces the poor from citizens to clients. It breaks up families, minimizes work incentives, blocks people from saving and acquiring property, and overshadows dreams of a promised future with a present despair born of poverty, violence, and hopelessness. (Gingrich 1995: 71)

This point of view is now part and parcel of Conservative rhetoric in Ontario. *The Common Sense Revolution* speaks of a social assistance system that "demands responsible behaviour from recipients of public assistance" (Ontario Progressive Conservative Party 1995: 9). The Harris government presents workfare as a measure to transform social assistance into an instrument of lasting progress rather than of temporary help; it insists that social assistance must not create "dependency," but encourage autonomy (Throne Speech 1995: 7-8). The goal is above all to support the "deserving" poor, i.e. "to help those most in need and those who genuinely want a hand up, not a hand-out" (Ontario Progressive Conservative Party 1995: 9). More than ever, "initiative and hard work are [to be] rewarded once again" (Ontario Progressive Conservative Party 1995: 4). For the Conservatives, like their neo-liberal cousins, social assistance is only acceptable if it targets the "truly needy." In the budget speech, this point of view gives rise to a policy by virtue of which seniors and people with disabilities already receiving benefits will get more favourable treatment than those who are deemed "employable." The Ontario government will not only move seniors and eligible people with disabilities off welfare, it will also create a new program (the Guaranteed Support Program), thanks to which they will enjoy benefits denied other social assistance recipients since July 1995: "a Plan that meets their needs, respects their dignity, and continues to protect their benefits" (Eves 1996: 7).

The 22 percent cut to social assistance benefits in 1995, as well as the workfare program and further social assistance cuts promised in 1996, show that the Ontario Conservatives have been keen students of American neo-conservative teachings: "The crucial goal should be to restrict the system (welfare) as much as possible, by making it unattractive and even a bit demeaning" (Gilder 1981: 117).

The Harris government implicitly subscribes to what Irving Kristol draws from Tocqueville, namely an inextricable connection between public relief and poverty: "A law which gives all the poor a right to public aid, whatever the origin of their poverty, weakens or destroys the first stimulant (the need to live) and leaves only the second intact (the desire to improve the conditions of life)" (Kristol 1995: 44). As George Gilder puts it: "In order to succeed, the poor need most of all the spur of their poverty" (Gilder 1981: 118). For Kristol, as for the "common sense" premier, the "welfare explosion"—whether in the United States in the 1960s or Ontario in the 1990s—can be explained by tried and tested behavioural theories:

> 1) The number of poor people who are eligible for welfare will increase as one elevates the official definitions of 'poverty' and 'need.'
> 2) The number of eligible poor who actually apply for welfare will increase as welfare benefits go up.... When welfare payments (and associated benefits...) compete with low wages, they outstrip them. (Kristol 1995: 47)

The Common Sense Revolution claims that Ontario "pays the highest welfare benefits not only in Canada, but anywhere in North America," and that this "is one of the reasons our welfare caseload has swollen to record levels" (Ontario Progressive Conservative Party 1995: 11). The Ontario Conservative Party shares Kristol's diagnosis: "A liberal and compassionate social policy has bred all sorts of unanticipated and perverse consequences" (Kristol 1995: 48). There was no need to be a prophet to understand what the Ontario Tories intended to do in the name of restoring "work incentives" and eradicating "perverse consequences" (see Hirschman 1991).

Today, as in the past, conservatism questions the validity of the social policies conceived at the end of the Second World War. According to Newt Gingrich, only one course of action can put America back on the road to prosperity and a sense of responsibility:

> we must replace the welfare state with an opportunity society...yet today too many Americans are bound in bureaucracies and antihuman regulations by which families are destroyed, the work ethic is undermined, male responsibility is made irrelevant, and young mothers find themselves trapped in a world where "income maintenance" replaces opportunity. (Gingrich 1995: 8)

Almost a decade after the Reagan era, the American Right is once again rallying America to a conservative holy war. The Ontario Conservative Party has heard the call and has adopted the program of the American conservative revolution: "The government needs to look at the changes in taxation, litigation, regulation, education, welfare, and government bureaucracies in order to encourage innovation and discovery" (Gingrich 1995: 60).

Opening Ontario for Business

Five of Newt Gingrich's six themes (taxation, regulation, education, welfare, and government bureaucracy) are taken up as the basic goals of the Ontario Conservative Party's electoral platform, *The Common Sense Revolution*: 1) to cut provincial income taxes; 2) to cut non-priority public spending (priority services being education, law and order, and health care); 3) to remove government obstacles to job creation, investment and economic growth; 4) to reduce the size of government; and 5) to balance the provincial budget. In addition to these basic goals, other objectives include reforming welfare, reforming education, and reorganizing the bureaucracy. The policies announced in the 1995 Throne Speech and the May 1996 budget are designed to implement these goals, which are both political and economic.

As for the deficit and the urgency of balancing the budget, the language and arguments used by Ontario Tories recall those of Newt Gingrich. They are the arguments most frequently put forward by North American conservative think tanks and by many politicians: "There are three essential reasons to balance the federal budget. First, it is morally the right thing to do. Second, it is financially the right thing to do. Third, each of us has a personal stake in it" (Gingrich 1995: 87). Economic and financial issues are never detached from the moral dimension in the conservative mind.

Under the strong influence of monetarism and supply-side economics, the Conservative Party claims that government regulation, payroll taxes "that kill jobs" (Eves 1996: 30), employment legislation—such as anti-scab laws—and even the income tax, are obstacles to job creation, savings and investment (Ontario Progressive Conservative Party 1995: 14, 15). The November 1995 *Fiscal and Economic Statement* is categorical on the subject: "Payroll taxes like the Employer Health Tax and workers' compensation premiums have also worked against job creation. So have artificially high minimum wages, legislated job quotas and other government intrusions" (Government of Ontario 1995: 6). As regards taxes, the May 1996 budget speech is uncompromising: "Unless we reduce our current levels of taxation, we will never create enough jobs to give Ontarians a secure future. We will never generate enough revenues to balance the budget" (Eves 1996: 30). "These tax cuts will mean more jobs for Ontarians. People will have more dollars to spend, more dollars to pay down their debts, more dollars to invest in new businesses, and more incentive to create jobs in Ontario" (Eves 1996: 32).

The goal of the Conservative crusade is to "free enterprise" from the government straitjacket: "the new government will restore prosperity, free the private sector to create jobs, and meet the challenge of renewing Ontario" (Throne Speech 1995: 1). The ultimate aim is to work at "unshackling business" (Throne Speech 1995: 2). "Restrictions that cannot be justified will be eliminated within 12 months" (Throne Speech 1995: 3). The treasurer could not have put it more clearly: "Ontarians want an economy that is freed from the burdens of red tape and overtaxation—where individuals have the opportunity and the means to set goals for themselves and for their communities" (Government of Ontario 1995: 1). "We must restore the environment that allows businesses to create jobs" (Eves 1996: 19). The idiom may not be new, but by contrast the ideological fervour is.

Conclusion

In attempting to explain why neo-conservatism was successful in the United States in the 1980s, but not in the 1960s, Irving Kristol points to the element that Ontario Tories have been able to exploit in the current context: "The new message—that dependency corrupts and that absolute dependency tends to corrupt absolutely—has given a moral dimension to welfare reform that it had lacked" (Kristol 1995: 379). For the first time in decades, Ontario is faced with a Thatcher/Reagan populist social conservatism that seeks to colour economic and social problems with a moral dimension. In Ontario, as elsewhere, this type of conservatism seduces the electorate, because it speaks to the heart. There has hitherto been a tendency to underestimate the psychological and political impact of the spiritual void this ideology seeks to fill. This moral dimension may be conservatism's great strength, but it may be its greatest weakness too.

Notes
1. Translated from the French by Paul Leduc Browne.
2. Intellectuals such as Alain Minc denounced the welfare state for "despoiling the sovereignty of the individual"(Minc 1987).
3. Trickle-down economics prompted John Kenneth Galbraith to remark that its proponents wanted to convince the public "that if the horse is fed amply with oats, some will pass through to the road for the sparrows" (Hobsbawm 1995).

Chapter 4

Deficitism and Neo-Conservatism in Ontario
Michelle Weinroth

Introduction

In a society governed by science and technology, statistics are not only endowed with enormous legitimacy, they are virtually sacred. Daunting and seemingly unchallengeable, such "facts" are all the more disarming when they surface in official fiscal statements like those defining Canada's current deficit. But while government figures on the economic crisis may appear absolute, they are inextricably bound to socio-economic perspective, political interests and ideological power.[1] That there have been conflicting views over these otherwise purely quantitative definitions of the national debt makes this amply clear. Indeed, while Paul Martin is content to bring the deficit down to 3 percent of GDP by the fiscal year 1996–97, right-wing ideologues and think tanks, credit firms and speculators deem the situation intolerable. At the other end of the gamut stand the Canadian Centre for Policy Alternatives and CHO!CES with their Alternative Budget. Registering the deficit as critical, these organizations nonetheless contest the neo-liberal and conservative prognoses as sensationalist, claiming that Martin's target suffices and can be reached readily without harsh measures.

As the debates rage on, Paul Martin struggles to make his official pronouncements seem consensually acceptable to all Canadians. Indeed, if the finance minister's ambition to balance the budget seems great enough, his need to *persuade* the public of his fiscal approach is just as significant. For his task and that of his neo-liberal colleagues is not merely one of devising new fiscal policies; it is also primarily a propagandist project in which his partisan views must exude an authority that can regulate public opinion.

So while the deficit can be readily quantified, it cannot be unequivocally qualified. Political debate on the matter draws on economic facts but functions as ideology. The sober recognition of proliferating debt grows amid right-wing pundits and politicians into a manipulative artifice of propaganda and social control. Call it *deficitism*, an exaggerated furore over our economic malaise that has acted as a catalyst of neo-liberal and neo-conservative hegemony. Appropriated by ideologues of differing persuasions, it reveals more about the respective ideological propensities and political motivations of its upholders than about the national debt itself.

Mike Harris's Common Sense Revolution is a case in point. In what follows, I shall argue that deficitism provides the litmus test through which to identify the premier's whole approach to achieving and maintaining political power. Harris used deficitism as a catalyst of neo-conservative hegemony thanks to precedents set by other governments, most particularly by the federal Liberals' consummate deficit campaign in 1994 and 1995. The latter not only helped form the matrix upon which Harris built his own electoral success, it engendered the nationalist fervour that enabled him to render austerity measures perversely acceptable to many Ontarians. But while the federal Liberals' deficit ideology furnished a preparatory ground for Harris's fiscal *coup d'état*, he did not carry forward their proselytizing efforts. He did not deploy deficitism in consensual fashion; rather he exploited it for the purposes of justifying a coercive authoritarianism and a hasty pragmatism that is now destroying large portions of Ontario's public sector. In his promise to reduce Ontario's debt, Harris has made deficitism an easy pretext for authoritarianism and prejudice against the poor. If allowed to hold sway, these two ideological forces which underpin his Common Sense Revolution will irrevocably change the face of Ontario.

Federal Deficitism
Deficitism

Deficitism emerges from an apparently pure definition of economic fact—that we are in the "red"—and develops into an ideological strategy for securing hegemonic dominance and political trust from the people. Voiced in the name of collective sacrifice—"we all have to pull together to save our country from bankruptcy"—it resembles the patriotic zeal and jingoism of war-mongering ideologues who in former times rallied young men to the trenches for God, Nation and Liberty. But like every form of right-wing nationalist rhetoric, it is duplicitous. There is always an oligarchy that preaches but does not practice its sermon. The rhetoric on the debt has become a *supra*nationalism dictated by a Canadian elite dreaming of a corporate New Jerusalem. It has transcended Canada's ethnic and provincial rifts[2], while retaining all the motifs of traditional nationalist furore: the impassioned and self-righteous mission to conquer a foe. Deficitism or corporate nationalism has come forth, apparently to defy the raging deficit, but in reality to reshape the configuration of postwar Canadian society.

Like every ideology, deficitism is most persuasive when it orchestrates a system of beliefs that play on the public's sense of guilt and fear, as well as its hopes for redemption. In lieu of rational argumentation, it creates an all-consuming political environment that compels the public to yield its critical spirit to the dogmas of debt culture. Thus the federal anti-deficit campaign presented an inflammatory picture of Canadian society in crisis, which unleashed the public's deep anxieties, fostered moral outrage over an enemy, and inspired fervent belief in collective sacrifice as a form of salvation from the country's economic distress. This discourse usurped the political stage and elevated "deficit-fighting" economics into a drama of palpable urgency.

Inflating the Crisis

By simulating the pressures of an objective force, the imminent threat of fiscal ruin, the Liberals were able to treat the deficit as a national emergency, a warlike crisis (Martin 1995; Flood 1994). They flooded the media with reports on the deficit, saturating the political context with a discourse of numbers that grew pervasively familiar to ordinary citizens. They made the deficit a popular, household preoccupation, no longer the exclusive interest of expert economists. Not that the average Canadian could really conceive of the magnitude or significance of overwhelming figures. Yet they seemed formidable and foreshadowed disaster. Pressure rose as the debt clock in Vancouver illuminated the figures of doom (Martin and Savidan 1994). Predictions of the debt's ceaseless proliferation instilled greater fear; comments like those of Peter Cook that by the year 2000, Canada's debt would reach one trillion dollars (Cook 1994) could only nonplus the quizzical public. In this heightened climate of crisis, cool intellect was forsaken as the government's alarm spurred individuals to believe in the necessity of swift action, in a conservative/neo-liberal agenda which had been declared inexorable and ultimately beneficial. Throughout, government rhetoric maintained its consensual force by using an all-encompassing and thus *seemingly impartial* question of fiscal distress to ensure its own rectitude in the face of public opinion.

The Elusive Enemy

The concept of a national crisis was also intertwined with the construction of an enemy before which the aggrieved Canadian community could witness its own peril. A useful scapegoat to account for the country's economic disarray, this adversary turned out to be multifaceted. On one level, it crystallized as a deficit gone mad, uncontrollably assailing the economy like an unstoppable torrent of debts. Economic collapse, which was continually projected in the ritual recitation of staggering statistics, turned into a virtually tangible, *external* force looming on the horizon beyond. Government officials and corporate executives pronounced with tones of desperation that the rate of the debt's growth was rapacious. Al Flood, chief executive officer of the Canadian Imperial Bank of Canada claimed that "the cumulative federal debt at the federal and provincial levels of government [was] growing at the rate of $60 billion a year" (Flood 1994). Paul Martin's 1994 budget broke the news that the deficit had swelled to $45 billion. "Only a few months earlier the deficit was reported to be $30 billion and the market types were warning that the end was approaching" (McQuaig 1996: 47).

On another level, the deficit was concretized through guilt[3] as an *enemy within us*, our complacent endorsement of "extravagant" government spending (particularly in the area of social programs), an "immoral," indeed "disgraceful" propensity towards fiscal mismanagement. This assumption was largely based on the popular myth that household and public sector debts are synonymous. Thus the reprehensible idea of "going into the red" misleadingly evoked the irresponsibility associated with poorly managed household finances.[4]

The Need for Collective Sacrifice

According to neo-liberal ideologues, the threatening presence of an enemy meant that Canadians had to subscribe to a common purpose and sacrifice themselves equally. Extreme crisis legitimized altruism and an unquestioning genuflexion before the public good. There lay the ideal ethic of national unity. If universally endorsed, it could guarantee the government substantial popular support. Yet this precept of collective sacrifice was spun out of a hollow morality that privileged the corporate aristocracy and penalized the average wage-earner. While thousands of Canadians in all areas of the public sector have reluctantly surrendered their jobs in the name of "downsizing," "restructuring," and "global competitiveness," there is no evidence that corporations forfeited anything. Both on the federal and on the provincial level, the "pious" mission to reduce the deficit was (and remains) ultimately two-faced and vacuous. For in reality, "the goal of austerity and government cutbacks is not to pay down the debt. It is to ensure that the world is kept safe for the money lenders who finance the debt" (Laxer 1996: 8).

As government rhetoric proves more and more duplicitous in its commitment to restore economic stability, the theatre of tragedy upon which deficitism was mounted turns into farce. Increasingly we see that neo-conservative and neo-liberal concerns about an imminent economic apocalypse were manipulative. While Canadians were summoned to surrender their privileges in the name of the commonweal, and with the earnest belief that it was imperative to do so at all costs, government and corporate ideologues secretly sought to sustain the deficit "crisis" as a catalyst of political and economic hegemony. The deficit is a pseudo-enemy: the real enemy turns out to be an entrenched welfare state. It is an obstacle in the entrepreneurial path of the corporate elite, a powerful and privileged group that would sooner not abide by the laws and ethical codes of civic obligation; it would rather chart the course of its financial success regardless of the human needs of other social classes. And since both neo-conservative and neo-liberal governments operate in close alliance with this corporate aristocracy, the welfare state is also the principal beast that they must kill by digging the political ground from under its feet and forcing it to collapse into its own grave. The masters of deficitism—government pundits and right-wing ideologues—have been the grave diggers and their ideological spadework (decrying the prevailing administrative infrastructure of the state) has dug up the turf beneath the public sector, creating an upheaval favourable for Mike Harris and his Common Sense Revolution.

Harris's Deficitism: Designing a Neo-Conservative Hegemony
Coming to Power

On June 8, 1995, Harris and his Progressive Conservatives seized Ontario triumphantly. In their political ascendancy, they brandished the sabre of "economic restructuring," promising to thrash the deficit mercilessly. Within three weeks of coming to power, the Tories cut $1.9 billion in government spending. Corporate and middle-class sectors in Ontario applauded this show of robust action. Welfare recipients and the unemployed, the unions and institutions acting on behalf of the less well-off saw the deficit-cutting sword as a chilling omen of things to come.

The conditions were ripe for Harris's victory. The federal Liberals had secured endorsement for the deficitist agenda. But there was also the political legacy of Bob Rae's Social Contract which caused a breach between the province's labour movement and the government. This factor weakened the unions' confidence in a political party that was capitulating to big business and to a dogmatic belief in deficit reduction that would only open the way for greater neo-conservative and neo-liberal legitimacy. Rae's political work ended in dispersal and failure. Arriving with the mission to restore order from the wreckage allegedly incurred by a previous government whose budget deficit went from $3 to $10 million a year, and whose provincial debt rose from $42 million to $92 billion, Harris was able to capitalize on the NDP's fumbles. Repeatedly he portrayed his predecessors as swindlers and squanderers.

> We inherited a provincial government that spends too much, taxes too much and wastes too much of taxpayers' hard earned money. That style of government has given us a debt of nearly $100 billion...one of the highest tax rates in North America. (Harris 1995a)

But whereas Harris and his colleagues cast aspersions on the Rae government, they refused to acknowledge that the debt did not originate in the latter's excessive spending, but in the Conservative policies of the Mulroney years: 1) former Bank of Canada governor John Crow's monetarist policy (he insisted that the rate of inflation be lowered to zero) forced interest rates to rocket, thus aggravating interest on the debt (Chorney 1989; Jackson 1990, 1990a);[5] 2) the recession of the 1980s and 1990s and the Free Trade Agreement with the U.S. caused a massive loss of jobs, especially in the manufacturing sector; the consequent rise in unemployment meant that government spending on social assistance and other programs (e.g. medicare) increased while less money went to the public purse in the form of tax revenues (cf. Barlow and Campbell 1991; Bellemare and Poulin-Simon 1994; Campbell 1993; Cohen 1995); 3) the federal government slashed its social transfers to the provinces and notably to Ontario, weakening Rae's financial power.

> The federal deficit-shifting onto Ontario in all forms since 1985/86, has increased the provincial debt by almost $23 billion through 1992/93. The provincial debt as of March 31, 1983 was $23.95 billion and was $68.60 billion as of March 31, 1993, an increase of $44.65 billion. Over 50 percent of this increase can be attributed to the federal deficit-shifting over the period.

Per capita debt in Ontario has risen from $2,752 at March 31, 1983 to $6,793 at March 31, 1993. Of the increase of $4,041, about $2,239, or 55 percent, can be attributed to "federal deficit-shifting."

In total, federal direct, indirect, and induced deficit shifting to Ontario and the associated financing costs will be about $9 billion in 1993/94. This is almost all of the estimated $9.5 billion Ontario deficit in 1993/94. In the absence of this shift, Ontario's budget balance would be in deficit by less than $1 billion. (McCracken 1993: 9)

For self-serving reasons, Harris eclipsed all mention of these crucial factors and placed the blame on his opponents.

The premier's deficitist politics also benefited from the path blazed by Ralph Klein in his unswerving mission to cut deeply into Alberta's public health, housing and welfare services. Over the past few years, Klein has become the point of emulation for many a conservative politician looking to the West for a utopian model of swift, unwavering elimination of the deficit.

Cursing the Enemy: the Leviathan of Government

"On behalf of all taxpayers, let me say clearly: Ontarians have had enough of high personal income taxes." (Eves 1995)

Harris never waxed lyrical or messianic over the deficit crisis. His main focus was on getting down to business (literally) and getting the "clean-up job" done. The pragmatics of reducing the deficit consisted in relentless cutbacks, delivered in sanguine fashion. Nonetheless, Harris's deficitist propaganda applied the basic paradigms of deficitism: he retained the crucial element of terror which underpinned the Liberals' rhetoric. Admittedly, he did not elaborate as fully on the national emergency as did the federal ideologues, but with spurious boy scout catechisms, he reminded Ontarians that we are "in this together," that "[w]e must all share in the sacrifices if we are to share in the gains achieved by getting Ontario back on track" (Harris 1995). Never mind that austerity measures "savage the poor today and reward the rich tomorrow" (Walkom 1995: A9). Finally he transposed the mood of terror from a discourse of crisis to that of taxation, into the formidable character of the "enemy of the people": the Leviathan of big government.[6]

The beast of bureaucracy was defined in terms of the two wings of economic administration: revenues and expenditures. Taxation has always struck a negative chord with Canadians (Cohen 1995). It has been perceived as one of the more punitive of government practices, a tithe inflicted on every citizen, a ritual sacrifice for belonging to the community/commonweal. Taxes and the very tedium associated with filing increasingly obscure income tax forms have rankled the public. Moreover, the rare occasion in which ordinary Canadians are in direct touch with public affairs, other than in referendums and elections, is through that fearful annual reminder that their hard-earned income is destined to be excised by decree. Increasingly, the notion of central government is received with public cynicism and disdain. Conscious of this widespread sentiment, newly elected government leaders have frequently sought to offset this imposition with an alluring compensatory note, the promise to reduce or to introduce few, if any new taxes. (Recall George Bush's "no new taxes.")

The second of the two tangents of government administration— expenditures—has more and more become linked with inefficiency, Kafkaesque labyrinths of wasteful and exasperating "red tape," and more remotely with the stultified forms of bureaucracy that used to plague former Eastern bloc regimes. The very notion of a time-worn and inoperative bureaucracy hints at failed socialist regimes and, closer to home, at wanting social democratic institutions such as the NDP. In denouncing overspending, Harris has exuded a scornful morality. In sculpting the menacing countenance of big government, he has criticized existing taxation and played on Canadians' fear that they will be ever more heavily taxed. His neo-conservative doctrine has focused on government's fiscally inefficient and punitive aspects. Under the pretext of balancing the budget, allegedly to "help get Ontario's public debt interest costs under control" and overcome administrative mismanagement and by "(protecting) taxpayers from never-ending tax increases" (Harris 1995: 12), he has postured as a type of saviour, shielding the taxpayer from the claws of government revenues.

Yet, in this rescue mission, Harris betrays the truth: that reducing the deficit is not about balancing the budget at all. Suffice it to look at his much-vaunted tax cut. The latter will "cost \$20 billion—every cent of it borrowed. But Harris and Eves care neither about arithmetic nor about the deficit" (Walkom 1996). Their aim has been to free business from the tangles of taxation and to relieve government of responsibilities for the public good. For them, the quintessence of Ontarian society should be commercial exchange. "Getting our finances in order is not an end in itself—only the start of the process of re-igniting our economy and restoring opportunity and hope to our province" (Harris 1995). "We will create partnerships with private businesses and open our administrative operations to outside competition, where this can save taxpayers money" (Harris 1995). So, as Thomas Walkom has noted, Harris has transformed the citizen into a taxpayer, eroding the concept of a common public interest and focusing exclusively on the individual's desire for private accumulation.

> [T]he public may possess interests that clash with those of private enterprise, interests that may for example, require government to regulate industrial pollution. But the taxpayer does not. His only interest is in paying less. (Walkom 1996: C1)

Thus as taxpayers pay less, the Ontario government abdicates its regulation of the public's interests, limiting the administrative powers of the state, and consolidating the role of the market as *the* regulator of societal relations. The ephemeral and illusory gratification of the tax cut ("more than half of the cut will go to the 13 percent of families with incomes more than $90,000, with the other half divided up among the other 87 percent" [Mackenzie 1996]) has constituted a prime assault on the Leviathan of government.[7]

Deficitism: From Common Sense to Prejudice

In exploiting the two perceived weaknesses of big government—heavy taxation and sprawling bureaucracy—Harris has contributed to the construction of an administrative beast deemed unruly and in need of massive constraint. In this myth-making, such neo-conservative discourse has also foreclosed the possibility of seeing any virtue in taxation and bureaucracy. He has thus effaced the important function of taxes as a source of revenue for the public purse, and has denied the usefulness of bureaucracy as a system of procedures that ensures fairness when citizens seek to defend their individual rights. As John Ralston Saul has argued,

> [i]t is...naive or disingenuous for those leading the fight against government to suggest that society will be reinvigorated by smaller government. Responsibility will simply have been transferred to an equally if not more sluggish bureaucracy in the private sector.... [B]y demonizing the public civil servant they are obscuring the matter of citizenry against the citizen's legitimacy and of the public good which only that legitimacy can produce. People become so obsessed by hating government that they forget it is meant to be their government and is the only powerful public force they have purchase on. (Saul 1995: 75–76)

But that is the point. Harris is keen to divest citizens of their public rights while seducing them with market options. His goal is to ensure that the idea of government will be utterly spurned. And thanks to the neo-conservative caricature of the welfare recipient as a parasitical dependent of the state, as the emblem of a system of a public service allegedly gone awry, the image of big government is, indeed, more effectively besmirched. The welfare recipient proffers the otherwise impersonal administrative structure of government an anthropomorphic identity through which to seed common sense prejudice. By harping on the welfare recipient, Harris has been able to sharpen feelings of acrimony and disrespect towards the Leviathan of government, exploiting the existing biases and discontents harboured by middle-class Ontarians towards the "dependants of the State." In this, he has revived the sentiment that the welfare poor constitute a dark, formidable "other," haunting the economic and ethical stability of the comfortably well-off. Not only has Harris's class prejudice marred the image of big government, depicting it as unjust in its "excessive charity" towards the welfare recipient, but it has also inflamed the moral outrage of the resentful tax-payer who sees his/her financial achievement diffused in the form of tax credits and social assistance benefits for the "indolent" unemployed. In this, he has tapped the aggrieved middle-class ego, fuelling ire over government "handouts," and intensifying selfishness as a necessary if not laudable individualism.

By splintering Ontarians into rivalling factions, primarily the business groups and employed versus the unemployed and welfare recipients, Harris has "played to the 87 percent of people who don't collect welfare against the 13 percent who do" (Skelton 1995). In his rhetorical appeals to the middle-class taxpayer and small businessperson, he has created a privileged community of likeminded Ontarians, addressing them as partners of mutual trust, with corresponding ethics of honesty and goodwill: "Partners don't mislead each other...and you can expect my government to give you the straight goods. Partners stand by each other...and you can expect my government to truly work with you and beside you" (Harris 1995a).

Meanwhile, as he has charmed one sector of society with business blandishments, the premier has instilled guilt into the hearts of those who have been unable to secure gainful employment, playing into the beliefs of traditionalists who see the lot of the underclass as a just desert or as no cause for complaint. Such widespread sentiments have prompted many members of the middle class to believe that it was "time to make welfare [a] less attractive option" (McDowell 1995); that "welfare...boils down to responsibility for one's own" (Gimpel 1995). The phenomenon of *deficitism,* which has convinced a certain mainstream public that drastic measures (indeed deleterious social and economic policies) were not only admissible but highly desirable "shock treatments" for an ailing economy, went hand in hand with a pervasive attitude: the state's dependants needed to be galvanized to work; they had to hoist themselves by their own bootstraps. But such beliefs could only survive if the groups that endorsed this self-sufficiency were themselves secure and well preserved from the buffets of outrageous fortune. Those cheering Harris's deficit-cutting mandate, and particularly his assault on welfare (*Toronto Star* 1995) were not likely to think they would be affected by the spending cuts, particularly as the promise of a 30 percent tax cut was dangled before them as a placating bonus. Indeed, "even the most draconian slash and burn tactics will leave a majority of people relatively unscathed—they still have jobs and can cope with social spending cuts" (Finn 1995). So there is a pervasive "I'm alright Jack" mentality, the attitude of middle-class citizens who think it acceptable to "declare open season on the rest of the province because they the comfortably well-off, are not being hit" (Daly 1995).

The origin of this selfishness resides in the prescriptions of the free market in which a principle of ambitious drive and self-sacrifice for ulterior reward marks the exemplary narrative of the capitalist, risen from rags to riches—a fundamental leitmotif of Harris's rhetoric which echoes the sentiments of his own electorate (Compton 1995). In this tale of ascension, which he portrays as his own trajectory, Harris delivers the morality lesson for able-bodied persons on welfare, glorifying the ideals of self-sufficiency and rugged individualism. Ontario, he has said, is open for business. Ontarians are consumers and partners; the free market proffers them opportunities otherwise thwarted by the "fetters" of government regulation. Yet this rhetoric of market freedom grows ever more spurious as the political measures implemented by the government reveal a highly authoritarian neo-conservatism unfolding daily before Canadians. The Omnibus Bill, for one, with its infringement on personal liberties and its curtailment of public services can only put into question the virtues of a renewed, commercialized Ontario.

Neo-Conservative Authoritarianism

Introduced in December 1995 with enormous haste, the Omnibus Bill (Bill 26) appeared as an awkward piece of legislation, an amalgam of many parts which even Harris and his ministers could not lucidly defend (Mittelstaedt 1995a). The bill

> is 211 pages long, has well over 400 clauses and contains 17 schedules that seek to enact or amend what looks like 47 separate pieces of legislation, many of which have not to do with each other...[the bill] is far too big and diverse for sensible debate. It mixes everyday housekeeping and some ready-to-roll innovations with some potentially profound changes to basic concepts of fairness and such icons as medicare. (Sheppard 1995)

The contents of the bill reflect the ruthless speed with which it was passed so as to preempt and preclude critical discussion. Many of its policies constitute a "surgical" cut through the "red tape" of a bureaucratic protocol which, while admittedly tedious, has often been a way of securing due process and preventing arbitrary decision making by high-ranking ministers. The Omnibus Bill purposely legitimizes and grants exclusive prerogative to such high-standing politicians.

> It will give the cabinet enormous, unilateral power to change the way public services are delivered from closing hospitals, to privatizing municipal transit systems. In effect, it legalizes and institutionalizes an imperial premiership in which the Premier or one of his ministers will have the power to make fundamental, far-reaching decisions without so much as a nod to the legislature, much less to the rest of us. (Vipond 1995)

Such authoritarianism within the administrative realm of public service resurfaces more aggressively elsewhere in Harris's hasty recourse to heavy police security protection at Queens Park. Through the Omnibus Bill, Harris revealed his harsher facets; his neo-conservative drive to crush all dissent and to wield an administrative power within the public service that would bleed

Ontarians of many of their democratic rights. The police force used to suppress dissenting views as measured as those of demonstrating kindergarten teachers (upholding decent standards of education) brought the authoritarianism of the bill to its logical conclusion: the punitive intervention of "law and order" (Coyle 1996; Sheppard 1996).

In its unstoppable will to forge ahead with this legislation, Harris radically diverged from the Liberals' use of deficitism as a hegemonic enterprise. Instead of deploying political manoeuvres to strengthen his hegemonic power, to sustain and extend it beyond the honeymoon period, he only flaunted the promises to cut massively throughout Ontario's public sector and bash the welfare recipient. Yet political hegemony is an ongoing process, never a *fait accompli*.

> [C]onsent is the essence of stable and legitimate democratic politics. Elections are obviously one benchmark of consent, but it is simplistic to think they crystallize and fuel a continuing mandate, if only because public opinion is notoriously volatile. That is why former governments of all stripes have wanted to win the consent of groups directly affected by government policy. Negotiations with 'stakeholders' were often messy and the compromises reached often costly, but through them continuing democratic consent was sustained, and that is hugely important. (Vipond 1995)

The Harris government, however, has shown no sign of conciliation. It has made no attempt to appease "special interest groups," which it has often denounced as irksome. Instead it has run roughshod over all those obstacles in its path, aiming to reinvent itself as swiftly as possible. In passing the Omnibus Bill, it exposed the true colours of the Common Sense Revolution: the desire of neo-conservative ministers to exercise their political power without consultation or real public discussion, justifying drastic measures on the grounds that voters gave Harris a mandate to reduce the deficit. In reality, the mandate has served as a fiscal pretext to launch the destruction of the welfare state (Vipond 1995).

The dismantling of state bureaucracy and the intensification of market-dominated social services have signalled the erosion not only of individual political rights but also the consolidation of a Conservative philistinism[8] that has favoured the use of gambling (Eves 1996: 26) as a way of paying the province's bills while breaking apart the educational infrastructure. But these political efforts to roll back the state, while introducing the rule of money-making enterprises, cannot be carried out unthwarted when little effort is placed on building hegemonic strength and reinforcing popular trust in the deficit-axing mandate. The negative reception of the Omnibus Bill indexed the impulsive and coercive character of the Conservative agenda as well as its poor timing. If Bill 26 is symbolic of Harris's superficial and technical approach to revolutionizing Ontario, his hegemonic success cannot have a long lifespan. On the contrary, his power and popularity have thus far depended on moments of extraordinary drama (i.e. the flourish of electoral victory, the deficit crisis, etc.). The political élan following his election, the spirit of intense animosity felt towards the welfare recipient, and the widespread resolve to bring down the deficit enabled him to act at a relentless pace. In the heat of such passionate moments of history, it is possible to execute political will with untrammelled force. But when normalcy sets in, when the routine of policy making unfolds, the public's corrosive cynicism and critical faculties are awakened as there is no blinding myth to obscure the facts. Ontarians are now slowly coming to their senses.

Conclusion

Unlike the federal tribunes, Harris could not exploit a nationalist sentiment as a binding force of consensus. Nor would it have been in his style to command a following with inspirational rhetoric. Harris rather derived political impetus from his predecessors. But like the federal Liberals, he deployed deficitism as a propagandist device which manipulated public sentiment and produced irrational acceptance of both destructive and undemocratic policies. If the federal campaign represented the crusade to fend off economic apocalypse, the neo-conservative revolution in Ontario constituted a war against the "dragons" of reason, intellect and associated "dissent."

As a hyped-up response to crisis, deficitism created the conditions through which Harris could justify two essential components of his Common Sense Revolution: authoritarianism and class prejudice. Under the pretext that crisis is fraught with urgency, Harris implicitly argued that there was no time for delay, for protracted discussion, analysis and all those "nasty" habits of a professional and intellectual elite, which he deemed both plaintive and ineffectual. With the ideology of deficitism at hand, he could readily dismiss the voices of discontent (those "special interest groups"), and judge their claims as self-indulgent. Similarly, the passing of authoritarian legislation such as the Omnibus Bill could be justified on the grounds that bureaucracy was duplicative, its red tape exasperating and convoluted. The arbitrary will of ministers could, in his eyes, effectively cut through the administrative tangles. Much of Harris's pragmatism tended towards simplistic and mechanical solutions to complex social problems. The quick-fix strategy to cut and cut ruthlessly is bound up with a philistine masculinism that refuses sophisticated and penetrating thought lest it introduce an effeminacy wholly offensive to the image of a "robust," conservative leader. But Harris's unswerving promise to keep a promise (a virtually unimaginable phenomenon given the empty vows of government leaders) became a dogged, indeed irrational pragmatism, abstracted from the real social and political needs of Ontarians. The promise became a symbol of political prowess and exceptional "virtue" such that the premier and his supporters could disregard the content of the promise and flaunt the mere act of doing so irrespective of its consequences.

As the ideology of crisis, deficitism has dictated the need for radical change, sacrifice and swift measures. In this, it enabled Harris's neo-conservative ministers to leap over the otherwise necessary stages of persuading the public of its punitive cuts, and use instead an empty logic—the electoral mandate—as the endorsement of their actions. Any opposition to Harris's policies, indeed, any evidence that his agenda was detrimental to the vulnerable social groups could be preempted in the dissemination of class prejudice against the poor and their supporting institutions within the public sector. Harris's denunciation of the welfare recipient as a social "other" served as a receptacle in which to eliminate all doubts, interrogations, and contestations of his policies. Fanning the resentments of the middle class against that most hated of government practices—heavy taxation—Harris solidified a prejudice against the welfare state and its recipients, using this antipathy as yet another commonsensical argument against his critics.

While most revolutions over the past two centuries have been associated with the triumph of reason (however instrumental) over the mysticisms of the Dark Ages, the Common Sense Revolution throws us back to a virtually premodern irrationalism, ruled by arbitrary power, "fortune," and the sharp polarization of social classes. Harris's neo-conservative project, like many a horror story, shifts out of real time and space, producing the bizarre and unbelievable. Take the example of little Chelsea and Samantha (five and six years old) from Mattawa Public School in Harris's riding. These two blithe little girls donated $21.97 from their savings to help reduce the deficit. Like sacrificial lambs, Samantha and Chelsea symbolize the epitome of those Canadians who have fallen prey to the religious power of deficitism. While government is being decentralized and deregulated and public service devastated by cuts, Mike Harris and Ernie Eves perniciously use the tender innocence of youth as the model of exemplary devotion to Ontario. The pure, but irrational childlike simplicity of two school girls comes to signify the deceptively saccharine side of Harris's Common Sense Revolution, the transformation of stinging sacrifice (cuts in public service) into sweet charity. Thus we witness the proliferation of charitable organizations and the pervasive belief that charity must substitute regulated public services, previously guaranteed as a basic right of needy social groups. Now, as the current philosophy has it, it is up to the corporate benefactors and well-endowed individuals to bestow their largesse on the poor. Yet, at a time when the very foundations of its economic survival are being threatened with cuts, user fees, health levies, etc., the under class is left with nothing more than the desperate hope that philanthropy and charity will come knocking frequently at its door. For just as Harris's cuts transform government services into privileges, so support for the needy is no longer a basic and regularly guaranteed right but a gift contingent on the whims of the wealthy. This is the dystopia of Mike Harris's revolution, and the ideology of deficitism, in all of its irrationality and political artifice, has made it pitifully possible.

Notes

1. As Harold Chorney has pointed out, "[i]t is fairly meaningless...to speak about the deficit as an absolute dollar figure. While talk of Canada's $30-billion deficit has a certain shock value, very little indeed is revealed about the state of the economy. The only meaningful way to assess the debt is to measure its size in relation to the overall size of the economy—the gross domestic product in the case of Canada and the gross provincial product in the case of Ontario" (Chorney 1992: 194). Linda McQuaig (1996: 49) shows effectively how "the deficit is essentially a measurement and its size can change according to what is included in the measurement. The Canadian government uses two different methods and comes up with two different size deficits, explains Stewart Wells, assistant chief statistician at Statistics Canada."

2. For another discussion of the way in which deficitism monopolized and transcended the discourse of existing nationalism, see Martin and Savidan (1994: 15): "This debt culture will make it possible to consign costly notions of national sovereignty or cultural identity once and for all to oblivion. ... The most marked oppositions would then dissolve before the unifying element constituted by debt culture."

3. Cf. John H. Hotson's discussion of debt and guilt which poignantly contrasts how the ordinary citizen is manipulated into paying up his/her debts, while the whole of market society is built on a system of debts and the perpetuation of debt (Hotson 1993).

4. Chorney shows effectively how public sector and household debt cannot be conflated (Chorney and Hansen 1992: 118). See also Laxer (1996: 8).

5. Not only does Lars Osberg deny that the deficit was caused by excessive government spending, he attributes the financial crisis to John Crow's monetarist policies. Osberg and his colleague, Quebec economist Pierre Fortin, argue that massive cuts in public spending will not solve the problem, whereas interest rates of 5 percent and a three-year freeze on public expenditures would reduce the debt from $550 billion to $150 billion in 15 years, and would bring unemployment down to roughly 7 percent (*Le Devoir* 1996: B2).

6. I am not claiming here that Harris initiated the critique of big government as a hateful Leviathan. Martin was also instrumental in attacking government and its structural problems.

7. "... [T]he tax cut benefits for very high-income earners are disproportionately large. A million dollar CEO will receive over $30,000 per year from this first instalment of the tax cut. When the tax-cut package is fully implemented, the CEO will receive close to $65,000; the tax cut for this one individual will eat up all the "savings" that resulted from Harris cutting the welfare of 17 single-parent families (mothers with two children)" (Stanford 1996: 3).

8. See Macfarlane (1996: 55).

Chapter 5

Rights and the Right: Ending Social Citizenship in Tory Ontario

Ian Morrison

Elected in June 1995, the Harris government has quickly embarked on the most aggressive campaign of slashing government services and benefits in Ontario's history. Behind these cuts is much more than a concern about government spending. The Tory agenda is an attack on the very nature and role of government itself, an attempt to redefine the limits of the state.

There are many ways to look at the impact of the *Common Sense Revolution* and the Harris' government's actions to date on the struggle for social justice and equality in Ontario. In this chapter, I will take the perspective of *social citizenship,* one of the foundational concepts of the "welfare state" which is now under attack. While we often take the concept of citizenship for granted, in fact the attributes of citizenship—the rights and privileges that we consider fundamental to participation in society—are historically very fluid. This is particularly so for those who live at the margins of privilege and advantage in society, whose citizenship has always been contingent and contested.

There is a curious section in the Ontario Family Benefits Act, enacted in 1968, which affirms that social assistance recipients are eligible to vote in provincial and municipal elections. What is curious, of course, is not that citizens of a democratic country should have the right to vote, but that as late as 1968 it was felt necessary to say so in legislation—a sharp reminder that not so long ago those on "poor relief," like criminals, were not secure in this most basic attribute of citizenship. In this chapter, I examine the origins of the concept of social citizenship, its links to political and civil citizenship, and the assault on social citizenship in Ontario today.[1]

Social Citizenship and the State

All collectively provided services are deliberately designed to meet certain socially recognized needs; they are manifestations, first, of society's will to survive as an organic whole and, secondly, of the expressed wish of all the people to assist the survival of some people. Needs may therefore be thought of as "social" and "individual," as inter-dependent, mutually related essentials for the continued existence of the parts and the whole. —Richard Titmuss, *Essays on the Welfare State* (1974)

Most discussions of social citizenship take as their starting point a famous 1949 essay by T.H. Marshall entitled "Citizenship and Social Class," in which Marshall investigates what it means to be a citizen in a modern nation state. Marshall argues that citizenship in liberal democracies has advanced in three stages. The first stage, developed in the eighteenth century, was the establishment of *civil rights:* basic legal rights to property, personal liberty and the principle of legal equality and due process. The second stage was the expansion of *political rights* in the nineteenth century: extension of the franchise and the right to hold political office. Marshall saw the twentieth century leading to the third stage of citizenship, *social rights*: the provision of basic social and economic security through such mechanisms as universal income transfers, social insurance, universal education and medical care.

For theorists like Marshall and Titmuss, social rights do not just derive from citizenship, they are constituent parts of it. Freeing people from immediate or imminent destitution makes possible their full participation in society, including their ability to exercise civil and political rights. This in turn increases social solidarity and enhances the meaning of citizenship. The measure of social citizenship, then, can be seen as the extent to which an individual as *citizen* is guaranteed access to the things seen as essential to basic dignity and participation in the society in which she or he lives.

Of course the provision of social entitlements affects other relationships in society, freeing people from absolute dependence on the labour market or familial relationships. For this reason, social entitlements always exist in a state of tension with pressures to limit this potential in capitalist and patriarchal societies. The actual forms that particular welfare states have taken in the twentieth century and the degree of social citizenship achieved in each therefore depends on many factors, including the relative power and organizational capacities of labour, the power and influence of women in and outside of the formal state, historical influences of national cultures and institutions, political organization and bureaucratic influence, and so on. The relative importance of these different factors in explaining welfare state outcomes is the subject of extensive debate among welfare state historians and theoreticians.[2]

Canada only ever achieved a modest degree of social citizenship compared with most industrial liberal democracies, particularly those of Europe. Canada, like the United States, has been called a "residualist" welfare state, reliant on private market ideology "in which means-tested assistance, modest universal transfers or modest insurance plans predominate" (Esping Anderson 1989). Nevertheless, in the decades after the Second World War major social programs proliferated in Canada. These included universal grants (such as family allowances) and social insurance programs (such as unemployment insurance), the preferred models for welfare state programs. During this period the federal government took on a major role even in programs administered directly by provinces, such as social assistance, health care and post-secondary education.

Neither Marshall's particular vision of social citizenship, nor the "welfare state" as it developed in reality, need be or should be accepted uncritically or nostalgically. If social citizenship is conceived only as reducing class inequality, other forms of inequality may easily be ignored or even assumed. For example, Marshall's history of liberal citizenship is the history of *men's* citizenship: it is not even accurate with respect to women's legal status during the same period (Fraser and Gordon 1992). Feminist theorists have pointed out the degree to which both liberal citizenship and social citizenship theory ignores the fundamental subordination of women (Pateman 1987) and the degree to which welfare state programs have both relied on and reinforced women's dependency within the family (Gordon 1990). Welfare state "citizenship" is also based on tremendous inequalities at the international level and racial and cultural subordination or assimilationism at the national level, and theories of social citizenship often obscure or even reinforce this (Gabriel 1996). Social entitlements often exclude at the same time that they support: for example, income support programs for people with disabilities often marginalize people rather than provide supports for social participation.

However, these critiques of social citizenship are directed at its under-inclusiveness and limitations. They do not challenge the basic proposition that progressive citizenship must include space in which claims of basic needs are not reduced to a dichotomy between "free" market provision and charity. Neo-liberalism, on the other hand, *does* represent a direct attack on social citizenship. It is widely accepted now that the Canadian "welfare state" is being dis- and re-mantled in accordance with a new dominant set of political, economic and social agendas, which include the enhancement of private market forces, reduced state economic regulation, shrinking social programs and reduced social spending.[3] In order to implement such an agenda, those propounding it must create political support, or at least minimize and fragment political opposition. In other words, neo-liberalism must in part work *ideologically*. The role of ideology in this sense is to make both the definition of problems and the proposed solutions seem simple "common sense" by constructing a vocabulary, a set of associations and ideational links which reduce complex realities to unquestioned responses. One of the most important parts of this ideological shift is in its discourse about social entitlements and the causes of need. While explanations of need have always been contested, the dominant understanding of poverty in welfare state policy assumed that the main causes of need were structural, rooted in the nature of the economy and factors largely beyond individual control. Neo-liberalism in all forms—and most of all in its particularly right-wing and doctrinaire manifestation in Ontario—has revitalized the dominant pre-welfare state ideology of poverty and need as based on individual inadequacy, whether this is expressed in the genteel language of "skills deficits" or the welfare-bashing rhetoric of "lazy scroungers." The point is to make one major group of the needy—those who are considered "employable" but who cannot meet all their needs through the market—seem less deserving of help.

A paradigmatic example of the rhetoric driving this ideological shift is the "problem" of "dependency" on government programs, which has become *the* main orthodoxy of Canadian social policy. The theme of "welfare dependency" has been taken up in various forms by governments of all political stripe in Canada, and was of course one of the most prominent themes in the 1995 Ontario provincial elections. The very word "dependency" reflects multiple assumptions about the nature of poverty and need, with its implications of moral degradation and individual fault, as Nancy Fraser and Linda Gordon have shown in their historical genealogy of the word in relation to social provision (Fraser and Gordon 1992). By easy association, the dependent citizen becomes, if not presumptively immoral, at least morally suspect. The moral anxiety thus created establishes a powerful demand that those in need continually and publicly prove their deservedness and their neediness. This feeds accusations of widespread fraud and abuse, the most time-honoured method for delegitimizing social provision. This then is the ideological climate in which a sweeping set of changes is being made to the landscape of social provision in Ontario, changes that I will discuss in more detail in the remaining part of this chapter.

Social Citizenship and the Common Sense Revolution

> Begin by recognizing that welfare is a...euphemism; when we talk about helping the helpless, we're talking about charity. Charity is not a dirty word, though it is treated as such by many of those on the receiving end; they prefer "welfare" because it suggests an entitlement with no need for gratitude. William Safire, *The Globe and Mail*, July 12, 1995 [reprinted from the *New York Times*]

Safire's conservative polemic raises a very important question: when the state helps people meet basic needs outside the market, does it help them as *rights-bearing subjects* or as *objects of charity*? Is such provision an *entitlement* or *largesse*? To answer these questions we must know what procedural, political and civil rights exist in the context of government programs; not just what the state provides, but also how government organizes provision of needs elsewhere, such as in the family or the private, non-profit sector. Safire is right about one thing. The answers matter a great deal.

In the rest of this chapter, I examine the status of social citizenship in Ontario from the perspective of *legal rights* to and in respect of social provision. The citizen/state relationship of entitlement is, almost by definition, articulated through legal instruments and institutions. In the final resort, if the most vulnerable citizens' claims against the state are not enforceable, they are not entitlements. I will suggest that the Harris government's actions with respect to social provision within and beyond the state must be understood as more than just reductions in available benefits and services. They are, in fact, a far ranging attack on entitlement intended to return those who cannot maintain "independence" in the market, or who are not legitimately "dependent" within families, to the status of charitable objects even within the parameters of state provision.

Social Rights within Canadian Federalism
A discussion of legal entitlement and social citizenship may begin with the legal context within which governments must act. One reason the Harris government has been able to act as it has is the lack of any legal framework for social citizenship within the Canadian federation.

The most fundamental legal constraint on government action is the Constitution, which includes both the division of legislative powers between the federal and provincial governments and the 1982 Charter of Rights. Unfortunately for the poor and disadvantaged in Canada, the Constitution contains no direct or express protections of social rights, and consequently has proved largely empty of content with respect to social citizenship. In fact, social programs are only mentioned in one section of the Charter of Rights, and that one mention is negative rather than affirmative: section 6 expressly protects the right of provincial *governments* to impose residency requirements for social programs.

The failure of the Charter to provide any real protection against the dismantling of the social safety net is hardly surprising. Our judges' understanding of the Charter is profoundly shaped by liberal legal ideology, within which the idea of positive social rights within the state—as opposed to negative libertarian rights against the state—being elevated to constitutionally protected status is almost literally unthinkable. Nor are most judges, overwhelmingly drawn from a politically conservative and economically privileged elite, much inclined to order governments to spend money on social programs. The courts might intervene to restrain the most egregious discrimination in distribution of entitlements (even here their record is not impressive), but there is no reason to expect that courts will be persuaded to use their most powerful weapon to defend any meaningful standard of social entitlement.

Lawyers have nevertheless argued that certain fundamental social interests should be protected under other sections of the Charter (Jackman 1988, 1994), but little has come of these efforts to date (although the glacial pace of the legal system means that many issues will not finally be resolved for years[4]).

Nor do any non-constitutional legal standards constrain provincial action around social provision. From 1967 to 1996, the federal government shared the costs of social services in Ontario, including social assistance, child care, legal aid and various other social services. The legal basis for cost sharing was the Canada Assistance Plan, or CAP. In order to receive CAP transfers, provinces had to sign an agreement committing themselves to a number of principles or conditions. While these standards were minimal in nature and regressive in some respects, they did include some important safeguards. These included an obligation to provide benefits to any person in need, an implicit prohibition on workfare, the

72

obligation to have a social assistance appeals system and a prohibition against discriminating against people from other provinces.

On April 1, 1996, CAP was replaced by the Canada Health and Social Transfer (which included billions of dollars in cuts to welfare transfers). All conditions were dropped except the prohibition on residency requirements for welfare—an ambiguous right to say the least, as protecting interprovincial mobility of desperately poor potential workers is quite consistent with the interests of employers. The federal government is also abandoning other social policy areas in which it was traditionally involved in social policy (for example, subsidized housing), which will further weaken any external constraints on provincial action. The only area where the federal government is determined to retain a real presence is medicare, the cost-shared program with strongest middle-class support. Thus, the federal government has effectively ended any national commitment to a social safety net with a bottom.

Citizenship, Law-Making and Democracy in Tory Ontario
If there are no legal guarantees for basic levels of social citizenship outside the provincial political process, then that process itself is obviously crucial. The Harris government notoriously has refused to consult, meet with or even acknowledge anyone who does not agree with its agenda. Government members including the premier routinely dismiss anyone who questions their vision or agenda as "special interests" or worse; it has even been reported that a cabinet minister threatened community groups that those who criticized the government's actions or agenda would be defunded (Toughill 1995).

It is difficult at the best of times for marginalized and disadvantaged people to have any public voice. Political participation is traditionally low among people who are already excluded from the social and political mainstream (Jackman 1994). Since the election of the Harris government, Ontario has also seen a truncated democracy specifically around access of the most marginalized people to the political process. The government has closed down various mechanisms that had been established by previous governments to consult with groups particularly affected by changes to social programs. Thus, for example, after the 1995 election Minister of Community and Social Services David Tsubouchi simply refused to meet with the Social Assistance Advisory Council (made up of social assistance recipients and representatives from community agencies) that was supposed to serve as a consultation body to represent recipient perspectives. This left the council no option but to resign. Internal documents indicate that the same ministry has deliberately adopted a policy that it will not consult with advocates and recipients.

While these are important *political* truncations of democracy, what is perhaps less obvious is the extent to which this has been accompanied by a *legal* truncation of democracy, by shifting large areas of law-making authority away from the legislature. For example, Bill 26, the notorious Omnibus Bill, concentrated enormous law-making power in the cabinet, in the form of regulation-making powers. Legislation—the official Acts of provincial legislatures and Parliament—must be debated, voted on and passed by a majority of the elected assembly. Flawed as our system of representative democracy may be, legislation cannot be enacted in secret and the legislative process provides at least a limited window for challenges to government policy. Regulations are subject to no such safeguards: they are not debated in the legislature and they can be passed in secret with no public consultation or advance notice. Where regulations primarily affect those with substantial political power, they will almost always be consulted and notified anyway. Politically weak and unpopular groups like welfare recipients can be and usually are ignored: the legislative process may be their only access to the formal law-making process.

Access to Justice and Legal Aid

Legal aid is a unique form of social entitlement, a social program which is entirely directed at making the exercise of other rights possible. In Ontario, legal aid has for many years been available to help people assert claims for income maintenance support (such as social assistance, unemployment insurance, workers' compensation), to resist evictions, and to seek spousal and child support. In the complex modern administrative state, having an advocate dramatically affects the likelihood of success in almost any kind of legal proceeding, even before supposedly informal tribunals (Mosher and Morrison, 1995).

The Ontario legal aid plan is in serious crisis. While the Tory government has temporarily backed down on an election promise to cut legal aid spending in half, due to intense opposition from lawyers, the issue is far from closed. At the time of writing family lawyers—who mostly represent women—have threatened a complete withdrawal of services, and "poverty law" services of all kinds are coming under increasing pressure. In the U.S., legal services to the poor have been relentlessly attacked by the political Right for more than a decade. Many U.S. conservatives argue that abolishing legal services should be a top priority, precisely because of the symbolism inherent in "welfare rights." The ideological stakes—and the relation between legal aid, legal entitlement and the rights of citizenship—have been made very clear in new restrictions now being imposed on American legal aid: legal aid lawyers will no longer be able to bring class actions against government agencies, challenge the constitutionality or legality of state welfare policies, or even to make submissions to legislatures or bureaucracies about proposed changes (Centre on Social Welfare Policy and Law 1995). If these restrictions are successfully imposed, the poor in the U.S. will not only be barred from effective participation in the political process over matters that affect their basic subsistence, they will not even be able to challenge the legality of government action. If the Harris government gets its way, similar policies may be imposed in Ontario.

Social Programs and Civil Rights

Another aspect of the erosion of social citizenship is the degree to which receipt of social provisions deprives people of common rights of citizenship. An important example here is the denial of privacy rights to recipients of social assistance. Privacy is widely viewed as a fundamentally important right, both in legal and in broader social discourse (Macfarlane 1995). Canadians consistently identify privacy as one of their most important concerns (Eko Research Associates 1993). Privacy is especially important for social assistance recipients who face discrimination, hostility and sometimes even physical violence if their identities become known (Steering Committee on Social Assistance 1994). The subordination of privacy rights is thus another indication of the status of social citizenship.

The Harris government has attacked the privacy rights of social assistance recipients with the reintroduction of mandatory random home visits, rule changes which invite and even mandate massive intrusions into privacy, and the introduction of a provincially-sponsored toll-free welfare snitch line. Ironically, protection of privacy legislation is routinely used to *deny* information to social assistance recipients, while providing little protection at all against the revelation of personal information, as we can see in the instructions given to snitch line staffers that callers are to be assured that their confidentiality will be respected. The problematization of social citizenship in relation to privacy issues is clearly expressed in the argument made by Evelyn Dodds, then a municipal councillor, later an (unsuccessful) Tory candidate and the first person Harris appointed to the Social Assistance Review Committee (SARC, the welfare appeals tribunal) in 1994, to a legislative standing committee reviewing protection of privacy legislation:

> For thousands [sic] of years it has been known that the greater the dependence of the citizenry on its government for support, the more liberty has to be given up. It's simply a fact. If you depend on the government to support you, you give up your right to privacy because the taxpayers' right not to have their money abused is greater. (Ontario Legislative Assembly, January 19, 1994: M-204)

Social Programs and Due Process

Another important component of social citizenship is the ability to actually enforce "legal" entitlements. The existence of entitlements in theory means little if disputes over entitlement cannot be resolved through a fair, accessible and independent mechanism, and if there are no external checks on the discretionary powers of those administering programs. A characteristic of the development of welfare state programs was the creation of a wide range of administrative tribunals to hear appeals and settle disputes about entitlements, on the theory that such tribunals should be cheaper, faster, more expert, more accessible and less intimidating than courts. The association between procedural rights and social citizenship in the welfare state can be seen in the mandatory condition under the Canada Assistance Plan that provinces have social assistance appeals tribunals as a condition of cost sharing.

In opposition, the Tories often verbally attacked the social assistance appeals system as complicit in "abuses" of the system. After election, they ignored the established recruitment process for SARC, appointing four Tory supporters to the board without even prior notification to the chair of SARB. Later, in an appearance before the Standing Committee on Government Agencies, the chair was subjected to openly hostile cross-examination by the leading government member (Ontario Legislative Assembly, 7 February 1996: A-135 ff.). With the repeal of CAP, most advocates expect that social assistance appeal rights will be restricted at the very least. Another government report has already raised the possibility of abolishing or sharply restricting the powers of the Workers' Compensation Appeals Tribunal, the independent tribunal that hears appeals in workers' compensation matters.

A more indirect but important challenge to process rights will arise if the Harris government proceeds with its threatened "workfare" program. Workfare will effectively lead to the privatization of broad powers to determine eligibility to basic benefits. Under mandatory programs of this nature a third party "employer" is necessarily given powers to decide whether the recipient is performing "adequately." The problems of having a fair and accessible process for resolving disputes over these kinds of issues would be enormous, even assuming the will to solve them. The government has also not addressed the question of how the various legal regimes governing workplace standards— Workers' Compensation, Employment Standards, health and safety legislation, Human Rights Code standards—will apply to workfare placements. If the province attempts to exempt workfare from the application of minimum protective legislation (however much remains), the "second class citizenship" of social assistance recipients will be even more clear.

Rights Beyond the State
Governments also have considerable power to shape social provision beyond the formal boundaries of the state, using techniques that range from laws that establish private support obligations and how they will be enforced, to the organization and regulation of the "private" voluntary and charitable sector through a whole host of legal mechanisms, such as leverage provided by direct funding, legal regulation of organizational forms, audit requirements, and delivery standards. Before the 1995 election, Ontario had been moving to regulate social provision beyond the state so as to grant clients of services specific rights vis-à-vis service providers, through legislation such as the Residents Rights Act, the Long Term Care Act, the Advocacy Act, the Substitute Decisions Act and the Consent to Treatment Act. Not surprisingly, the Tories in opposition

vehemently opposed most of this legislation. They have already repealed or gutted some of it and, at the time of writing, legislation has been introduced to remove more of these rights. There is a clear link between the truncation of rights with respect to social provision through the state and the dismantling of legal protections outside the formal state apparatus. The link lies in the imperative to re-inscribe all social provision to the marginalized and vulnerable, both in law and in the social imagination, as charitable.

Conclusion

If massive cuts to social programs and social services signal a determined effort to undo the welfare state at one level, the truncation of legal entitlement is a corollary strategy at the level of the citizen. Neo-liberalism does not just undermine, but in some senses inverts key concepts of social citizenship as these had come to be understood. If social entitlement was a defining measure of citizenship in the welfare state perspective, neo-liberal discourse has attempted with some success to make "entitlement" a *problematization* of citizenship by equating it with dependency. The discursive space for *interdependence*, as Titmuss used it, is collapsing into a dichotomy between dependence (only legitimate within the "private" family) and independence (through the market). Rights of citizenship are those that attach to the mythical "law-abiding taxpayer," to use the ubiquitous phrase that replaces "citizen" in most speeches by members of the Ontario government, while good neo-liberal citizens are defined by their distance from claims on the state and absence of claims rooted in personal identity (Brodie 1995: 57). The creation of a "two-tiered" citizenship in reality, within the liberal legal mythology of equal citizenship, is advancing quickly in Tory Ontario.

Notes

1. Various labels have been attached to the set of political, economic and social agendas that make up this attack on the welfare state: "conservative," "neo-conservative", "new right," etc. I prefer the word "neo-liberal" because of its association with the dominant *laissez faire* economic liberalism of the nineteenth century, which has been revived as economic orthodoxy. Neo-liberalism may or may not be associated with moral and social conservatism as more commonly understood.
2. There is a substantial literature both on the origins of the welfare state in particular countries and on international comparisons of welfare state development. Two very good literature reviews from the feminist perspective are Gordon (1990) and Orloff (1993). For a thorough and careful review of competing influences in the development of welfare programs in Ontario, see Struthers (1994).
3. There is already a very large and growing cross-disciplinary literature examining restructuring and the neo-liberal agenda. For a variety of perspectives on this issue, see Brodie (1995, 1996), Jessop (1993), Teeple (1995), Drache and Ranachan (1995), Johnson, McBride and Smith (1994).
4. Because of the length of time required for the litigation process and the extraordinary resource requirements of constitutional litigation, very few of the most basic

questions arising in the Charter around social rights have finally been resolved. Only the Supreme Court of Canada can give a definitive answer to legal questions. However, there have been very few successes to date in attempts to achieve social rights through constitutional litigation at lower court levels. Hopes for Charter constraints on the dismantling of the welfare state are particularly dim in Ontario, where the Ontario Court of Appeal has refused leave to appeal the dismissal of a legal challenge to the October 1995 21.6 percent welfare rate cuts: *Masse et al. v. Ontario* (February 8, 1996) Ont. Divisional Court; Court File No. 590/95.

Part Two

Unmasking the Impacts

Chapter 6

Social Assistance in the New Ontario
Allan Moscovitch

Introduction[1]
In their first year in office, the Harris Conservatives have moved rapidly to institute many of the changes to welfare promised in their *Common Sense Revolution* (Ontario Progressive Conservative Party 1995). As a package, these changes represent a significant reversal of the direction of welfare reform of the last ten years. They run counter to the recommendations of the independent Ontario Social Assistance Review Committee, which heard submissions from over 1500 groups and individuals across Ontario from 1986–1988 (Social Assistance Review Committee 1988), and which both the previous Liberal and NDP governments had begun to implement. More importantly, on the first of April 1996 they overturned some of the key principles of the federal Canada Assistance Plan, which had guided the administration of provincial social assistance since 1966. This chapter begins with a brief review of the history of federal and provincial welfare reform. What follows is an outline and analysis of the substance of the changes to welfare proposed in the Common Sense Revolution and the legislative and administrative changes instituted by the Ontario Conservative government since election in 1995.

Ontario Social Assistance Before the Tories
Until the 1950s, municipalities in Ontario handled the administration of minimum income programs for the mainstream population. Mother's benefits were provided in 1921 and in the other provinces between 1916 and 1930. Federal legislation to provide cost sharing of benefits for physically disabled persons appeared in the 1950s. The 1956 Unemployment Assistance Act offered federal cost sharing for provincial benefits to the "employable unemployed" who were not eligible for unemployment insurance. In 1966, the Canada Assistance Plan (CAP) consolidated federal funding and included single parents, disabled persons, the able-bodied unemployed, and anyone else in need in one comprehensive piece of legislation. Through CAP the federal government cost-shared all provincial minimum-income programs.

By the end of the 1960s, most provinces and territories had a consolidated system of provincial social assistance administration. Ontario retained a two-tiered system of administration. Under the General Welfare Assistance Act, the municipalities administered "short term" income assistance while under the Family Benefits Act, the province itself administered "long term" income assistance.

In practice, this has meant that the Ontario government administers income assistance for single parents and disabled persons, while the municipalities run social assistance for everyone else who does not have sufficient income to survive. CAP required participating provinces to grant social assistance solely according to demonstrated need. The need principle has existed in direct conflict with the older principles of deservedness and private labour. Towards recipients who are classified as employable (a classification that varies considerably from province to province) all provinces have adopted an approach of coercing the presumably reluctant and undeserving worker into rejoining the paid labour force (Myles 1988). In Ontario, provincial and municipal social assistance administrations have required recipients who are classified as employable to undertake a regular job search. But under the provisions of CAP, they have not been permitted to require employable recipients to work as a condition of receiving assistance. Unemployable recipients, such as certain disabled persons, have come to be accepted as deserving of public support; in effect they have been paid to stay out of the labour market.

Recent History of Social Assistance Reform in Ontario

For much of the ten years before the Conservative government was elected in June 1995, successive provincial governments, both Liberal and New Democratic, were concerned with reforming the social assistance system. In July 1986, the Liberal government of David Peterson appointed the Social Assistance Review Committee (SARC) to conduct an independent public review of social assistance programs in the province of Ontario (Social Assistance Review Committee 1988). The 624-page *Transitions* report was released in September 1988. It outlined 274 recommendations grouped into 5 stages of reform. At the centre of Stage Two was the drafting of new social assistance legislation. After the release of *Transitions* a widespread consensus emerged in Ontario on the importance of the report and the need for reform. The report also helped to revitalize community-based social action. Local SARC committees sprang up around the province, forming a network.

Transitions was released in the midst of a mini economic boom in the province, with unemployment below 5 percent, particularly in the areas of high population in southern Ontario (Ontario Ministry of Finance 1995b: Table 7). At the same time, the restructuring of the labour market in the 1980s created a growing level of dependency on social assistance: rates grew from 4.5 percent in 1981 to 6.4 percent in 1988 (Advisory Group on New Social Assistance Legislation 1991: 19).

In the spring of 1989, the Liberal government packaged several of the *Transitions* recommendations in what it called the Supports to Employment Program (STEP). The package was estimated to cost $415 million, a figure chosen to coincide with the estimated cost of Stage One predicted by the SARC report (Advisory Group on New Social Assistance Legislation 1991: 24).

One year later in May 1990, the minister of Community and Social Services of Ontario appointed an advisory group on new social assistance legislation to provide him with advice on the drafting of new social assistance legislation. When the New Democrats were elected in September of 1990, they asked the advisory group to prepare an interim report so as to fulfil more quickly their mandate of improving the conditions of the poor in Ontario. In January 1991 (before the interim report was released) the government committed to several increases in welfare rates. Two months later, in the spring budget, the NDP government implemented roughly two-thirds of about 100 recommendations from the advisory group—a commitment of over 200 million new dollars. This financial commitment grew larger very rapidly as the Ontario economy entered more deeply into recession after the spring of 1991, with unemployment reaching 9.6 percent (Ontario Ministry of Community and Social Services October 1995; Ontario Ministry of Finance November 1995: Table 7).

In line with their conservative agenda, the federal government and the Bank of Canada followed policies which made reducing inflation the primary purpose of federal economic policies. One result was higher unemployment, which led to more claims on unemployment insurance and cost-shared provincial social assistance. Another result was a growing federal deficit and debt, despite the federal government's rhetoric of cost containment. In an effort to limit expenditures, the federal Conservative government instituted a cap on the Canada Assistance Plan funds available to the three "richest" provinces, Ontario, British Columbia, and Alberta. Implemented in 1990 and extended to 1995, the cap significantly limited the funds available to the Ontario government to pay the costs of a recession which federal policy exaggerated.

The recession hit Ontario the hardest (Cross 1993: 8). Unemployment rose rapidly after 1989, leading to greater dependency on both unemployment insurance and social assistance. Unemployment was the most important reason for the increase in the percentage of Ontario citizens dependent on social assistance; it rose rapidly from 6.4 percent in June 1988 to 8.1 percent in June 1990 and 13.1 percent in June of 1991 (Advisory Committee on New Social Assistance Legislation 1991: 19). This meant that, by March of 1992, more than one million people in the province used welfare as their primary source of income (Human Resources Development Canada 1995: Table 361).

To respond to their political agenda of reducing poverty and inequality in Ontario, the New Democratic government nonetheless increased social assistance rates. They increased basic needs allowance by 7 percent and the maximum shelter allowance by 10 percent in 1991; increased them again by 2 percent and 3 percent respectively in 1992, and increased both by 1 percent in 1993. These increases built on a 6 percent increase implemented by the Liberal government in 1990 (Ontario Ministry of Community and Social Services. 1995).

The NDP government moved ahead more slowly to implement the recommendations of the *Transitions* report. In June 1992, *Time For Action*, the report of the advisory group, was released. It contained details on how to create a single-tiered social assistance system under one piece of legislation and one set of administrative rules. At the centre of the proposed reforms was an elaboration of Opportunity Planning, an idea first raised in the *Transitions* report. Under it, the social assistance administration would be oriented to helping people move on in their lives, including into employment.

Because of rising welfare rates, constrained federal cost-shared funds and provincial tax revenues, the provincial government responded cautiously. It took a year, until July of 1993, for the ministry to release *Turning Point*, a 26-page document outlining the government's support for the principles of the advisory group's report. But it made no promises to proceed to substantive reform.

During the three years leading up to the election in June 1995, the government emphasized expenditure restraint and training, including for social assistance recipients. In 1992 the STEP program was cut back and the working poor could no longer receive an income supplement or other benefits unless they were on welfare when they started employment. Recipients were transferred to other income security programs (especially CPP Disability), for which they were eligible. To counter accusations that the NDP was soft on welfare fraud, the government announced a program of "enhanced verification" as part of the government's expenditure control plan in April 1993 (Ontario Ministry of Community and Social Services 1994).

Also in 1994, the government announced its Joblink Ontario program, with a modest $25 million budget to develop eight resource centres around the province and 4000 more training places for social assistance recipients. It looked like a very limited move towards the opportunity planning concept promoted by previous welfare reform reports (Ontario Ministry of Community and Social Services 1994).

The number of beneficiaries of social assistance in Ontario peaked at 1,379,000 at the end of fiscal 1993–94 but in the spring of 1995, just before the election, the numbers still remained high at 1,344,600 (Human Resources Development Canada 1995: Table 361).

The New Conservatives' Agenda
During the 1995 election campaign, the provincial Conservative Party made the reduction of the deficit and the debt key issues. More disturbing is the support they appear to have garnered by attacking welfare recipients. In the *Common Sense Revolution* document the Conservatives argued that:

> Ontario pays the highest welfare benefits not only in Canada but anywhere in North America. This is one of the reasons our welfare caseload has swollen to record levels. The simple fact of the matter is that we can't afford it. (Ontario Progressive Conservative Party 1995: 11)

They thereby implied that above average benefits, and not the recession or unemployment, were the principle reason for the rapid increase in social assistance cases since 1989. Their plan called for a reduction of welfare benefits to "10% above the national average of all other provinces" (Ontario Progressive Conservative Party 1995: 9, 11).

The Common Sense Revolution made much of alleged widespread welfare fraud and overpayments. According to the document, the previous government had "already admitted to the existence of massive overpayments in welfare benefits. One estimate runs as high as $247 million since 1990" (Ontario Progressive Conservative Party 1995: 10). This would amount to $49.4 million or roughly 0.8 percent a year for five years, a minuscule fraction of the total annual cost of welfare in Ontario. As for fraud, the document states that "estimates of welfare fraud have ranged from a few million to hundreds of millions of dollars" (Ontario Progressive Conservative Party 1995: 10). Provocative but without substance, the document could not point to any evidence. Were the estimates per year or, like the overpayments, was this an estimate over five years? What the Conservatives didn't say was that even $200 million a year amounts to roughly 3 percent of the cost of welfare in Ontario, a relatively small percentage loss in a large administrative system. We can all agree that the provincial government should have sound administrative practices to ensure that social assistance funds are not wasted (Ontario Progressive Conservative Party 1995: 10). But, it is costly to eliminate all mistakes and fraud in a large administrative system, and it is likely not cost-effective to try to do so.

The Conservatives also committed to spend $500 million on "new and innovative programs to help those most in need and those who genuinely want a hand up, not a hand out" (Ontario Progressive Conservative Party 1995: 9). It turned out that the increased funding would be for obligatory workfare and learnfare programs in which "able-bodied recipients—with the exception of single parents with young children" would be required "either to work, or be retrained in return for their benefits" (Ontario Progressive Conservative Party 1995: 9). The implication is that there are large numbers of recipients who could be working or training for work but who are refusing to because they are lazy. The Conservatives ignored the close to 10 percent unemployment, the large numbers of people working in jobs which pay little more than welfare, the considerable number of recipients who are employed (and receiving a welfare top-up), and the large waiting lists for training programs.

The Common Sense Revolution did promise to guarantee social assistance rates for disabled persons and seniors at current levels and eventually to take them out of the welfare system entirely. Implicit in this promise is the view that only these groups are fully deserving of assistance, because they are "unable to work" (Ontario Progressive Conservative Party 1995: 10).

Lastly, for children the major proposal was to introduce nutrition programs for school-aged children but with "private sector and volunteer support," they expected to do it at "little or no cost to taxpayers" (Ontario Progressive

Conservative Party 1995: 10). The document also proposes better child support enforcement through a compulsory mediation program, a program of paying welfare bonuses to young, single parents who stay in school, and a program of encouraging the formation of youth centres staffed by volunteers to help with homework. The commitment of someone else's time and money makes two of these proposals hollow.

The Conservatives in Power

One of the first acts of the new government was to release a mini-budget on the 21st of July 1995 entitled *Ontario Fiscal Overview and Spending Cuts*. In the document, the finance minister reiterated the Conservative message that "governments must stop acting as though the problem is one of insufficient revenues." Based on the view that they had "inherited a severe spending problem," the government announced a series of measures which were intended to cut $1.884 billion from expenditures. Consistent with their pre-election message, many of these measures were directed at poor and low-income Ontarians. Heading the list was a record reduction of 21.6 percent in social assistance rates on October 1, 1995, "so that they are on average 10% higher than the average of the other nine provinces (Ontario Progressive Conservative Party 1995: 11). This change was projected to save the Ontario government $469 million in the rest of 1995–96 and $938 million in 1996–97, the first full year of the change. The reduction in social assistance expenditures for 1995–96 was projected to be 24.6 percent of the total and 34.7 percent of the program spending reduction. There was no mistaking the government's intention to reduce spending at the expense of the poor. The statement did note that recipients who undertake employment would be able to earn back the amount of the cut (Ontario Minister of Finance 1995: 2–3, Table 1).

The province's approach to rate cutting was based not on the Canada Assistance Plan criterion of need in the administration of welfare, but on the older criterion of deservedness. The mini-budget reiterated the Conservative Party's pre-election promise that "benefits for the support of seniors, persons with disabilities and their families will not be reduced" (Ontario Minister of Finance 1995: 3). Conversely, benefits were reduced for the able-bodied unemployed and for single parents since, in the view of the provincial Conservatives, they are not deserving.

In a *Backgrounder*, the Ontario Social Safety Network argued that the government went deeper than it needed to in responding to its election promise. It argued that 1995 data on provincial social assistance rates would have suggested a cut of 17 percent. Instead, the government used 1993 data to justify the higher rate cut. The *Backgrounder* also suggested that much of the difference in rates between Ontario and the rest of the country has to do with the generally higher costs of shelter particularly in Toronto where the highest percentage of welfare recipients is located. The government provided no indication of the potential for personal and social disruption that might result from so drastic a change (Ontario Social Safety NetWork 1995: 3).

The mini-budget also indicated that new measures would be taken to "tighten eligibility and reduce fraud...to ensure that welfare goes to those persons who are truly in need" (Ontario Minister of Finance 1995: 3).

Over the summer of 1995, the government announced it was instituting a fraud telephone line to encourage people with complaints about potentially fraudulent relatives, friends and neighbours to call in. Announced as a triumph of the Common Sense Revolution, there has since been no indication of whether the promised $15 million in savings has been realized. The promised savings are a small fraction of what was claimed in the *Common Sense Revolution*. Nothing more has been heard about fraud since the opening of the "hotline."

According to the government's own calculations, it intended that 60.7 percent of its $850 million in program savings would come from reductions to welfare-related programs. It also intended that 32.2 percent of its $500 million in operating expenditure savings would come from the Ministry of Community and Social Services, through cutting payments to social service agencies funded by the province by 2.5 percent on the first of October and by another 5 percent in 1996–97 (Ontario Minister of Finance 1995: Tables 4, 5).

The jobsOntario training program was cancelled; the special provincial programs to help municipalities fund high welfare caseloads were cancelled; a moratorium was placed on the development of new non-profit housing; major infrastructure capital programs were reduced or eliminated, cutting many potential or actual jobs in the construction industry.

Tightening Eligibility

In October 1995, while the rate cuts were being implemented, the province circulated a training manual entitled *Eligibility and Entitlement Initiatives* to income maintenance staff (Ontario Ministry of Community and Social Services 1995). It noted that cuts in the allowance would affect the basic allowance, the maximum shelter allowance and the board and lodging allowance.

The new *Eligibility and Entitlement Initiatives* also widened the definition of living in a spousal relationship. Previously a recipient living with a person of the opposite sex had up to thirty three months to decide if their relationship was spousal. After October 1995 it is an income maintenance worker who will determine if an applicant or recipient is living in a spousal relationship; the length of the relationship will no longer matter. The key issues now are residence, financial interdependence and social and familiar factors.

The clear intent of this change is to make it more difficult for a single person on assistance to progress into or try out a relationship, a choice available to people not on assistance. It is based on the idea that if a man is present in the home of a single female, then he should be paying if he has an income. The change will generate some savings (how much is not estimated), but its primary purpose appears to be both moralistic and punitive. The message is that (heterosexual) single people who "play house" should not be supported by the state. If they do, the state will punish them by cutting them off welfare.

A second major element is a change in what is called the "quit–fired" policy. Under the old rule, the applicant or the recipient of general welfare could be refused benefits for one month if they refused or resigned from employment without "just cause" or if they were dismissed because of "wilful misconduct, disobedience or wilful neglect." However, if welfare administrators considered the penalty too harsh, they could simply reduce but not terminate benefits (Ontario Ministry of Community and Social Services 1995: 72).

Under the new rule, the quit–fired penalty was raised to three months and the administrator was no longer able to exempt any cases. In the case of a family dependent on the welfare and income of an applicant/recipient, the welfare would be available for the dependants only. The argument utilized for this rule change is that it will stop workers from using welfare as a bridge to a better job. Now they will have to stay with the job until another is available. It is another way to reduce the capacity of workers to refuse or to quit inadequate or abusive employment.

A third element is a change intended to make it more difficult for 16- and 17-year olds to obtain welfare. Attendance at a school or training institution will be mandatory as a condition of receiving welfare unless there is "medical evidence verifying a need for treatment" (Ontario Ministry of Community and Social Services 1995:4).

There is no doubt that youth on welfare is an emotive and controversial issue. At what age does a youth make the transition to adulthood and independence? On this, there is no consensus in Ontario or elsewhere in the country. For example a youth may drive at 16, vote at 18, and drink alcohol at 19. Child welfare legislation applies to children up to the age of 16. In moving to reduce their access to welfare, the Harris government is stating that 16- and 17-year-old youth should be subject to parental care. Will the government review other child-related legislation for consistency with this view? Or is this another cost-cutting measure which will force more youth to remain in abusive homes or to take to the streets?

The Fiscal and Economic Statement

On November 29, 1995, the Ontario minister of finance released a document which, he stated, was to form "an essential part of our program to renew Ontario" (Ontario Ministry of Finance 1995: 1). The document asserted that the problems of the previous decade were due to overspending, high taxes, and deficit financing, all of which were barriers to job creation (Ontario Ministry of Finance 1995: 2). The document signalled the government's view that the priority for the government would be cutting expenditures, taxes and regulations. It claimed this would create jobs and a balanced budget within five years.

The statement noted that federal reductions in transfer payments to Ontario for health, education and social services would total $2.2 billion over the subsequent two year period.[2] These cuts would be taken into account in the provincial government's calculations. In order to bring about further expenditure reductions, the province announced a series of measures which included a reduction of $290 million in transfers to the municipalities in 1996-97 and a further cut of $262 million in 1997–98 (Ontario Ministry of Finance 1995: 17–18). While the government noted that these reductions represented roughly 2 percent of the total municipal budgets per year they did not note that the total cut in the provincial transfer (including that made necessary by the transfer payments) would amount to 22.4 percent in year one and almost 43 percent over the two-year period.

These cuts have forced municipalities to review and reduce their budgets. Since social assistance spending is a major portion of local spending, it was inevitable that municipalities would make changes in their welfare budgets. Since they are obligated to continue to pay for a portion of the cost of general welfare and must administer it according to a framework set by Queens Park, the easiest part of the welfare budget to cut is discretionary benefits. In Ontario, municipalities deliver a discretionary program of special and supplementary benefits for both general welfare and family benefits recipients. Under these programs, municipalities pay a major portion of the cost of moving expenses, special medical expenses (particularly for persons with disabilities), emergency travel, special furniture and clothing expenses, and expenses related to death. These programs have come and will increasingly come under pressure as municipalities, facing further reductions in transfer income, attempt to reduce their expenses.

The government continued to reduce the incomes of low-income Ontarians with its proposals to reform the Ontario Drug Plan. From the first of June 1996, social assistance recipients and seniors receiving the guaranteed income supplement (seniors must have relatively low incomes to qualify) have been required to make a co-payment of $2. per prescription. Further, seniors earning over $16,000 individually, or as a family earn over $24,000 per year, would be obligated to pay the first $100 of drug-related expenses and to pay the pharmacist's dispensing fee. The statement estimated that a further $225 million would be saved at the expense of low-income Ontarians (Ontario Ministry of Finance 1995: 23).

The Ontario Budget 1996

The first Ontario budget (Ontario Minister of Finance 1996) featured the *Common Sense Revolution*'s promised tax cut. The reduction in the provincial income tax rate would be 30.2 percent, to be implemented over a three-year period. While the government noted that 520,000 modest-income taxpayers would benefit, a percentage reduction is bound to provide its largest benefits to people with higher incomes. It could be argued that it was the reductions in social assistance spending which made the tax cut possible, an example of the Conservative version of Robin Hood—taking from the poor to give to the rich.

The budget also made mention of an expected Ontario Support Plan for seniors and disabled persons, a plan intended to take these groups out of welfare, and a school nutrition program which would be started in partnership with a non-profit organization. Both items were promised in the *Common Sense Revolution*. Lastly, the budget took credit for a drop in caseload of 129,000 between June 1995 and March 1996, although without any evidence as to why the government's policies should have been responsible.

Ontario Works

On June 12, 1996, the Ministry of Community and Social Services announced the Ontario Works program according to which, welfare recipients would be obligated to work for their welfare cheques. Disabled persons, seniors, and single parents with young children would be exempt. Echoing the *Common Sense Revolution* (Ontario Progressive Conservative Party 1995), the ministry news release suggested that workfare would "break the cycle of dependency created by the previous administration." Twenty communities had consented to become involved; the ministry announced it expected all communities to be involved by 1998. Of the $1.3 billion in social assistance savings which would result from previous cuts, $450 million would be reinvested in obligatory workfare (Ontario Ministry of Community and Social Services 1996b).

Six days later the ministry announced a reorganization of employment programs which provided more detail on the free enterprise involvement in the program. Job-ready recipients would be referred to commercial or non-profit placement agencies who would be paid an up-front fee of $200 per recipient and a percentage of the savings up to a maximum of $1200 per recipient. Community groups were invited to sponsor local projects for which Ontario Works would potentially cover the costs. Welfare recipients would be expected to work an average of seventeen hours a week (Ontario Minister of Community and Social Services 1996; Ontario Ministry of Community and Social Services 1996a; Ontario Ministry of Community and Social Services 1996b).

According to the ministry, workfare would take a number of forms: job-ready recipients would be referred to placement agencies; some recipients could be involved in work-oriented training (but not in university since the government had previously announced that university students could not collect welfare); some recipients would become involved in community projects; a few may become involved in starting their own business. Many questions were left unanswered by the publicity. Would recipients get to choose among these options? How much of the $450 million would be spent on these twenty pilots? What kind of personal and financial support would be available? How long would recipients be obligated to participate? Will the emphasis be on people who are job-ready, as in many of the U.S. workfare programs? Will any funds be available for literacy training? Will there be penalties for non-attendance or nonparticipation? And since the program is publicized as "results-oriented" will any effort be made to evaluate the effectiveness of the program?

Conclusion

In their first year in office, the Ontario Conservatives have moved swiftly to implement their agenda of cutting expenditures and reducing government and taxes. It is clear that they have been busy getting done what they promised to do in their pre-election document. They have stuck to the script offered by the *Common Sense Revolution* even to the point of using the language of that document in presenting their legislative and administrative changes. They have faced some significant labour opposition but so far it has had no significant impact on their program. Further, it appears that in carrying out their program they have until now remained popular.

They have cut welfare rates relative to those prevalent in other provinces, ignoring the relatively high cost of housing in many parts of Ontario. The cuts have resulted in many hardships for individuals and families who have been forced to accept poorer housing conditions. Instead of setting a standard for decency in the treatment of the poor, they have argued that Ontario should be less generous because the standard in other provinces is lower.

Born of the bitter experience of the Depression, Canada's welfare laws since the 1960s have prohibited compulsory work for welfare and supported the principle that all people demonstrably in need should have access to social support. In reducing eligibility, the Conservatives have moved the administration of welfare farther away from the principle that the community should support all people in need, not simply those whom the government judges to be more deserving. In introducing workfare, they have contradicted the 30-year-old principle that desperate people should not be forced to take a job in order to get the support they need. In doing so they have not found a new and more efficient way of running a welfare program. They have simply begun the process of returning us to the past.

Welfare under the Conservatives will be more punitive, less generous and less supportive. For social justice organizations who oppose this Conservative vision of the future, the task ahead is to re-establish in Ontario a vision of an economically stable society within which a greater sense of social solidarity and generosity will again be possible.

Notes

1. The author wishes to thank Matthew Deline for his assistance in locating many of the documents used to complete this chapter. Thanks also to Ruel Amdur for his explanation of changes in the administration of social assistance, to Linda Lalonde for her explanation of the impact of the changes, and to Diana Ralph and Nérée St-Amand for their patience and for their editing of the text. Any errors or omissions are the sole responsibility of the author.
2. In the 1995 budget, the federal government announced the termination of the Canada

Assistance Plan effective 1 April 1996. It was replaced by the Canada Health and Social Transfer which consolidates into one block fund federal transfers to the provinces for health care, social assistance, social services and post-secondary education. In early 1994 the federal government had announced plans to reform social security in Canada by revising the way the existing envelope of funds could be spent. By the time of the federal budget in 1995 this commitment to maintain funding had changed to a substantial reduction in federal funding of provincial social assistance for 1996–97. The 1996 budget indicated federal plans to further reduce federal transfers for 1997–98 and to stabilize them at this reduced level until into the next century (Government of Canada 1996: 12; Government of Canada 1995: 25; Government of Canada 1994).

Chapter 7

Tory Welfare Policies:
A View from the Inside
Linda Lalonde

Impacts on Housing

The welfare cuts were announced in July 1995. We knew after the election that something was coming, but we didn't know how much or how bad. Many people were hit harder by the cuts due to actions they took around their housing before the cuts came out. For example say you are a single mom with one child. Before the cuts, $652 was the maximum amount you could get for rent before the cuts. You had signed a lease on June 1, 1995 for two years, on the reasonable expectation that you were going to get at least the same amount for shelter. So you signed a lease for $625, which left you some money for hydro or other expenses. That would have been a reasonable activity on the first of June, and if you had any brains, you signed for two years, locking yourself in at that amount, so that you would be protected if rents went up. Now their maximum rental allowance is $511. So those people who were doing a responsible thing are coming out the worst, because they are stuck in those leases. The landlords are not going to let them leave unless they can produce a sublet, but where are you going to get a sublet? From someone in the same position as you?

Other people had their names down for various forms of subsidized housing, such as co-op housing, and planned to move into them this year. As a result of Harris's freeze on non-profit housing starts, that co-op is not going to be built. And now they are stuck in a place that they can't afford or which is sub-standard. And they can't afford to move.

Rooming House Landlords Profiteering from the Cuts

If you look at rooming house prices for the past twenty years, you will see they increase lock-step with the welfare rates for single people. So if the rental allowance was $300, the rooms also went for around $300. Then when the allowance went up to $325, rooming house rates again went up. When the allowance was at $414, rooms were renting at about $425.

Rooming house landlords have done two things since the cuts to welfare. Some have put their rents down, although usually not by as much as the cuts. You had $414 in shelter allowance and after the cuts you had $325. So you saw rents drop from $425 to $375. I don't think anybody brought it down to $325. Other landlords have taken single rooms and put in bunk beds. Where there were six rooms in the house with six people living there, sharing one or two bathrooms and one or two kitchens, now there are twelve people. Let's say the room would have rented for $400 before, it's now renting to two people for $275 each. So the landlord is actually ahead of the game with $550. You are still able to live on your welfare, but you are living in what is basically a powder keg. You don't have room to turn around, you can't even close your door and be alone.

In some cases it is a buddy with whom you are sharing. What happens when your buddy moves out? They are not going to let you keep the room for $275. Obviously the landlord is not going to roll his rent back to $325 from $550 with only one person in the room. They are going to move someone in with you. I would not want to be around some of those places on a hot summer day. I think there are going to be some social problems coming out of these places.

I know one landlord who said he would help you find someone else to move into your place, but the biggest place he has is a two bedroom. Where there was a mom and two kids in an apartment, i.e. the mother in one bedroom, and the kids in the other, he has moved in another single mom with one kid, under the guise of helping single moms meet their rent. But, in fact, what he is doing is making sure his place is filled. He doesn't give a damn about what is happening in the life of the families. And obviously if you take two families and put them together, you are going to have conflicts, whether between the parents or the kids. Again you are asking for trouble.

We have seen situations where a recipient has found someone with whom to move in. Each family can only access the moving allowance once a year, so they have used it and moved in with Joe or Susie. It doesn't work out and they are trapped there. So they end up taking money out of food in order to move out into another place. Remember that they have to come up with first and last month's rent. What they originally thought was going to be a money-saving move ends up costing them money. People have not got a lot of manoeuvrability when they have several mouths to feed.

I was in the landlord–tenant court early in 1996. Of the people there who didn't have representation, two-thirds identified themselves as being on social assistance. The reason they gave for non-payment of rent was the welfare cuts.

In the first two weeks of January 1996, seventeen people came into our office homeless because of the cuts.

Forcing Recipients to Quit School
Many people on assistance have quit going to school. They were saying "okay, I can afford to live as a single parent, and I can look after my kids and go to school, and I can get by with OSAP (Ontario Student Assistance Program) topped-up by welfare." Then the welfare cheque was reduced, and the provincial government said people could go out and get a job to make it back. If you are going to school and raising three kids, obviously your school work is going to suffer. So some people have said: "I'm not going to take the chance of messing up my school record." No one wants to drop from a B+ average, to a C- and then have to explain to a potential employer or graduate school that the reason was the welfare cuts.

That is a permanent mark on your academic record. So there were lots of people who quit school as soon as the cuts were announced. Some of them are going part-time, but a lot of them are out permanently. It has hit people who were on a career path through education, not just those doing upgrading but people who were going to college and university.

Now the provincial government has announced that people will not be able to attend school while on welfare. They will have to apply for OSAP. Although OSAP will be increased, this effectively will make welfare into a repayable loan if people want to better their education. Unless she is prepared to put herself into serious debt, a single mother will have no choice but to stay on welfare.

Cuts to Municipalities

The most devious cuts to programs made by the Harris Tories may be those to lower levels of government. These have been an excellent way for them to force someone else to take the flack for the Tories' dirty work.

The worst of these cuts was to child care. Amended in July 1995, the new legislation took effect the following October. For the previous few years, the NDP government had created new child care spaces only through the jobsOntario (JOT) program which had as its other components training, community economic development and job creation. Although child care spaces are normally funded 80:20 by the provincial and local governments, the JOT spaces were funded 100 percent by the province. This was to allow social assistance recipients to participate in training or start employment even if the municipality could not afford its share of the cost. This spread the social safety net more evenly over the province. There were approximately 14,000 of these spaces across Ontario. Any subsidized spaces in a new daycare centre opened in the last few years would be entirely JOT spots.

Then the Tories announced half-way through the municipalities' fiscal period that at the three-quarter point of their year, they would lose the extra funding and have to pick up the 20 percent for the rest of the year. It is vital to note that *by provincial legislation*, a municipality cannot run a deficit. The only ways those spaces could be maintained would be to impose a special tax levy (right before Christmas?), to divert the fund from an existing program (and potentially kill or cripple the other program) or to offer a reduced subsidy to the parents (thereby increasing their daycare fees, often out of their reach). Many municipalities chose to close the spaces, in some cases putting the viability of the whole daycare centre in jeopardy. But if you ask any Tory MPP, they will tell you they have not closed a single daycare space—those decisions were made by the municipalities. And, they will say, these were probably good decisions made by the people closest to the situation and best able to judge whether those daycare spaces were necessary or not. Of course, there was no consultation with the experts, i.e. those parents who had to quit school or work because they had no child care.

It is important to remember that these spaces were created for people on social assistance who had gotten jobs or gone into a training program. These are people who are actively trying to get off the welfare system—just the sort of people one would think a government with the stated goal of getting folks off assistance would want to support and use as role models. If, however, the Tories' real goal is to punish and humiliate people and destroy any chance the "thems" have of becoming "us," a good way to do it is to hack away at the supports that enable people to become self-sufficient.

Opportunity Planning versus Workfare

The Tory government is presenting workfare as the employment program of the future. They have stepped over or around many years of research and study, some of it conducted by their own ministry or their municipal partners. The Social Services Department of the Regional Municipality of Ottawa–Carleton, for example, has been involved for the past four years as a partner with social assistance recipients and community agencies including the Social Assistance Recipient (SAR) Council, in a pilot project to test the concept of Opportunity Planning (OP) for recipients. This is one of nine pilot projects around Ontario, each of which is testing a different model. This pilot was developed as the culmination of years of work with the community in the employment area, involving not just deliverers of employment programs but social service agencies and clients as well. I have been involved with the pilot project from the start and have chaired its community management committee for the last three years. The model chosen involved a partnership between the welfare worker and the recipient to develop an action plan which identifies the recipient's barriers to employment and sets out a plan to overcome them. If a client needed specific services in the community and could not otherwise access them, the pilot had funds to provide them. These included counselling, resumé writing, training, transportation, and child care, as well as specific equipment needed for training or employment. Social service workers were given extensive training in assessments, community resources, computers and other areas to enable them to respond to their clients' needs appropriately. In addition, caseloads were reduced from 1:105 to 1:90 to enable them to spend the necessary time with each client.

Although, in the fall of 1995, the Tories disbanded the evaluation unit that was studying the nine pilots across the province, the Ottawa pilot arranged to have its own evaluation done (Michaud 1996). The results were amazing. Over the first two and a half years, the pilot saved the province and the region $1,500,000 per year in direct social assistance costs. People who went through the pilot had a lower rate of re-application than the control group. In addition, both the workers and the clients expressed a high degree of satisfaction with their experience. Ottawa–Carleton Regional Council, in the spring of 1996, endorsed the OP model and its principles and recommended it to the province instead of workfare. Because OP does not punish welfare recipients but rather supports them, does not send them into pointless busywork but involves them in an organized approach to employment preparation, does not blame them for their poverty but encourages them to find ways out of it, this provincial government will not examine it as an alternative, let alone adopt it across the board as a way to get recipients permanently off social assistance and into good, well-paying jobs. It is completely opposite to the retrograde and punitive programs they favour such as workfare.

Impacts on Health

The Harris cuts will have serious effects on people's health and well-being. First among these will be the results of simple deprivation since folks won't have adequate food and shelter without adequate income. In many cases, this will mean poor maternal health, since mothers will often deny themselves before their children. It will be difficult if not impossible to track these situations and attribute them directly to the cuts. If a mum has six colds instead of two next year, was it the weather? Was she taking care of herself? Did she get caught in the rain a lot? Couldn't she afford a raincoat and boots or did she fritter her money away on food for her kids?

The cuts to hospitals and health care in general will impact much more severely on the poor than on the wider population. It is well known that the poor require health care more intensely and more often than other segments of society. This is a result of poorer nutrition, lowered resistance to disease, living in more cramped quarters and substandard housing, less access to recreation, fatigue and, in some cases, unstable employment. They also tend to have more serious accidents and self-inflicted injuries than people who are not so poor. So they wind up using emergency wards and having health crises that require (expensive) hospitalization more often. The rich have access to health care options such as American hospitals and specialists, or private nurses, which are not available to the poor. They also have the choice to eat properly and generally to preserve their health better than their poorer compatriots.

Poor children often begin life less pleasantly than the children of the rich. The incidence of low birth-weight with all its attendant risks is significantly influenced by economic class. The Ontario Ministry of Health, under the Tories, is promoting early discharge from hospitals, including maternity patients, as a cost-saving measure. The early discharge of mothers and their newborns as soon as twenty four hours after birth puts both at risk, but particularly the child. Most poor women are not going home to a nurse or nanny and often they do not even have a spouse who could help take care of both mother and baby. In fact, Mum may be going home to care for other children and returning to work very soon because she can't afford to take time off.

The most critical time in the establishment of breastfeeding is not in the first day but several days down the road. If Mum does not have access to help and advice, it is all too easy for her to abandon nursing and resort to the bottle, thus depriving her baby of the health and social advantages of breastfeeding. Bottle feeding is also more expensive than nursing, further contributing to the family's troubles.

Drugs

One of the most dangerous and insidious cuts is to the Ontario Drug Benefit Plan. The government is adding a user fee, euphemistically referred to as a "co-payment," to every prescription provided to a senior or social assistance recipient in the province. The amount of the user fee varies, depending on your age, from $2.00 to $6.11 per prescription. While this may not seem a significant amount, it has the potential to seriously affect people's health. The other danger, of course, is that what starts as a minimal sum can increase dramatically once it has achieved a certain level of acceptance and become the status quo. For example, the government of Quebec has recently announced that seniors in that province who had been paying that "minimal" amount of $2.00 (sound familiar?) will soon begin to pay 25 percent of the cost of their prescriptions up to a ceiling of just over $300 per year. But don't get them wrong—minimal payments are nothing to fear!

Every Tory has a story, so they have found two reasons why they have no choice but to cut service—it will cut down on over-use/misuse of medication and it will help save the health care system and particularly the drug program for the future. I think they have slightly missed the correct target for action. If a doctor gives someone six prescriptions, two of which are unnecessary, surely it is the doctor, not the patient, who needs to be corrected.

In many cases, medicines interact with or interdepend on each other and it could be dangerous for the patient not to take one or the other. For example, the doctor may have prescribed five grams of medicine A and ten grams of medicine B. Both are essential. He has also give five grams of medicine C because the combination of A and B will have undesirable side effects. The three have to be taken together and in the right dosage or the entire process is useless and potentially life-threatening.

At the same time, people may not be able to afford the drugs when they need them. Single people on assistance get only $195 to cover everything over and above their shelter allowance. This includes paying any part of their rent that is above $325. A family may have two or three members sick at the same time. Picture a parent making the choice on the 26th of the month whether to spend their last $20 on drugs for the kids or on milk and bread for the family.

Sick people face costs other than prescription drugs such as over-the-counter drugs, bus fare to the doctor's office and the lab, specific foods, etc. None of these costs is subsidized. Some people are on assistance due to their medical condition and it is their medication that is keeping them out of hospital. Common sense would indicate that the government should pay the drug costs since they are lower than the costs of hospitalization. Somehow when you capitalize the "s" in "sense," as in Common Sense Revolution, it changes all that.

Emotional Impacts of the Cuts

We are seeing a growing level of desperation since the cuts. People have gone through that time where they could scrape by, and even manage, but now they are getting into the time where their flour is running out.

One woman came into our office and said that she has had to put her kids in care with the Children's Aid Society (CAS). She knows that if she puts her children in care, they will be fed, clothed and sheltered at a middle-class level, and that the best she can do for them is little more than keeping them alive. She said, that as a responsible parent, she should put them into care. CAS says to her, that they can't take them because she's not abusing them. They are in a safe housing situation; they are going to school; they are clean and they have appropriate clothes. She told us that if she drops them off enough times in the lobby of Children's Aid, they will take them. "If that doesn't work I will drop them off at the cop shop; if that doesn't work, I will drop them off at the Children's Hospital." Obviously that has to be affecting her relationship with the children.

Forcing Women and Children to Stay in Abusive Relationships

We know of situations where women are staying in abusive situations because they have looked at what they can afford on $511 a month in rent and they are not prepared to take that particular leap. If they knew that they were going to continue to get $511, that might be different. But the way that the government is talking, there is no guarantee that the support is going to be there next year or even next month. Normally, they would say "I can swing that somehow." But people can no longer count on even that level of support. They are trying not to put themselves in the situation where the second or tenth round of cuts can hit them again. They won't go to a place where they are only borderline able to manage, but not much more. I think that is what is motivating women who are staying in dangerous situations.

Why the Numbers on Welfare Are Dropping

Although the welfare rolls are dropping, the Tories are carefully not tracking where people are going. If they believed that their programs were getting people jobs, the very first thing they would do is jump up and down from roof tops and fly those figures around. So if they choose not to do the tracking that would tell where those people went, it is because the answer is not one they want to have. After all, freedom of information laws might provide those answers to the public and put the lie to their claims that they are de-welfaring Ontario.

We know that a lot of people are no longer collecting welfare. But that doesn't mean they have improved their situation. Large numbers of people are going off assistance because they can't sustain their housing. When they become unable to sustain their housing, they stop being counted as welfare recipients. For example, when someone goes into a shelter, they go off social assistance.

Sometimes to survive, a mom has found a job as a waitress. But the job won't sustain her and the child, and allow her to live in decent housing. So she has gone to live on her friend's couch, and has sent her kids back to their father, who may or may not be abusive. I'm not suggesting that every situation like this is wrong. Sometimes the kid is better off with dad than with mom. But what that shows is not that the family is broken up, but that mom went off welfare. All they are tracking is the drop in cases.

If you are a student and you have OSAP to cover your other expenses, you are not on welfare anymore; you are on another form of government assistance. But that form of government income is going to see you walk out of school with a high debt. You may have to move back in with your parents, with whatever problems that brings.

People Are Dying Because of the Cuts

Starting last September and early October, we had many calls from people who said: "I have sat down and done the numbers, and I can't live. I don't have enough money to survive." I remember one particular gentleman calling in and saying "I'm trying to decide, and I want to ask you are these numbers right? Is this what I'm going to have?" And he basically said "the decision I have in front of me now, is that I know I don't have enough money to live on starting in November, so there are two ways I can die. Do I jump off a bridge or throw myself under a train, and do I do it now so I don't have to live in deprivation, or do I wait, knowing that ahead of me is that same solution; that either I starve to death, or in three months' time, I'm going to do myself in. And I'm asking why wait for spring? Why not do it now?"

A psychiatric hospital had three patients whose families had called in for help over the 1995 Thanksgiving weekend, and it took those people off its out-patient roll on Tuesday. They had committed suicide. That is in one weekend.

Psychiatric Patients Are Particularly Vulnerable

We have people calling in and saying "if I do this, will I be okay?" and trying to figure out how to live inside the new smaller box. In a lot of cases, these are psychiatric patients who can't get the right note from the doctors to qualify for long term disability. They can't hold down permanent jobs; if you are an alcoholic, you may be able to work for three or four days, or until your first pay cheque, and then you fall off the wagon. You have a history of 400 jobs, but they have only lasted a week. A lot of people are going out and getting these jobs that only last a week, so it's not as if they are not trying to do something. But they need that support in the middle when they bottom out. Welfare needs to be there to support them.

People with psychiatric illnesses run into bureaucratic hassles. Unless you are sick the day you go to ask the doctor to sign the forms to say you can't work, you can't get on long term disability. If you have an episodic illness, you may be having a really good day when you see the doctor, and he or she can say that you are at a level where you can work again. That person doesn't see you when you are in the depths of despair. Or the doctor sees you when the medication is working and doesn't see you when the medication is not working. So you may be able to go and get a job. But after four days, you are going to lay out the foreman on the floor. That's not really recommended for your long term career prospects. Those people know that while they may not be able to verbalize, they are not really employable. They know that they are going to have this sort of up-and-down history. They are sitting there saying "there is no way that I can go out and get a job that would make up the difference. I might be able to do a little something here and a little something there. Maybe my brother-in-law will hire me to fix his car or whatever." They know that they are not going to be able to rely on their own resources.

The Myth of the Lazy Welfare Bum

The effort people are making to get off social assistance doesn't really fit in with the popular image of sitting at home with smokes and beer, and running out to bingo. I think I have met only one person in eighteen years who wanted to be on welfare. I would say she had other problems that contributed to that decision. In Ottawa–Carleton, we can demonstrate that for every single program to get people off welfare, whether it's a job-finding club, or resumé writing, or life skills, or upgrading courses, there are people lined up down the street to get into it. These programs are always over-subscribed. I have seen people with literally no chance of employment, going out and applying for job after job after job, because they didn't want to sit at home on welfare. There is that stereotype, but it's just not realistic. Most people want to work. You don't look through many school yearbooks and see many people who said "I want to be a welfare bum." Some people, because of alcohol problems, illnesses or family responsibilities, may give the appearance to the outsider that they are sitting at home chugging back that beer and collecting that welfare cheque, but this is not accurate.

Welfare Abuse

There *is* abuse of the system. I won't deny that. I know several people who are abusing the system. A few of them are doing so maliciously; most others are doing it as a way to survive, because they don't know of any other way. I'm not going to say to a mom who can't afford to pay for shoes for her kids "don't go out and wash Mr. Richman's floors one afternoon a week so that you can afford to buy shoes for your daughter." That is not malicious abuse. I think there is a difference. You need to distinguish between people who abuse the system with criminal intent and those who are trying to survive. If someone is collecting welfare in Ottawa, Edmonton, Montreal, Vancouver, Halifax and Toronto, and wherever else in between, I have a problem with that. A mom who goes in with her six kids to collect welfare, and then lends four of her kids to her sister next week to go in and apply for welfare, I have a problem with that too. But, people who are stretching the limits to be able to live are not committing the same kind of abuse.

Poor-Bashing Ideology

I think that people need to understand that Harris's welfare policies are a question of ideology. It has nothing to do with improving people's lot in life or saving money for the system. It is purely and simply ideological. And it's not going to work. It is not going to produce people who suddenly get the vision and say "I too can get a full-time job. What am I doing sitting around at home? Thank you Mike Harris for pointing that out to me."

The Harris anti-social policies do not in any way deal with the underlying problems of why people are unemployed, and why the individual is not able to get a job, or why the economy is not able to provide these people with jobs. If we want long term solutions, we find out why that person is not able to hold down a permanent job, or is not able to get a job.

Conclusion

The activities of the Regressive Preservatives—or do I mean the Progressive Conservatives?—under Michael Harris should not come as a surprise to anyone. Their intensions were very clear in both the *Common Sense Revolution* (Ontario Progressive Conservatives 1995), a document which they distributed to almost every home in the province, and in their speeches both before and after the election. They intended to change the face of Ontario, to reduce welfare rates, to introduce workfare, to unload public housing and take government out of the housing business, to cut government spending and to free up business from government restrictions.

The difference between the Tories and other governments we have known is that the Tories implemented the program that they advertised. They have also acted on a policy of "hit hard, hit fast and take no prisoners." They, in fact, declared war on Ontario as we knew it. They have set out to entrench their philosophy throughout the government in such a way that it cannot be dislodged even if they are not re-elected. This presents unique dangers to poor people.

The first targets of the Tories were people on social assistance and those who depended on community social services. I would suggest this is because they perceive them to be the easiest targets and the least able to defend themselves. The poor have traditionally been difficult to organize and many years of poor-bashing have made them vulnerable to society's disdain. Cuts to community agencies made some of them as vulnerable as those they serve and, in some cases, unable to support their communities in fighting the other activities of the Harris Tories.

The Tories are destroying the services we had and thereby drastically lowering the standards to which we can aspire. By establishing a lower base point, they make it much harder for us to support our previous arguments for how things should be. Let's say we were previously at 20 on a scale of 1 to 30—we could set a 25 percent increase as our goal and work towards reaching 25. When they move us back to 10, an improvement of 25 percent only gets us to 12.5 and we would be portrayed as unreasonable in reaching for 15, never mind 20. The status quo is now established at 10 and anything over that is now an improvement. So if in four years the Tories give welfare recipients a 2 percent increase, people will see it as having more money to buy the necessities of life as opposed to its being still less than recipients got in 1985, fifteen years earlier.

Creating a new status quo early on means it will become accepted by people and less easily challenged by groups now firmly labelled as "special interest." This means we are no longer running to stay in the same place; we are running to keep that place from disappearing from view entirely. For the poor who often run barefoot and on gravel roads, the race is over before it has really begun. We are becoming outcasts in our own communities, rejected by the government which is itself the author of many of our misfortunes. By attacking our health care system, income security programs, education opportunities, housing options, child care choices and community supports the Ontario Tories have declared open season on the poor and fired the first shots.

Chapter 8

"Common Sense" Assaults on Families

Brigitte Kitchen

The Growing Divide: The Sixty-Forty Society

Canada is a profoundly, and increasingly, inequitable society. This reality is reflected in the declining share of market incomes accruing to families in the three lower-income groups, which comprise 60 percent of Canadian families. Their share of income fell from 41.1 percent in 1981 to 40.1 percent in 1992 (Centre for International Statistics 1995). This widening of income inequalities is a socioeconomic phenomenon observed in every G-7 country. Globalization and the neo-conservative agenda of shrinking government have created 60–40 societies where the "triumph of capitalism" (to borrow a term from Gary Teeple 1995) has benefited the top 40 percent of families while diminishing the economic prospects of modest- and low-income families. In the past, federal and provincial social programs like unemployment insurance, social assistance and workers' compensation have prevented the widening of income inequalities between families. In Ontario, the Harris government's social policy agenda, set out in its Common Sense Revolution election platform, aims to scuttle the effect social programs have on income distribution. The Harris government's agenda demands that the widening of income inequalities in the market no longer be controlled through political action.

From its New Right perspective, the Ontario government attributes to the market the ability to create a more economically healthy society than could ever be achieved through the intervention of government. In Harris's Ontario the inability of individuals and their families to meet their subsistence needs is defined as a personal flaw when it is in fact the result of downsizing and restructuring. That Ontario, more than any other province, is caught simultaneously in a cyclical as well as a structural job crisis that has robbed families of their ability to provide for themselves in the labour market does not seem to disrupt the New Right's blind faith in the market.

This chapter argues that the Harris government's moral fervour for small government, low taxes and a diminished, "affordable" welfare will destabilize the basic floor of material security on which family life depends. It points out that the cuts to social programs and services signal a redefinition of government's responsibility for family life. Lower social assistance benefits, the reduction of child care services for working families, the re-introduction of the "spouse-in-the-house" rule, and changes to the Ontario Family Support Plan increase stress on the most economically vulnerable families, particularly those parenting alone.

While Ernie Eves is fond of claiming that "for the sake of our children...we must put our fiscal house in order" (Pascal 1996: A23), his government's policies in fact constitute an outright assault on families in Ontario.

The Market Assault on Family Life

Raising children requires money, energy and time; pre-requisites that are scarcities for the majority of families, and compounded for sole support parents who have to compensate for the loss of the other parent in all three areas. Unfettered market forces which throw people out of work or diminish their salaries make it difficult or impossible for many to provide for their children. They also generate an individualistic self-interest which is destructive to family life and separates families from one another—each competing for jobs, higher wages and other material resources (De'Ath 1983: 50). The New Right policy orientation of the Ontario government also aims to establish the independence of families from the state. It expects families to take primary responsibility for themselves and not rely on government to protect their standard of living against market forces. The freezing of the minimum wage at $6.85 an hour is one measure this government considered crucial to achieving this goal.

The minimum wage has always been an important factor protecting the purchasing power of those working in the low-wage labour market, where women and young workers are mainly concentrated. By reducing the protective powers of unions, cutting the funds for retraining, and decreasing the funds to colleges and universities in Ontario, the Harris government aims to create a low-paid economy in Ontario. This is an agenda that counteracts and undermines the stability of family life. To make ends meet both parents have to hold down a job. In only 27 percent of husband–wife families is the husband the only income earner (Vanier Institute of the Family 1994: 71). This means that the vast majority of parents have less time to spend with their children and have to add the costs of child care to their limited household resources. The Statistics Canada Survey of Family Expenditures for 1992 found that, despite their considerably lower incomes, sole support parents spent almost as much on the necessities of life as childless couples did—91 percent as much on groceries and 84 percent as much on housing (Centre for International Statistics 1995).

Bill 26 (the Omnibus Bill) allows cities to charge for library cards and the use of skating rinks and swimming pools, and increase fees for recreation programs in parks and community centres. These additional charges have to come out of the already strained pay cheques of low- and modest-income families—those with incomes of $40,000 and less. With these changes, their struggle to make ends meet will become even more difficult.

The high consumption needs of children make parents the primary spenders in the Canadian economy. Consumer spending makes up 60 percent of the economy in Canada. If parents cannot find jobs, or can land only low-paying jobs that do not pay enough to support their families, the economy suffers from the lack of family spending power. The more efficiently produced goods and services of downsized companies remain unsold on the shelves, and business profits fall. Furthermore, families can only cut their budgets to a certain point. The way they spend their money often causes major disputes, undermining already shaky marriages and contributing to marriage breakup. Paul Atwell from the Graduate School of City University in New York points out that couples out of a job divorce at a rate 30 percent higher than the norm for their age, education and family background (St. George, Feb. 24 1996: B3).

Gender Matters

The current government's destruction of Ontario's social infrastructure represents an abrogation of our collective responsibility for the social and economic well-being of all citizens. It is by no means gender neutral. While the economic prospects for almost all families raising children in Ontario today are dismal, sole support mothers and their dependent children suffer more than men from measures undermining the welfare state. Their risk of living in poverty is five times greater than that of two-parent families (National Council of Welfare 1996: 17). The reasons for their poverty cannot be attributed to their sole parenting but are directly related to their gender. Men raising children on their own do not experience the same degree of poverty, nor do they remain living in poverty for as long (Kitchen 1992: 12). The economic vulnerability of mothers is a reflection of their disadvantaged position in a labour market that is increasingly segmented into high-skilled, well-paying and low-skilled, low-paying jobs. Women are overwhelmingly found in the low-paying jobs, and even when they work at higher-paying jobs, women receive only two-thirds the payments of men. The Common Sense Revolution ensures that women's economic situation is not likely to improve.

Employment and Pay Equity

In a gender-segmented labour market the Harris government has increased women's vulnerability by abolishing employment and pay equity provisions. Section J of Bill 26, the Omnibus Bill, either eliminates or changes some forty pieces of social legislation, including the proxy method for determining pay equity. Both the Equity Commission and the Advocacy Commission introduced by the previous government have been scrapped. About 100,000 Ontario women will lose $81 million in pay equity payments because they have jobs at which men traditionally do not work (Walker, Oct. 6 1995: A1). The government argues that a direct comparison between their pay scales and those of men is impossible. The insistence that wage levels are determined by the market and not by government regulation discriminates against women working in traditionally low-paid service sectors such as child care, nursing homes, cafeterias and domestic work.

Women's participation in the labour market on an equal basis with men depends on the scope and adequacy of services provided by the state. Because of women's continuing primary responsibility for child care, women either do not participate in the workforce or work part-time. As a result, their pay scales and job advancements fall considerably below men's, or they are dependent on the earnings of a man in their lives, and failing that, they become dependants of the state. Employment and pay equity are important measures supporting women's efforts to gain self-reliance. For women in particular, the systematic impoverishment of the public sector by the Ontario government can only mean that the limited economic power and control over their lives that they had been able to gain is put even more in jeopardy. Employment and pay gender equity would go a long way to break women's economic dependence on men and government. A 1977 U.S. government study found "that if...women were paid what similarly qualified men earn, the number of poor families would decrease by half" (quoted in Feldberg 1986: 164).

Child Care

The Harris government has made much of its commitment to break the dependency of families, particularly of sole support mothers, on social assistance. It is, however, not prepared to invest money in child care to enable parents to enter the labour market or to take up training opportunities that would make them more marketable. Provincial transfer payments to the municipalities are to be reduced by a staggering 47 percent. The reduction has put the funding at risk for subsidized child care, which enables low-income parents to participate in the workforce, secure in the knowledge that their children are well looked after. Are they to quit their jobs to take care of their children? Or are they to risk the safety of their children by leaving them in the care of individuals untrained in child development? It costs up to $1200 a month to have a child cared for by qualified staff in a day-care centre.

The government's position is that it cannot afford a publicly-funded, licensed daycare system. What it does not say is that child care is yet another social program that runs counter to the New Right agenda of the Common Sense Revolution. An internal discussion paper by the Ministry of Community and Social Services suggests that government withdraw entirely from child care for school age children, leaving it entirely to parents and the private sector. Child care centres are to be licensed once every three years instead of annually and to be monitored while they are licensed by a self-regulating body (Philp 1996: A5). These plans, if carried out, would reverse the progress made in twenty years of public policy on child care in the province. Child care is one area in which the Harris government is likely to encounter vehement resistance to reduced public funding. A threat to cut the wage supplements of about 12,000 child care workers in July 1995 brought out the first major demonstration against the Harris government. More than 1000 daycare workers, parents and toddlers joined together to protest the cuts. Surprisingly, this government which has proved to be unmovable on any other issue, abandoned the idea of the cuts.

If the wages of child care workers have been protected, the loss of subsidized daycare spaces as a result of provincial cuts is still a threat to their jobs. As many as 14,000 daycare subsidies across the province are in jeopardy because of the Ontario government's decision to reduce funding from 100 percent to 80 percent. Municipalities are expected to fill the gap left by the province, which they cannot do without an increase in property taxes. Both Premier Mike Harris and the Minister of Community and Social Services David Tsubouchi suggested that parents in the workforce rely on family members, friends and neighbours to look after their children. This caused a great deal of public outrage and anger even among many Harris supporters. Parents are deeply concerned about the future of child care in the province. The government has responded to parents' concern by setting up a review of Ontario's child care system (Toughill Feb. 4, 1996: F1). Many parents understand that child care is not just a support service for those of them in the workforce. They realize the crucial importance child care plays in the intellectual, emotional and social development of their children. The question is: will the government?

Sole-Support Mothers

Low marriage rates and a rise in the number of sole-support parents seem to coincide with periods of economic decline (Blumstein and Schwartz 1983). Divorce is a fact of life in Canada. For every 2.4 couples marrying in 1990, one couple divorced (Vanier Institute of the Family 1994: 47). More than one-third of all mothers are expected to be single mothers at some point. Ontario has the second largest number of sole-support parents, after Quebec: 19.3 percent of all families (Statistics Canada 1991). Roughly two-thirds of sole-support mothers (200,000 out of 342,800 in May 1995) are supported wholly or in part by social assistance benefits (Ontario Social Safety NetWork Backgrounder #1 1995: 3).

Since taking office, the Harris government has pursued an agenda of social program cutting and changes in welfare eligibility that punish poor parents and children instead of helping them. Using the pretext that government spending in Ontario is out of control, and claiming that social assistance payments provide a standard of living beyond the comfort level, the government of Premier Mike Harris has singled out poor families as the group whose financial support it can cut with widespread public approval. In October 1995, it cut social assistance benefits by 21.6 percent. Having lost one out of five dollars, a sole-support parent with two children on family benefits now receives a basic needs allowance of $532 and a maximum shelter allowance of $707 (Statistics and Analysis Unit 1996). This gives such a parent and her children a maximum income of $1239 a month or $14,868 a year. The poverty line for a family of three is $22,000 a year in a mid-sized city (Campaign 2000 1995). A social assistance family of that size will now be living $7132 a year below the income level considered necessary for a decent standard of living. They are reduced to struggling to get by with $5.91 per person per day.

In metropolitan Toronto, a group of nine prominent citizens, politicians and media persons experimented with living on the reduced welfare rates for one week. They found it tough. For East York Mayor Michael Prue, it was a gut-wrenching experience "leaving him not only physically hungry but lethargic and even a little aggressive" (Gombu 1996: A4). These are feelings that are damaging and destructive to the ability of sole-support parents to care for their children. Parents have to be able to afford a healthy diet and have enough financial and emotional security in their lives to live up to the challenging demands of parenting. Exhaustion and aggression may cause parents to physically and emotionally neglect or even abuse their children. The future moral and social costs to Ontarians in terms of the damaged lives of children are more than likely to exceed current savings from social assistance cuts.

The impact of the social assistance cuts on recipients with some paid employment was somewhat less drastic. Those with earnings are allowed to keep a portion of their earnings. This is not a new "common sense" provision of the Harris revolution. It was also a policy of previous governments. In the context of New Right orthodoxy it is, however, part of the government's strategy of dividing those on social assistance into deserving and undeserving recipients. Arguments against social assistance are framed in terms of its understanding of common sense: "He (a taxi driver) gave me the answer in 17 words, stop paying more people more and more money just to stay at home and do nothing" (Workfare Today and Tomorrow 1996: 4). Apparently, raising children and looking for non-existent jobs—at a time when Ontario is facing its most serious employment crisis since the 1930s—is considered doing nothing.

The get-tough approach of reducing monthly welfare cheques to mere survival levels was challenged before the court by a group of social welfare advocates and community legal aid workers. The court ruled against granting an interim injunction to prevent the implementation of the cuts, but heard evidence as to whether the cuts deprived social assistance recipients of the basic means of subsistence. In January 1996, a panel of three judges ruled that the level of social assistance payments was the responsibility of government and not of the court. In fact, this ruling says that the poor cannot count on the courts to protect them from government-imposed hardship.

The Family Support Plan
The Ontario government is increasing the difficult financial situation of sole-support mothers even further with its plans to introduce substantial changes to the Ontario Family Support Plan, which ensures that non-custodial parents punctually and regularly meet their court-ordered support obligations towards their dependent children after separation or divorce. The plan currently keeps about 78,000 women and their children off social assistance. In the fiscal year 1995–96, the plan is expected to recoup $49.8 million that non-custodial parents owe sole-support mothers on welfare, thus reducing the costs of Ontario's general

welfare and family benefits programs. However, child support payments are deducted from social assistance benefits, leaving women and children no better off than if the father had not met his financial obligation (but saving taxpayers money). "Ontario has the only maintenance enforcement program in Canada which fully offsets the cost of services and provides a similar amount as net return to the government" (Dranoff 1996: A21). It is also the most cost-per-case efficient program of its kind in the country. To further cut operating costs, those on the plan are to be charged a user fee of $2 per call to a caseworker. This is a cost women, desperately short of money because of the non-compliance of a court order by the father of their children, can ill afford. Given the cost efficiency of the program, it seems puzzling that the Attorney General is calling the program unsuccessful and planning to drastically cut its budget and to lay off staff.

The Family Support Plan is certainly not without flaws. Because of serious understaffing, women seeking enforcement of a support order often have to wait an unreasonable length of time before a caseworker responds to their request for help. If the plan is to operate with even less staff, more women will have to wait even longer. How will they feed their children during that waiting period? Some of them may have to resort to social assistance while they are waiting to have their court-ordered support payments enforced. Taxpayers are also affected by the understaffing of the plan because the recouping of social assistance payments is put in jeopardy. The interests of mothers and their children coincide with those of taxpayers in the effective operation of the Family Support Plan. While the well-being of vulnerable people is of little significance to the Harris government in its pursuit of a balanced budget, jeopardizing a social program that has benefited taxpayers appears to be a contradiction of its political agenda.

The Spouse-in-the-House Rule
The revision of the "spouse-in-the-house" regulation of the General Welfare Assistance Act and the Family Benefits Act, that became effective October 1, 1995, represents the Harris government's clearest attempt to enforce a monolithic form of "the family" emphasizing uniformity of experience and universality of structure and function. The regulation is a manifestation of the deeply entrenched gender stereotyping of women as dependants of men. It implies that a man has to pay for the sexual and housekeeping services he receives from a woman (Kitchen 1984: 13). It defines men as providers and women as dependants in "the heterosexual family" whose function is the nurturing and socialization of children. Same-sex couples are exempt from the "spouse-in-the- house" rule. To apply the rule to them would in fact constitute an implicit recognition that they are a family. In this instance, the government is hoisted with its own petard by prescribing compulsory heterosexuality. In the case of same-sex couples, the Harris government's gendered ideology about family life clearly clashes with its class ideology.

In the class war against the poor, the "spouse-in-the-house" rule provides further opportunities for harassing and stigmatizing social assistance claimants and recipients. Before its amendment by the Liberal government of David Peterson, the "spouse-in-the-house" rule had remained the most sexist discriminatory welfare legislation in place. Applicants for social assistance were deemed ineligible when they were found living with an unrelated person of the opposite sex. Recipients who were discovered in violation of the rule were charged with the criminal offence of fraud and required to repay the assistance they had received. Although the rule applied to both men and women, sole-support mothers were most affected by it. Since a married woman living with her husband cannot apply for social assistance for herself and her children, a sole-support mother living with a man could not be allowed to receive public income support either. The Charter of Rights and Freedoms allowed the Women's Legal Education and Action Fund (LEAF), in conjunction with Canadian Civil Liberties Association, to enter a Charter challenge in the courts against the rule on the grounds of its "adverse-impact discrimination" arguing that:

a. the definition of "spouse" was too broad;
b. it denied assistance without proof that the sole-support mother was financially supported by the man she was living with, despite the fact that there was no legal obligation to do so;
c. it constituted an invasion of privacy;
d. it violated women's equality rights; and
e. it jeopardized children's entitlements to benefits.

The government of David Peterson accepted that the cohabitation regulation was discriminatory and amended it in 1987 by bringing the financial support obligations between spouses and for their children in line with the Family Law Act. Sole-support parents could live now with a member of the opposite sex up to three years before they were considered to be living in a spousal relationship that implied support obligations. The onus was placed on the welfare administration to prove that a spousal relation existed before they could cut recipients off benefits.

The foremost reason given by the Harris government for its reversal of the cohabitation rule is its concern with reducing the Ontario budget deficit. Savings of about $45 million a year are anticipated by removing the time factor from the definition of a spousal relationship in the determination of eligibility for social assistance (Constante 1996: 25). In fact, since the Harris government reintroduced the cohabitation rule 6947 women, more than twice the number that had been expected, have lost their social assistance benefits (Constante 1996: 23). Other arguments cited in support of the rule were: public perception that sole-support mothers on assistance living with a man were receiving an economic windfall for three years to which they were not entitled; and that seven out of ten provinces enforced the cohabitation rule without allowing a couple a minimum period of living together to test the strength of their commitment (Constante 1996: 14).

The requirement that sole-support parents provide evidence that they are not in a spousal relationship with the man or woman who lives in the same house with them re-opens the door to administrative harassment. It requires massive bureaucratic intrusion into the most intimate realms of relationships, and thus threatens "the family" which many New Right supporters consider to be the most significant institution in society. The success of the cohabitation rule in breaking up relationships will lead almost inevitably to an increase in the number of children growing up with only one significant adult in the house. The regulation jeopardizes the chances for children to grow up in stable family relationships. According to child development experts, this is an important factor in maintaining healthy, stable and well-adjusted children (Gee 1993). For the Harris government, of course, facts about the potentially undesirable outcome of the breakup of a family cannot be allowed to affect its fiscal imperative to cut government spending.

The "spouse-in-the-house" regulation, like the social assistance cuts, has been challenged in the courts under sections 7 and 15 of the Charter of Rights and Freedoms. Section 7 protects persons against violations of life, liberty and security. Section 15 guarantees equality by protecting members of identifiable groups against discrimination. The new rule clearly discriminates against children. They can only receive social assistance through the agency of another person. If their mothers are denied eligibility because they are deemed to be living with a man who has an obligation to support them, so are the children.

Conclusion
The Common Sense Revolution makes Ontario an unequal and divided society and cruelly destroys the family life of poor people. The free market agenda does irreversible damage to family life in the province, leaving poor and modest-income families devastated. The allocation of material resources to meet consumption needs takes place in the context of three major social institutions: the market, families and the state. The market, however, continues to fail families. Family breadwinners lose their jobs so companies can earn higher profits. Unemployment statistics provide one of the clearest indicators of the polarization that has occurred in the province between those with and those without jobs. The burden of unemployment and social spending cuts has fallen particularly hard on young people in their childrearing years. In Ontario, the New Right policy agenda of the Harris government is punishing parents for being without jobs and sole-support mothers for being without a male breadwinner to support them. While these families bear the brunt of the slashing of social programs and services by the government of Ontario, other better-off families cannot escape from the devastating consequences of the policy decisions of the Ontario government. They can pay for the services that are no longer provided by government, but they

cannot disregard the devastation the New Right agenda has brought to the lives around them. They will encounter increasing numbers of homeless and hungry families in the downtown streets of our urban centres and they will hear about the crime, abuse and neglect afflicting children.

Since it does nothing to create the jobs that parents need to be self-reliant and to support their families, the political legacy of the Common Sense Revolution will be a socially and economically destabilized Ontario, with a mass of devastated families living on the margins of Ontario society. Its extreme individualist philosophy, with its aim to produce self-reliant families, in fact distorts and fractures families—and all other social relationships—in an increasingly divided Ontario (Seabrook 1990: 50).

Chapter 9

The Racist Face of "Common Sense"

Jean Trickey

Introduction

How do we begin to discuss racism in the context of Progressive Conservative Ontario? It is not easy to talk about racism at the best of times. Racism moves insidiously in and out of everyday reality, intersecting with class, gender, ability, and sexual orientation. It plays itself out in the lives of Aboriginal peoples and ethnocultural and racial minorities at every level of existence. The belief that racism consists primarily of individual acts, such as harassment and name calling, clouds our view of the more systematic practice of racism embedded in our society.

Anti-racism educator Philomena Essed (1991) moves us away from an individualistic perspective by showing how racism functions as ideology, structure, and process. It is *ideology* because "inequalities inherent in the wider social structure are related, in a deterministic way, to biological and cultural factors attributed to those who are seen as a different 'race' or 'ethnic' group" (45). It is *structure* because "racial and ethnic dominance exists in and is reproduced by the system through the formulation and application of rules, laws, and regulations and through access to and the allocation of resources" (45). And it is *process* because "structures and ideologies do not exist outside the everyday practices through which they are created and confirmed" (45).

Racism is one of the many strategies used to distract people from the full-blown disparity between rich and poor, and the real shortage of jobs. Under the Harris government, the poor are experiencing a dehumanizing process similar to racism that designates them as a category, classifies them as unworthy, and promotes ill treatment toward them. This sort of domination, power over and blaming are essential components of the neo-conservative agenda in Ontario. While certainly not invented by the Harris Tories, racism is a convenient tool of this government.

The Harris government promotes the resurgence of racism through: 1) *ideology*—using idealized images and coded language; 2) *structure*—cutting programs and services for immigrants and racial and ethnocultural minorities, and eliminating equity programs; and 3) *process*—tacitly inciting racist sentiments by abandoning anti-racist leadership.

Racist Ideology

In the silent ideology of white supremacy, the Ontario power elite insist that white, middle- and owning-class people are the norm. They promote racism through images that portray other groups as "the problem." These images interweave themes in a process similar to that used by neo-conservatives in the United States.

> [R]ace played a considerable role in the building of a new hegemonic alliance based on rightist social, cultural and economic principles.... What has been accomplished is a successful translation of an economic doctrine into the language of experience, moral imperative, and common sense. The free market ethic has been combined with a populist politics. This has meant the blending together of a 'rich mix' of themes...nation, family, duty, authority, standards, and traditionalism—with other thematic elements that struck a resonant chord. (Apple 1993: 24)

Today in Ontario, that metaphorical mix exploits the insecurity many feel in this period of economic uncertainty. Tough economic times have often provided a fertile terrain for ideologically constructing "other" people as drains on the system, as special interest groups, or as illegitimate or fraudulent immigrants (Cashmore 1987; Essed 1991; Dominelli 1988; Henry et al. 1995). The mixing and restatement of themes play on these insecurities to justify right-wing positions such as the Reform Party's anti-immigration policies, the "Quebec old stock" disdain for "others" and opposition to Native land claims. These themes contribute to skewed images of what constitutes Canada. This rhetoric paints a picture that excludes some and incites fear and opposition towards the "other." For example, Harris has issued a stream of rhetoric playing on the contradictory anti-immigrant myths that immigrants are taking all the jobs, and that immigrants are a drain on the welfare system.

Inciting racism is a part of a broader strategy of the Common Sense Revolution in Ontario. The Harris government uses innocuous-sounding language, which is in fact a system of coded, symbolic, culture-specific representations which silently polarize groups into regressive them-and-us scenarios. Media sympathetic to the Tories support these idealized images by publishing full-faced pictures of black criminals and pseudo-psychological treatments of the pathologized immigrant family.

The current neo-conservative hyperbole contrasts cheerful golf vignettes (Major 1996: A4) with riot police fending off the dangerous masses (Di Matteo 1996: 18). On the one hand is the fervent fantasy, and on the other "common sense" is besieged. Such images form a cultural imperialism that is "exclusionary, monocultural, ethnocentric, and homogeneous" (Henry et al. 1995: 299). They portray the "others" as dark, sinister, or criminal. There are no pictures of the persistent poverty of Aboriginal peoples, the de-skilling of immigrant women, the hungry children. In images of the Common Sense Revolution, there are no barriers to access, no predisposing conditions behind poverty, unemployment and crime. The invisible poor or coloured deserve their state because they have not worked hard enough or assimilated. Cashmore (1987) in his discussion of similar conditions in Britain concludes:

> The emphasis on the individual ethnic groups as perpetrators of their own problems reveals a faith in the power of minorities to modify themselves out of abjection, if only they have the 'urge and drive'. Seen in this light, anyone can bootstrap their way up the social ladder. It is as if we should acknowledge the obstacles erected by white racism...yet never concede that they can impair a minority's progress. The only true impairment, the reasoning goes, lies within the group itself. (163)

Racist Structure

In contrast to these images, Harris has actually furthered racism in several ways. He has eliminated equity legislation and programs. Minorities are caught in the trickle-down effect of federal, provincial and municipal cutbacks; losing programs such as jobsOntario and the youth employment program. The 21.6 percent cut to social assistance left those with less power to flounder in their own poverty.

One of the more blatant acts against fairness in employment was the repeal of the Employment Equity Act, which included the employment equity components of both the Police Services Act and the Education Act (Ontario Legislative Assembly 1995: 592). This withdraws support for women, Aboriginal peoples, racial and ethnic minorities and those who are disabled. The loss of standardized hiring criteria leaves these target groups with diminished opportunity to overcome systemic barriers in the workplace.

This repeal has ramifications beyond just jobs. The Employment Equity Act was part of an evolution of legislation and was not the end process of redress on equity issues. Ontario has been a site of considerable effort by minorities in the struggles against racism and anti-Semitism over time (Henry et al. 1995: 5). Legislation to address some aspects of the problem has included:

- the first provincial anti-racist legislation, the *Racial Discrimination Act* in 1944 to prohibit the display of signs and symbols with racial or religious discrimination;
- the *Fair Employment Practices Act* in 1954;
- the *Fair Accommodations Practices Act* in 1955, to discourage discrimination in housing and other accommodations;
- the *Anti-Discrimination Commission* created in 1958, changed to the *Ontario Human Rights Commission* in 1961.
- the *Ontario Employment Equity Act* in 1993.

The repeal of the Employment Equity Act effectively stalls responses to workplace inequity. It also counters the spirit and intent of the past legislation, which recognized racism as a systematic rather than individualized component of Ontario society. This is made clear in the statement by Minister of Citizenship Marilyn Mushinski at the second reading of Bill 8, the *Job Quotas Repeal Act:*

> This bill, when passed by the Legislature, will repeal job quotas and will restore merit based employment practices in this province. It will also restore hope to all people who want to compete for job opportunities based on their qualifications, based on their ability, based on merit.... (Ontario Legislative Assembly 1995: 481)

Just whose hope is being restored in this action? Meritocracy is consistent with the Common Sense discourse on reverse racism which insists that power is being usurped by the unworthy. This popular doublespeak proposes that the success of one group means the demise of the other. It also implies that women and designated minorities are unqualified, pushing out the best candidates. Such statements promote the belief that women are not equal to men or that education outside Canada is of little or no value. Charges of reverse racism are common responses to efforts to begin to redress inequities. What is the rationale for the order to destroy all workplace survey data collected by employers as part of employment equity? Could it be that this destruction of all data makes it impossible to evaluate the workplace conditions of targeted groups? The government claims that these data are of no significance in the new climate of the "non-legislative equal opportunity plan" (Ontario Legislative Assembly 1995: 258). But the Ontario Human Rights Commission is now the designated body to deal with workplace discrimination, and it is an organization driven by individual complaints. The responsibility for resolution of equity issues is no longer on the state; individuals must provide proof of incidents—proof which has just been destroyed by edict of the state.

Human rights commissions have been criticized as inadequate to deal with racism issues at the best of times (Henry et al. 1995: 263). The recent staff reductions at the Ontario Human Rights Commission were roundly criticized by anti-racism advocates. Avy Go, spokesperson for the Urban Alliance on Race Relations said the Tories are trying to make an already weak commission even less effective (Welsh 1996: A8). Another spokesperson for the Ontario Public Service Employees Union concurred that the staff reduction "is just another signal of how they [the Harris government] are trying to get rid of all the protection people of Ontario have for the elimination of racism" (Welsh 1996: A8).

The loss of pay equity has a drastic effect on women in lower-wage jobs. The considerable effort expended over the last few years to arrive at an approximation of equal pay for work of equal value raised expectations among women, particularly in sex-segregated employment. Immigrant women and other marginalized peoples are often employed in sex-segregated and racialized positions such as nurses aides, office cleaners, factory workers, child care and food service employees (Henry et al. 1995: 293). To make matters worse, these jobs are the first to be contracted out to private employers; and the Conservative government's changes to the *Employment Standards Act* rescind previously negotiated agreements and union rights when a company sells a contract to another company. This legislation effectively ends union continuity, wage and benefit obligations (Eber 1996: 2).

It is important to place this in the perspective of an increasingly shrinking job market. "The restructuring of the global economy is squeezing out good occupations and producing jobs with little security and inadequate compensation. Employment of immigrants in these jobs will result in a visible underclass in Canada's largest cities" (Stafford 1992: 68). Women of colour from developing nations and Aboriginal women are traditionally underemployed, with employment rates and income levels considerably below the national average (Frideres 1993: 162).

The cuts to social assistance, coupled with the other cuts to services for marginalized segments of the Ontario populace, create a substantial shortfall in the lives of minorities. The decreased shelter allowance increases the potential for landlords to discriminate against non-white social assistance recipients. It is now easier to ghettoize racial and ethnocultural groups in substandard housing. Does the speculation that a U.S. firm is considering the purchase of the Ontario Public Housing Corporation (Boback, 1996: B4) also forecast the creation of even larger racially segregated urban housing ghettos for Ontario?

In 1994, MacLeod and Shin researched needs of immigrant women in Ontario. In their report *Like a Wingless Bird: the experience of immigrant and visible minority women,* they discussed some of the difficulties educated, refugee women experience as welfare recipients.

> The erosion of self-worth, dignity and a belief in one's potential, which is so common to the experiences of people forced to accept welfare, is magnified many times for refugees who bring with them to the welfare system a deep sense of displacement and uncertainty. What this means is that women with higher educational backgrounds and professional degrees can find themselves dependent on welfare, and can find it as difficult as people with less education to move out of the "welfare trap." (32)

The issue of policing is an ever contentious one among minorities. Police are at the forefront of the enforcement of the Common Sense Revolution. Harris has ensured that the police, decked out in riot gear, maintain a high visibility during his term of office.

The implications of this visibility and the apparent Harris "friendship" with the police have particular significance to minorities. At the best of times, minorities have shaky relations with the police. According to Henry et al., "in many ways, relations between the police and the racial minority communities can be seen as the flashpoint, the means to gage the general temper of race relations in Canada" (1995: 109).

The Ipperwash blockade is a prime example of such a flashpoint. In September 1995, a 38-year-old Aboriginal man, Anthony (Dudley) George, was killed in the confrontation between the Ontario Provincial Police (OPP) and the blockaders. Hall, in a critique of police/native relations contends, "[we] have time and time again witnessed the invocation of police powers to defend and protect the resource claims of non-Indian title holders..." (Hall 1996: 9). Criticism also came from Assembly of First Nations Chief Ovide Mercredi who said: "It was not necessary for anyone to die here.... Mike Harris has the power to resolve this peacefully" (Fennell 1995: 22).

To date, Harris has resisted demands for an investigation into the confrontation at Ipperwash. Richard Powless, an Aboriginal leader, stated: "We've been calling for a public inquiry on the shooting, and we can't get it. We can't get a response. Is that racism?" (Welsh 1996: A8).[1]

The 1995 Report of the Commission on Systemic Racism in the Ontario Criminal Justice System, condemned the over-representation and differential treatment of Black people at all levels in the justice system (Commission on Systemic Racism 1995: i–xi). The commission further reported that Black and Aboriginal men and women are over- represented in prison where "the criminal justice system has its harshest impact" (1995: 95). A typical response to reports on racism is denial. This denial usually frames the victims of racism as the cause of the problem, questions people's ability to judge their own experiences, and proposes alternate explanations for the racist acts they experience. The Harris government has neither endorsed the findings of the report, nor proposed any action to redress this injustice. Instead, it has pursued a U.S.-style "get tough on crime" campaign.

Poverty is not a crime. However, high employment levels among minority youth promote instability among that group. What will be the possible outcomes of never having a job to go to? What are the implications of higher police surveillance in low-income neighbourhoods? If the number of minority youth arrested and convicted of crime is high at the present time, what are the implications for the future? Is there a greater demand for protection of property in lean times?

The Harris era will generate more problems than solutions for the marginalized residents of Ontario. One hint of its ultimate effects is privided by a New Zealand social worker, who analyzed the impacts of her country's economic and social restructuring—chillingly similar to that taking place in Ontario today. She concluded that the changes were most damaging to the Maori, immigrants, and women (Dobbin 1995a).

Racist Process

The slashing of the Ministry of Citizenship and Culture Anti-racism Secretariat (ARS) sent a clear signal of the government's disinterest in anti-racist initiatives. ARS served as a funder for anti-racist programs and as the "centralizing body for initiating and implementing anti-racist programs for the province" (Toronto Coalition Against Racism 1996). Small grassroots community organizations were energized by the support on racism issues. Anti-racist programs made it possible to attract volunteers to the organizations, with benefits to both. ARS helped to facilitate discussion and anti-racist activity, research and exchange of ideas. Whether or not there was adequate funding to meet the tremendous need for anti-racist programs, ARS did serve as an "internal consulting body to government and minor funding bodies to organizations" (Henry et al. 1995: 293). The Secretariat was instrumental in keeping the dialogue open. Among the groups concerned with the loss of ARS is the Toronto Coalition Against Racism. Their factsheet (1996) lists the following concerns about the Citizenship cuts:

- programs specific to immigrants and refugees have been drastically reduced in resettlement programs such as language training and interpreter services as well as multilingual access programs in areas such as health;
- funding for special projects and services under the Native Community Branch and Aboriginal Economic Development has been cut drastically; and
- in the arts, cuts have endangered the work of First Nations and community of colour artists and organizations.

In challenging a move by the Ontario government's withdrawal from direct services for immigrants and refugees, MPP Tony Ruprecht (Parkdale) stated to the Minister of Citizenship and Culture, "you've just killed a number of significant programs, including the welcome houses across Ontario which train newcomers for jobs and provide English classes" (Ontario Legislative Assembly 1995: 146). Similar programs such as the Cultural Interpreter Pilot Projects were also supported by the Settlement and Integration Unit, as part of the ministry. For years the programs have been invaluable to thousands of newcomers who speak neither French nor English (Estable and Meyer 1992: 9) and they have also provided employment to immigrants.

Since the Harris government has withdrawn from anti-racist initiatives, it functions as a racist government. The dismantling of progressive policies and programs is an abdication of the leadership necessary in a complex, multicultural society. Just as the Harris government's images have moved us toward fear and resistance, anti-racist images could have led us in the opposite direction. The wholesale dismissal of anti-racism initiatives makes racism more intractable. In the interests of all its citizens, the state must take the initiative in dealing seriously with racism. As Henry et al. (1995) argues:

> The influence of state policies and practices at various levels (federal, provincial and municipal) is critical to the eradication of racism and the promotion of racial equity. As such, the state has a special responsibility to assert leadership. (260)

Instead of providing leadership, the Harris rhetoric and actions have served to manage, divide, conquer, and effectively divert our attention from our commonalities and potential for living and working together.

The splintered response of the communities that are the sum of Ontario is predictable. Racism is real, alive and a tool in the divisive intention of the Harris strategy. Serious thought must be given to how quickly attitudes toward particular groups have shifted. This book concerns the actions of the Harris government, but it must be remembered that he and his majority government were elected. They apparently struck a "resonant chord" with many voters. The fact is that this government orchestrated the undoing of many years of advocacy by minority and other communities for an equitable Ontario. The actual cuts will continue to have negative impacts on the residents of Ontario long after Harris is gone.

Conclusion: Rebuilding an Anti-Racist Agenda

In my work and day-to-day interactions with students, friends, family and organizations, I have observed horror and shock in response to the policies of the Harris government. What strikes me is the indignation tinged with unbelief that this could happen here. Essentially we were absorbed in our own myth of ourselves as tolerant and moderate. As a result, much of the leadership has been caught off guard, isolated.

To dig ourselves out from this condition, we must make the tremendous effort required to build meaningful coalitions. We need to *share* ideas and strategies. And, using Freireian theory, we must ask ourselves how we can develop truly popular leadership in this first-world situation. The concept "popular" is crucial to this work. The image of leadership in the white mainstream is one of personal autonomy and privilege, which overshadows popular leadership. This image is culturally specific, and serves to maintain power in the hands of a few who espouse meritocracy and right to rule.

We need to develop a collective response to oppression, however small. Governments and multinationals conspire to persuade us, on the one hand, that we are helpless and unable to influence events and, on the other, that our "interest groups" have the power to erode "traditional values." To make the most of the power that we have, we need to ask ourselves some questions: what have other groups done in the past? What are some effective sites of resistance and how can they be expanded? How is it possible to reroute the complicity, the smugness, in order to form opposition? And might it be an ability to tap into everyday experience that distinguishes between leadership and domination? The immediate social difficulties require leaders who listen, drawing from knowledge and analysis of the past (not just the white past) and present, in order to meet the challenges of the future.

There are experienced veterans among us from around the world who have struggled and lost, and struggled and won. It's time to ask them what they know.

Note

1. The situation remains unresolved. However, the Toronto Coalition Against Racism has launched a fundraising campaign to help in the payment of legal fees for the band members (Toronto Coalition Against Racism, 1996).

Chapter 10

The Franco-Ontarian Community Under the Harris Counter-Revolution

David Welch

Introduction

When listening to nostalgic discourse from the Harris government, Franco-Ontarians might well ask the question: would we want to live as we did in the 1950s? In spite of numerous contradictions remaining both within the community and in its relations with the English-speaking majority, Franco-Ontarians generally recognize that they are better off today. Not very long ago, individual and collective choices were far more limited and general well-being was far less widespread, especially for women, the working class and those living in peripheral regions.

In this chapter the Harris cuts will be presented in the context of a particular community, that of the Franco-Ontarians. Firstly, the historical development of some of their community institutions will be presented, most notably those in schooling and in the social and health services, with particular emphasis on developments in the past thirty years. I will focus on Franco-Ontarian resistance to policies imposed by the anglophone majority as well as their internal community resistance to practices imposed by the elites. Secondly, I will examine how the cuts of the Harris government have affected the Franco-Ontarian community, especially its most vulnerable sectors. Finally, I will examine a few practices now being developed within the Franco-Ontarian community that are alternatives to the existing ways of doing things.

The Development of Social Institutions in French-Speaking Ontario

Since the beginning of permanent European colonization in Ontario during the eighteenth century, Franco-Ontarians have played an active role in the economic and political development of the province (Jaenen 1993; Welch 1993).[1] Founding relatively homogenous villages, the French Canadians who moved to Ontario preserved many of their unique cultural forms. In many regions there were enough Franco-Ontarians to establish schools, parishes, social organizations and, later, cooperatives and *caisses populaires*. These autonomous institutions in turn gave the community a distinct social life and the means to distribute resources within the community. Though they were a minority within the province of Ontario, Franco-Ontarians continued to see themselves as being part of a larger French Canadian society with links to French Canadians elsewhere, including the Franco-Americans of New England.

From the eighteenth century onwards, French Canadians established their own autonomous schools. As restrictions were placed on these schools in the 1880s and later, especially between 1912–1927, Franco-Ontarians undertook large-scale campaigns of civil disobedience. This resistance to state oppression allowed the French-speaking Catholic Church to become far more active in the social and economic life of the community, becoming in a sense the main governing institution. At the same time there was some resistance to models imposed on the community by the Catholic Church, especially when this led to higher taxes for the largely impoverished population (Welch 1993: 334). These various contradictions continued largely unchanged until the 1960s. Due to continual resistance on the part of the community against state sanctions on schooling matters, the provincial government was forced over time to recognize that there could be some limits to its own state power.

For social and health services, Franco-Ontarians relied heavily on the volunteer work done largely by women in both urban and rural areas and on the mutual aid or charitable societies, such *l'Union St-Joseph* and the *St-Vincent-de-Paul*. As well, the community established various charitable institutions— hospitals, orphanages, and shelters for the aged usually under the direction of female religious congregations. Situated mainly in Ottawa and Sudbury, they remain even today prominent institutions in the larger community. For instance *l'Hôpital général d'Ottawa* (the Ottawa General Hospital) was founded to serve the Catholic community, largely Franco-Ontarian. It was the interaction among these three types of community social practices that laid the framework for today's French language social services in Ontario.

Most of the social and health services that developed in Ontario, other than those administered by French-speaking religious congregations and charitable organizations, were unilingual English. Often these services were administered by non-profit organizations such as the Children's Aid Societies that functioned almost entirely in English, regardless of their funding sources, even in cities such as Ottawa and Sudbury which had large Franco-Ontarian minorities. French language services became more marginalized with time as new state-funded services were organized, particularly affecting the most vulnerable sectors of the community (Carrière 1995). This indifference to francophone needs can be understood when one remembers that French Canadians remained excluded from positions of economic and political power, never rising above the level of foremen, forever remaining the subsistence farmers, lumberjacks, servants, semi-skilled railway workers and surface workers for the mines. The inequalities of capitalism along with hostility against French Canadians excluded them from positions of any influence over the wider socio-political institutions of the province.

Accelerated Urbanization and Transformations
in Franco-Ontarian Institutions

The period during and after the Second World War, with its rapid industrial expansion, saw the complete transformation of the economic and socio-cultural face of Ontario. Ontario completed its transformation to industrial capitalism, becoming more and more integrated into the North American economy. These changes had an important impact on the Franco-Ontarian community. In the space of only a few years, the community went through a massive displacement of population within the province—from the countryside to the regional cities of the north, and from the north to the industrial cities of the south. Parallel to these demographic changes, thousands of Québécois and Acadians settled in the manufacturing cities of the south and in some of the mining cities of the north.

This increased proletarization led to new identities, embodied for instance in unions, that led to new social relationships within the community and to frequent conflicts between the various elites with differing class interests. Frequently the traditional Franco-Ontarian elite did not give support to miners and lumber workers as they fought to improve their working conditions; in some cases they openly supported the mine owners (Arnopolous-McLeod 1982; Pelletier 1987). To help temper these changes, Franco-Ontarians established new institutions (schools, *caisses populaires*, recreation centres, etc.). However, generally speaking, for more specialized services the Franco-Ontarians tended to use the social and health services of the majority, operating almost solely in the English language. Schooling fared a bit better since in the northern and eastern parts of Ontario Franco-Ontarians frequently dominated the separate school boards. In the south, new schools were created only after heavy opposition from the existing boards. For instance, in the 1960s in Toronto, about 500 Franco-Ontarian school children were crowded into one school. When parents asked that a new school be built to accommodate the increasing population in the suburbs, the local separate school board initially refused. A group of mothers then set up a school outside in the spring weather in order to force the school board into building a new school.

The Franco-Ontarian Community and New Relationships with the State

In almost all sectors of social and economic life, the Ontario government, like the government of the other provinces, became far more interventionist in the 1960s. In the name of reform and the improvement of society, the Ontario government spent millions of dollars to transform educational, social and health services across the province. The 1960s also brought about greater recognition of Franco-Ontarian rights, most notably through laws 140 and 141, that allowed the establishment of solely French language elementary and secondary schools. The federal Official Languages Act (1969), following the recommendations of the Royal Commission on Bilingualism and Biculturalism, also contributed to increasing the bilingual presence in federal government institutions, especially in the Ottawa area.

These changes led to an historical change in the attitudes of the Franco-Ontarian elite towards the state. Traditionally, the religious and secular elites turned to the family and to religious institutions for the protection of Franco-Ontarian identity and the development of schooling and social and health services. Secularization and increased state intervention increased the distance between the elites and their community as people looked outside the community for resources (Carrière 1993; Juteau and Kimpton 1993). In the future, the rights won from the state and delegated by it, would determine to a large extent the power and influence of the Franco-Ontarian elite and the degree of autonomy it would retain.

Even with the right to new schools, struggles continued between Franco-Ontarian parents and their various community organizations and the many English-speaking Ontarians and the government for another fifteen years, before a relatively complete network of French language secondary schools was established across the province. These struggles in such places as Kapuskasing, Penetanguishene, Iroquois Falls, Sturgeon Falls, Windsor, and Mattawa to name only a few, in turn led to many divisions within the Franco-Ontarian community during vicious fights over the control of ever decreasing resources (Welch 1991). It took twenty-five years to establish three French language community colleges in the province.

In the arena of social services it was really only in the 1970s in eastern Ontario and in the early 1980s in northeastern Ontario that the provincial government began to allocate funds for French language social services. Since there were no obligations to give services in French, both the government agencies and the private state-subsidized agencies did little to increase services to the French-speaking population (Carrière 1995). The Franco-Ontarian community remained dependent on the limited French language services, offered on a voluntary basis and, ever decreasingly, by religious institutions. However, even here there was a price to pay; for more and more of the old French language or bilingual hospitals, usually in areas of concentrated Franco-Ontarian population, were being replaced by new facilities that gave better services but tended to function far more in English than in French. Thus in some cases, in the name of modernity, Franco-Ontarians lost the control of institutions that they had controlled for generations.

Franco-Ontarians also lost control of their neighbourhoods. For example, in the name of urban renewal and in spite of large-scale opposition, large parts of Lower Town in Ottawa, once about 80 percent French-speaking, were demolished. The establishment of low-rental housing brought in non-francophone people; other renovations brought in a wealthier English-speaking population. Lower Town is now only about 40 percent francophone. In the process, the social fabric of the neighbourhood was destroyed, eliminating many of the projects of collective self-help. The same process happened in the Moulin à Fleur neighbourhood in Sudbury and in the Sacré-Coeur parish (Cabbagetown) in Toronto. In the new suburbs of Ottawa, Sudbury and Toronto, it became difficult to recreate a similar community life, for there is now greater dispersion of the population, and greater distances between schools and community centres. New cultural practices have tended to be centred around middle-class interests, leaving less for the original working-class culture that once flourished in the inner cities (Stasiulis 1980: 26).

In some ways, the French Language Services Act (1986) was an important step forward for the Franco-Ontarian community. A victory after years of pressure from the Franco-Ontarian community, it assured that in certain designated areas of the province, provincial government services would be provided in both English and French. Its application showed a somewhat greater respect for the 550,000 Franco-Ontarians in the province, and had as a secondary effect the creation of hundreds of jobs for community members in the public and semi-public services. However, all municipal services were excluded from the Act and non-government agencies receiving government funding were left to decide for themselves if they wanted to apply for designation. Even in cities such as Ottawa, which has declared itself bilingual, the services are often not clearly defined and are left to the goodwill of public servants. Frequently, designated positions remain frozen due to the cutbacks of the past ten years or are filled by people speaking very little French.

New Visions, New Social Practices

Out of the many reforms that directly affected the Franco-Ontarian community since the 1960s, new social practices began. As the state was pushed to allow greater recognition and space to the Franco-Ontarian community, many Franco-Ontarians turned away from the more traditional elite to a more "modern" one advocating the importance of working with the government to bring about what were perceived as needed reforms. Others went even further and sought parallel French language services (based in part on the New Brunswick model), rather than spending huge amounts of energy on attempting to "bilingualize" existing English language services. Out of these various mobilizations, some social activists began advocating for the establishment of totally new services that were not simply translations of English language services with all their "professionalism" and lack of citizen participation, but rather proposed original, more democratic social practices that reflected the culture and needs of the community, especially its more vulnerable members (Groupe C'est le temps 1981: 112; Tissot 1981: 95).

Among these new services have been four community radio stations, established in more peripheral regions of the province. Over twenty-four popular literacy programs, self-help groups of all kinds and more recently, community economic development projects have added to the community involvement. For example, Franco-Ontarians were very active in the recent worker/management/

community/private sector (Tembec) take-over of the Spruce Falls pulp mill in Kapuskasing. And some of the most dynamic alternative projects have come out of the various women's organizations: the need for better daycare, shelters for women victims of violence, and immigrant information services for women. In some cases these were new organizations, such as *les Ontaroises de l'Est, Franco-femmes* in the North and, *le Réseau des femmes du Sud de l'Ontario* in the South (Cardinal and Coderre 1990). In other cases some of the more traditional women's organizations reorganized their activities with new perspectives and objectives.[2]

Social activists recognized the importance of the welfare state in financing the multitude of projects that were cropping up in French-speaking Ontario. Franco-Ontarians were not only trying to "catch up" to the anglophone majority, but were proposing new ways of looking at and doing things. Though this led to frequent tensions among Franco-Ontarians as to what should be prioritized, few people questioned the ever greater reliance of the community on the financial resources of the provincial government. Few questioned the fact that large numbers of the most active people in the Franco-Ontarian community were enticed into jobs with state agencies, thereby at times creating a "brain drain" away from the various regions toward the government ministries in Toronto. Even those who continued to work independently frequently found themselves dependent on the government for the continued funding of their activities, making them vulnerable to any cutbacks.

Due in part to openness on the part of the Peterson Liberal and the Rae NDP governments, few questioned the tendency of the provincial government to impose conditions. This facilitated an increase in government power to define what might be considered proper boundaries for Franco-Ontarians, and to determine, to a certain extent, what were and what were not acceptable practices. This greater dependency or even co-opting, made it more difficult for Franco-Ontarians to work out their own compromises, or to adapt to rapid changes within and outside the community, and in turn to create their own collective solutions. Most of the demands of the community did little to question established notions of the social, economic and political order.

The Harris Counter-Revolution and the Franco-Ontarian Community

The election of the Harris government and its program of massive cutbacks have hit Franco-Ontarian social and educational institutions, as well as community-based projects, particularly hard. Once again, they are learning that changes do not come without struggle, both to retain what has already been won and to achieve even more. On a number of levels, Franco-Ontarians remain vulnerable. For instance, the functional illiteracy rate within the community is about 30 percent and many are poor. Though the vast majority of Franco-Ontarians are urbanized, many live isolated and dispersed in small towns, far from the main networks of services.

As in any minority situation, overall schooling costs for Franco-Ontarians tend to be higher, though their budgets are often smaller. For instance, transportation for schooling eats up a significant part of the budgets. French language books are more expensive, and schools tend to be smaller, leading to higher per capita costs. With a more limited schooling tax base due to inequities in the taxation system, any cuts in government funding can be very harmful. For instance, the French language school boards in Ottawa receive between 50 and 70 percent of their funding from the provincial government, whereas the Ottawa Board of Education is self-sufficient.[3]

In spite of the progress made, Franco-Ontarian institutions, being younger and less wealthy, have fewer reserves than those of the majority. Many, such as the *centres medico-sociaux communautaires* (French language community health clinics), have only recently been created, with limited and often special funding. Other services, such as shelters for battered women, usually consist of one French language institution to cover a large area. When the sole service is cut, the French-speaking population finds itself with only English language services. For example, in November 1995, all funding for social services was cut at the Toronto's local *centre médico-social communautaire,* leaving 1200 French-speaking persons without any services in French. It has been estimated that only about 5 percent of the former clients have the financial resources to consult with a social worker in private practice. Similar cuts occurred in Hamilton and Welland.

When cutbacks occur, French-speaking employees suffer disproportionately. Unless a position is designated as French language, French speaking employees (who often have less seniority) are laid off or transferred and replaced by those speaking only English. The ability to speak French and to possess an understanding of some cultural aspects of the local community is over-ridden, in bureaucratic organizations, by other considerations such as seniority.

Franco-Ontarians in some cases have been slower to profit from the greater openness of previous governments in funding new initiatives, because they frequently do not know about or do not have people in the right places. For instance, Franco-Ontarians were establishing several new housing cooperative projects just when the Harris government cut almost all funding.[4] French language non-profit daycare is far less developed than that existing in English, and therefore is more affected by cutbacks.

The trend of the provincial government to cut funding and then leave the decisions on what to cut to the local communities has meant greater divisions. People must decide: do we cut salaries or jobs? What services should be kept and what ones should be dropped? Since many of the parallel services established in recent years by Franco-Ontarians are relatively small, this has led to some bitter divisions among social activists (particularly in smaller communities).

Financial cutbacks are not the only means by which to marginalize a community, or at least certain sectors of it. Closely linked to the actual cutbacks is a vicious neo-conservative discourse that presents all demands that are contrary to a particular and narrow view of society as being from a "special interest group." The Harris government has broken any commitment to debate with large sectors of civil society, refusing the intermediary role that social organizations have historically played in Ontario. For instance, in June 1996, the government abolished without warning the 25-year-old *Conseil de l'éducation franco-ontarienne*, a Franco-Ontarian advisory agency on all matters pertaining to schooling, including the post-secondary level. Now all decisions on schooling will remain in the hands of politicians and educational bureaucrats, leaving broad sectors of the community out in the cold. In the future, the government will accept certain requests but treats others as not being representative, thereby leading to further divisions within the community. Those seeking greater equality, notably women, children, low-income earners, people with disabilities and visible minorities, are given the least legitimacy. In this context, Franco-Ontarians will not all be affected by cutbacks in the same way, for there exists important class, gender, racial and regional differences.

For all of the above reasons, the Harris government will likely leave the French Language Services Act alone. Why change something that already has so many exceptions to it? A better way is simply to limit funding, or cut it, and to allow the service to wither. An example of this trend was the cut in March 1996 of 35 percent of the annual budget of *l'Office des affaires francophones*, the government commission that has as its mandate to protect the gains under the French Language Services Act. Another danger for the community is for the leadership to concentrate its energies on the protection of the French language Services Act while the Harris government cuts in areas such as welfare, education, social housing, community services, or transfers to municipalities, thereby affecting the most vulnerable in the Franco-Ontarian community.

The cutbacks certainly have led to an initial feeling of hopelessness within the Franco-Ontarian community. Because so many Franco-Ontarians work directly or indirectly for state-funded institutions with the aim of improving French language services, family incomes are left extremely vulnerable to cutbacks.[5] More recently, Franco-Ontarian activists have begun voicing their opposition to government policies by refusing to participate in doing the government's dirty work of deciding who and what will be cut. For instance in March 1996, a representative from the social services department of the Regional Municipality of Ottawa–Carleton came to speak to a group of French-speaking community workers to talk about what role they might play within the context of the Harris government's plans regarding workfare for those receiving social assistance. The community representatives present angrily made it clear that they were unwilling to do the government's work and betray the very population with whom they have been working for years. They told the regional government that in regard to workfare or any other program perceived to be coercive, they were on their own. However, community spokespersons, except for some women's groups, have tended to be low-keyed in their criticism, as if by their silence they might go unnoticed and therefore be less affected by the cuts.

Still other Franco-Ontarians have begun to propose that instead of trying to catch up to the majority by recreating the same services in French, the community should begin looking at new alternative solutions that depend less on government funding and more on community creativity and resources. Are some alternative projects less vulnerable to government cutbacks than others? How can new social practices emerge from social organizations and not be imposed by the state? Finally, what role should the state play in the continued development of the Franco-Ontarian community? Still others have suggested that new alternative forms of social practices should be developed that avoid the alienation that has existed in anglophone or even some francophone services. How can the notion of professionalism be looked at differently?

Franco-Ontarian Alternatives to the Harris Counter-Revolution

Contrary to what the neo-conservatives proclaim about the Left, progressive social activists and professionals have not all been blind defenders of the status quo in education and social services. On the contrary, few have been more critical of the ever greater bureaucratization and dehumanization of the state and its actors than people working directly in communities, be they teachers, community activists or social workers. In recent years, the notion that social issues are merely "technical problems to be resolved administratively by experts, instead of political issues to be resolved through a democratic process by service users and providers" (Browne and Landry 1995: 111) has been contested.

At least since the 1970s, some Franco-Ontarian social activists have been critical of the welfare state, not limiting their criticisms to inadequacies in the provision of French language schooling and services. However, while criticizing government as being too rigid, hierarchial and impersonal, they have continued to defend the notion that the state has an important role to play, by means of the tax system, in providing the financial means for organizations to provide services as defined democratically by the community. In recent years, they have been supporting the struggle for less government, but at the same time rejecting the transfers of service provision to the private sector. Many Franco-Ontarian activists realize that the private sector, with its for-profit motives, makes many of the vital services needed in the community simply uneconomical except to the wealthiest. Rather they defend the idea that the funds should be provided largely by the state, as well as in part from those benefiting from the service, and that these funds should be transferred to the community-based groups. In practice, this can lead to a greater number of options, since the community-based groups would be competing with state agencies, and thereby providing "the advantage of the qualitative (flexibility, proximity to clients, capacity for innovation, etc.) and quantitative (expected lower costs)..." (Browne and Landry 1995: 370). As pointed out previously, Franco-Ontarian community service providers would also give a service that better respects both the language and culture of the community.

One example of this newer approach to state-community-based group relations can be seen in the actions of *L'Union des cultivateurs franco-ontariens (UCFO)*, founded in 1929 as a French language farmers' union. Its turnaround began in 1983 when it founded the bi-monthly newspaper, AGRICOM, to help break down the isolation of the Franco-Ontarian farmers and to serve as a tool for socio-economic development in rural French-speaking Ontario. There are now 5300 subscribers with 1200 in Québec. Under the *Loi de 1993 sur l'inscription des entreprises agricoles et le financement des organisations agricoles,* the UCFO is now recognized as the only representative group for Franco-Ontarian farmers, allowing it to receive funding from a form of dues check-off, capable of financing the Union and 70 percent of AGRICOM. In 1989, it founded the first two *Groupements de gestion agricoles de l'Ontario* in eastern Ontario and in 1993 another one in northeastern Ontario. Financed 50 percent by the government and 50 percent by the farmers themselves, these collectives allow each group of forty farm families to hire their own farm management specialists (and agronomists) to assist them in the management of their farm production. Costing less than government agronomists linked to the rapidly disappearing Ministry of Agriculture, the agronomists working directly for the farmers are accountable to the farm families themselves and not to the government. In early 1996, the Harris government, in its plans to decentralize the Ministry of Agriculture to Guelph, proposed to subordinate the three regional agricultural colleges to the University of Guelph. In turn, the UCFO proposed that a special partnership between the *Collège d'Alfred* and the University of Guelph be established whereby the management of the college be undertaken in partnership with an autonomous board of directors appointed by the community, totally independent from the Ministry of Agriculture—something not allowed until now. These examples of developments in the socio-economic organization of Franco-Ontarian agriculture show that it is possible to better use government funding, assure greater democracy and accountability to those using the services, and respect the particular language and cultural needs of the community.

In other areas of the province, Franco-Ontarians are looking for new ways to cope with cutbacks. In Sudbury, women's groups are combining their services, not only to save money but to provide support for women directly affected by the government's measures. A women's work cooperative is being initiated to create new jobs for women based on local needs and talents. In Hearst, a women's cooperative tree nursery called the *Maison Verte* was founded in 1981, under the direction of a local women's group called *Parmi-elles*. Originating with some federal government funding, the project provides eight full-time jobs and about thirty five part-time jobs. The participants in the project are now growing millions of tree seedlings and garden plants, and building new greenhouses to begin tomato growing for the local market.

These few examples show that the institutions of the Franco-Ontarian community, not unlike many other communities living in Ontario, are up to the challenge of assuring new forms of services and job creation. Starting from grassroots initiatives, they have sought government funding but have attempted to avoid the over-professionalization of state agencies. They have been confronted with the challenge of avoiding within their own organizations these same tendencies to becoming too bureaucratic and professionalized, and in the end anti-democratic. A final challenge remains—the need to avoid becoming inward-looking, thereby developing other forms of intolerance and exclusion. The groups must find ways of uniting their actions with those of other communities who have common interests. It becomes a "struggle between very different values; the logic of competition versus the logic of community; the logic of machines and machine efficiency versus the logic of people trying to make a life for themselves and participate meaningfully in their society" (Menzies 1996: xv). In the end it becomes a question of whether "the local [will] be an extension of global uniformity, or the global [will] be an extension of local diversity" (Menzies 1996: 19).

Notes
1. In the eighteenth and nineteenth centuries, before French Canadians came in large numbers from Québec to work in agriculture and the timber trade, the French Canadian presence was concentrated on the western Great Lakes and around l'Assomption (Windsor). Here people were linked closely to the fur trade thereby creating a particular symbiotic relationship between the Native people (women) and the French Canadian fur traders. By the late eighteenth century, a new nation, known as the Métis, was emerging around the Great Lakes, a people who were neither French Canadian nor Native, but who spoke French as well as Native languages, were Catholic and worked for the fur companies.
2. For more indepth analysis of the transformations in the Franco-Ontarian women's movement see: Cardinal (1992a, 1992b); Cardinal and Coderre (1990, 1991); Coderre (1995); Juteau-Lee (1983); Juteau-Lee and Roberts (1981); Pelletier (1980, 1987); Proulx (1981).
3. This inequity is due to a number of factors. Separate schools still do not receive their share of commercial and industrial school taxes, forcing them to depend on government special grants that can be cut at any time. Most French language schools, especially at the elementary level, for historical reasons, are separate. Furthermore, if French-speaking ratepayers in Ottawa do not declare themselves as "francophone," their taxes go to the English boards. Also, Québecois living in Hull, Québec and operating a business in Ontario, cannot send their school taxes to the francophone boards since they are "out of province." Regardless of their wishes to support francophone schooling, their taxes go once again to the anglophone boards. Finally, the anglophone population being generally wealthier, own more highly assessed homes and therefore pay more taxes.
4. The *Coalition franco-ontarienne sur le logement* estimated that only about 2 percent of the co-op housing projects have been directed towards francophones whereas they form 5 percent of the population. However, in 1994 in Ottawa, it was estimated that

about 50 percent of the new cooperative housing projects accepted by the NDP government that year were directed towards the French-speaking community, whereas the community formed about 25 percent of the total population (Pilon 1994). Of the 385 projects stopped by the Harris government, 13 were for francophones (Racine 1995).

5. It has been estimated that about 32.5 percent of Franco-Ontarians work in the public and parapublic sectors as opposed to 25.4 percent of anglophones (Grenier 1996).

Chapter 11

Ontario Workers Take On the "Common Sense Revolution"

Steve Watson

On election night, Ralph Klein, Mike Harris's Conservative counterpart in Alberta, is said to have called Harris and urged him to "move fast, move hard, and don't blink." Harris was clearly acting on this advice in his drive to create a cheap, low-waged, non-union labour force and a reserve army of desperate unemployed to undercut the bargaining power of those who still have jobs.

The repeal of Bill 40 (Ontario Labour Relations Act as amended by the previous NDP government) and the passing of Bill 7 (Labour Relations Employment Statutes Law Amendment Act) at record speed in October 1995, were clear-cut attacks on collective bargaining rights which workers had attained over years of struggle in Ontario. The Harris government also has slashed many other workers' rights, and is planning to cut even more. Pay equity has been slashed and allowable payments capped. The employment equity legislation has been repealed.

Less obvious is the connection between the Tory welfare cuts and the attack on the bargaining power of workers and their organizations. This chapter describes some of the direct and indirect Tory government assaults on the rights of Ontario workers and describes initial resistance to them by organized labour.

Social Wage Under Attack

The Harris win on June 8, 1995 tells us that more than a few union members fell for the line that there were too many welfare cheaters living off the taxes workers pay. All paid workers, however, have a stake in what happens to income support programs. Jim Stanford, an economist with the Canadian Auto Workers (CAW), makes the connection between slashing unemployment insurance and welfare benefits and workers being bullied into accepting lower wages and deteriorating working conditions:

> having a class of destitute Canadians abandoned by both the labour market and by government serves a useful purpose for right wing governments and for business: it serves to constantly remind other Canadians of the terrible things that can happen to them if they fall out of favour with their employers. In other words, the attack on welfare is very much part of the same overall strategy to increase the insecurity of all workers, and to achieve lower wages and a more "disciplined" labour force. (Stanford 1995: 11)

Only a third of all unemployed workers actively looking for work now qualify for unemployment insurance benefits, compared with 90 percent in 1989 (Wiggins 1995: 93). Changes to UI qualifying rules and benefit periods, not a booming job market, have cut the numbers of workers collecting UI benefits. Unemployed workers who either exhaust their UI benefits or no longer can qualify often have no place to turn except welfare.

Ontario social assistance rates were cut by 21.6 percent, as of October 1, 1995. The minister responsible, David Tsubouchi, released a welfare diet that a single person should be able to live on for $90 a month (Ontario Tories' Welfare Menu Substandard: Poverty Groups 1995: A11). An Ontario Federation of Labour (OFL) information bulletin said that his recommended menu was so nutritionally deficient that if he were feeding a prisoner of war on this diet, Tsubouchi would be in contravention of the Geneva Convention. The rules of war do not apply to class war.

Welfare bashing has come home to haunt union workers in unexpected ways. In August 1995, Tsubouchi announced that his ministry was creating a province-wide welfare fraud line. He encouraged the good citizens of Ontario to call a toll-free number and tattle on neighbours they believed were cheating the welfare system. When society officially condones informing on one's neighbour, it doesn't stop with those least able to defend themselves. It can be turned against workers in a powerful union.

In September, only a month later, in a move too similar to the welfare fraud line to be mere coincidence, General Motors (GM) Canadian president, Maureen Kempston-Darkes, announced a GM toll-free line that employees could call to report on other GM employees they believed were acting contrary to "company policies." CAW president, Buzz Hargrove, denounced this as an idea inspired by the Harris war on the poor, and union members at GM staged a protest at corporate headquarters against the "rat line" where they burned thousands of snitch cards distributed to them by the company.

Workfare is another Harris government policy which indirectly targets Ontario workers, threatening their wages, their bargaining power, and their jobs. Under its provisions, "employable" welfare recipients will be forced to demonstrate that they have worked seventeen hours a week or risk having their welfare benefits cut entirely (see Moscovitch Chapter 6). The resulting flood of desperate people forced to work without any salary or labour rights will undercut the wages and bargaining power of those currently employed. If workfare jobs are real jobs, they should be paid and protected by labour legislation. If they are not, critics ask, "why is anyone being forced to do work that is not necessary"? This amounts to punishing the poor for the crime of being poor. As Tory workfare plans unfold, one wonders how much appetite Harris will have for them when welfare recipients organize as workers and demand their rights, as relief camp workers did in the 1930s (Brown 1987).

The promised 30 percent cut to provincial income tax rates will benefit the rich disproportionately and at the expense of the poor. The Harris tax cut for one millionaire will eat up all the savings attained by cutting the welfare of seventeen single parent families (mothers with two children). So Harris must impoverish fifty one people to give the millionaire his 30 percent tax cut (Stanford 1994).

The Harris tax reform will further deplete provincial tax revenues, force the government to borrow more to cover the deficit, and cut more programs to pay the resulting interest charges. The OFLcontends in its alternative budget submission that the net borrowing needed to finance the Harris tax cut will be $20 billion (Ontario Federation of Labour 1996). The end result will be higher municipal property taxes and user fees as the province cuts subsidies to the municipalities, universities, colleges, school boards and hospitals.

Bill 7 Rolls Back Collective Bargaining Rights

If a growing reserve army of more and more impoverished and desperate unemployed was not enough to discipline Ontario workers into accepting less on October 31, 1995, the Tories passed Bill 7. It included sixty three last-minute amendments most members in the legislature had not read. During the election campaign, Harris promised voters he would repeal Bill 40, the changes that the previous NDP government had made to the Ontario Labour Relations Act.

The NDP's Bill 40 had been about making the Ontario Labour Relations Act live up to its stated purpose; to encourage collective bargaining between workers and their employers. Before Bill 40, an employer could use the labour code to break a union. The way Eatons defeated an organizing drive in five Toronto area stores in the 1980s illustrates how that worked.

When Retail Wholesale union organizers began signing up low-paid workers at the Eatons stores, a group calling themselves Stop the Union, instigated by the company, handed out anti-union literature in the workplace during working hours. When union organizers tried to distribute literature at the store entrances inside the malls, the property owners called the police to have them evicted for trespassing on "third party" property. After the union filed for certification, the board had to hear petitions from workers who had a "change of heart." During those long delays, the company conducted open warfare against the union in the workplace. Although the labour board eventually certified the union, the workers had to strike for a first collective agreement. Eatons answered with strikebreakers. The Canadian Labour Congress organized a national boycott of Eatons to push the company to negotiate. Pressure was building on Eatons. However, once the strike approached the six month mark, it was the union that was under pressure. The union had to sign a collective agreement in order to guarantee that the union workers would at least be able to return to their jobs. Under the pre-Bill 40 Labour Relations Act, the employer did not have to reinstate striking workers if the strike or lock-out lasted more than six months. With the union over the barrel, the company dictated the terms of a one-year agreement. The union had won few real gains for the workers. As the one year agreement came due, it was a foregone conclusion that the inevitable decertification petition against the union would succeed. Eatons had provided a case study in how to use the Labour Relations Act to break a union (Currie and Sheedy 1987).

Bill 40 aimed to remedy what took place at Eatons. It did away with the six month deadline for reinstatement after a strike. It banned scabs and barred further petitions after the union filed for certification. It allowed for limited organizing and picketing on third party property. It opened the door to first contract arbitration thirty days after a legal strike date. It guaranteed orderly reinstatement of union workers after a strike or lock-out. With expedited hearings and interim orders, Bill 40 gave more effective remedies from "unfair labour practices" like firing of union supporters during organizing campaigns and first contract bargaining. Bill 40 also saw to it that an employer had to negotiate an adjustment agreement in the event of mass layoffs or plant closure. A standard adjustment plan means retraining for laid-off workers, enhanced early retirement pensions, and enhanced severance pay.

Bill 40 also said that when private contracts for cafeteria, security or cleaning services change hands, the new contractor had to offer the jobs to the workers employed by the old contractor and honour their previous working conditions. Before Bill 40, it was common for workers in these poorly paid service jobs to find themselves on the street with no notice and no job, only because the service contract had changed hands.

Bill 7 repealed all those provisions. But it went farther. For example, petitions to decertify a union are nearly always behind-the-scenes work of the employer. Yet the labour board must now hear decertification petitions and order a quick vote, where in the past they would likely have been dismissed because of employer involvement.

Bill 7 not only wiped out the provisions of Bill 40, but it also did away with sections of the act dating back to 1950 and, ironically, to previous Conservative governments. With the passage of Bill 7, gone was the provision whereby the labour relations board had to certify or recognize a union if the required number of workers properly signed union cards. Bill 7 calls for mandatory votes. These mandatory votes give the employer yet another chance to threaten workers into voting against the union. Often employers simply tell workers that the plant will close and move elsewhere if they vote yes. Hargrove reported that in the CAW's last campaign at the Michelin tire plants in Nova Scotia, for example, 500 workers who had signed union cards voted against the union in a mandatory vote.

The mandatory vote is one feature of the U.S. National Labour Relations Act. Stephen Lerner, a consultant with the AFL-CIO Organizing Institute in Washington, D.C. reported to a staff conference of the Public Service Alliance of Canada that U.S. unions now lose so many of these votes that only 11 percent of U.S. workers are union members today, compared with 30 percent in 1950. As a result of this serious erosion of union strength, U.S. workers have suffered a series of serious setbacks[1].

Was all this necessary? Harris had told the voters he would repeal Bill 40 arguing that its provisions stifle the economy and kill jobs. However, since many Bill 40 amendments were only a matter of simple fairness, the economic catastrophe predicted by business never materialized. In fact, profits recovered during the period that Bill 40 was law. Nevertheless, Bill 40 stood in the way of the business aim of creating a cheap, non-unionized labour force. Harris's corporate backers wanted everything in Bill 40 to go, not because they had proven their case against Bill 40 but because, with a Harris majority government, they simply had the power to get what they wanted.

Workers' Compensation and Safety Rights Threatened
On August 8, 1995 the Workplace Health and Safety Agency was disbanded. Many of the workplace health and safety and minimum employment standards inspectors have been laid-off. The Ontario government is also considering proposals to weaken the worker's right to refuse unsafe work, a cornerstone of all worker's safety rights on the job.

In February 1996, Cam Jackson, minister responsible for workers' compensation, released a report which, if implemented, would gut past, present, and future compensation benefits to injured workers. Jackson proposed to limit the right to appeal and time period in which to appeal. Benefits which are now 90 percent of net earnings could be reduced to 75 percent. The report talks about turning the entire system over to private insurers. Employers would control payment of compensation claims for the first six weeks of injury. Employers then could exert more pressure on the worker not to file a claim when injured, and instead use sickness or vacation days. Negotiated collective agreements would be invaded and overruled. Employer top-ups of certain Workers Compensation Board (WCB) benefits would not be allowed. The WCB would be the insurer of last resort. Workers could have to use up other benefits like private disability, UI, sickness, and Canada Pension Plan disability benefits. Redefining work-related injury would mean repetitive strain injuries, strains, sprains, chronic pain, back pain and occupational stress could be next to impossible to claim. Jackson would eliminate the Office of the Worker Advisor.

Jackson justified all these regressive proposals by pointing to an "unfunded liability" crisis, out-of-control benefit costs, and high employer premiums. But at the same time, the WCB has $7 billion in the bank; employers have been receiving millions in rebates; the board has never borrowed money; employers' premiums are lower than they were in 1988; and benefits expense per claim is the lowest it has been in ten years (Toronto Injured Workers Advocacy Group 1996).

Harris Backers, Not Bill 40, Are the Real Job Killers
On May 26, 1995, Harris released a list of 100 chief executive officers (CEOs) who backed his Common Sense Revolution (Mittelstaedt 1995: A5). Among them were Peter Munk of Horsham Corporation, Trevor Eyton of Brascan and

John C. Eaton of Eatons Canada. They have ample reason to support the Harris agenda. Horsham, for example, enjoyed an effective tax rate of 1.4 percent on profits of $190 million U.S. in 1994 (Turk 1996). But Harris's pitch obviously struck a responsive chord with a lot of people who feel insecure about their future and who want to believe that his solutions might work. Reward business enterprise and initiative with lower taxes and higher profits, and they will surely create jobs.

However, this theory doesn't stand up to scrutiny. The corporations have had it all their way. They wanted the Canada/U.S. and North American Free Trade Agreements. They got them. They wanted the unemployment insurance program cut back, Bill 40 repealed, workers compensation cut. They got it all. So, where are the jobs? General Motors of Canada made a record profit of $1.39 billion in 1995, and cut its work force by 2500. Bell Canada made a profit of $502 million and cut 3170 jobs. Inco made $227 million and cut 1963 jobs. Petro-Canada made $196 million and cut 564 jobs. Shell Canada made $523 million and cut 471 jobs. Imperial Oil made $514 million and cut 452 jobs. The Bank of Montreal, the TD Bank, and the Canadian Imperial Bank of Commerce, with total 1995 profits of $2.8 billion, cut 3071 jobs (Ip February 6, 1996: A1).

With Harris joining others in the job cutting, there are virtually no employers to whom Ontario's youth can turn for secure, life-time employment. This trend is no accident. Stock market speculators reward corporations that announce mass layoffs by buying their stock and driving up their shareholder values. They punish those that are slow to cut jobs by selling shares and driving down their stock prices (Ip March 23, 1996: B1). Harris's claim that Bill 40 was a job killer is hard to support. On the other hand, when one looks at how the stock market players push corporations to cut jobs, we can see that the real job killers are the very investors who back Harris.

For example, GM has successfully lobbied the Ontario labour minister to introduce amendments to the Employment Standards Act to permit a 56-hour work week in line with practices in U.S. plants, instead of the present Ontario maximum of 48. A longer mandatory work week will deny job opportunities to the unemployed.

OPSEU's First Strike Provoked by Bills 7 and 26

Under Bill 7, when the government privatizes public services, crown employees lose their union successor rights. This was one of the issues that provoked the Ontario Public Service Employees Union (OPSEU) strike which began February 25, 1996. Harris planned to cut between 13,000 and 27,000 public service jobs, largely by contracting out to private companies work now done by government employees. Bill 40 had required that the new employers had to employ the government workers affected, and recognize their service, seniority and collective bargaining rights. Bill 7, by contrast, says the government does not have to honour successor rights.

Another key OPSEU strike issue had to do with the new powers the government gave itself through the Omnibus Bill (Bill 26). This bill amended over forty provincial laws, repealed some and created new ones. Only civil disobedience by an opposition member in the legislative assembly forced the government to grant public hearings on the bill that was tabled when the press was in the traditional lock-up studying the budget. Bill 26 became an OPSEU strike issue because it took away the right of crown employees to enhanced early retirement benefits in the event of mass layoffs, a standard feature of workplace adjustment agreements.

Since the anti-scab law (Bill 40) was repealed, union members may have found some unexpected friends. For example, Paul Walter, president of the Metro Toronto Police Association refused to escort "replacement" workers through OPSEU picket lines:

"What difference does it make whether ten people are allowed into a building to do clerical work if the possible result of that is that we have broken bodies and tens of thousands of dollars worth of damage? You've got to draw a common sense line in the ground.... It is not a criminal offence for people to picket, for people to demonstrate. In fact, it's our right as Canadian citizens. If certain acts by an employer, like using replacement workers, would cause potential for violence, then obviously as police officers we can not support that." (quoted in Toughill February 16, 1996: 2)

After five weeks on strike, OPSEU won a major improvement over the government's "final" offer. OPSEU won back certain pension rights endangered by Bill 26. The real significance of the outcome lies in the fact that the government had to make its first compromise on an agenda it was determined to push through without compromise. Moreover, the Harris government had to negotiate seriously with an organization they thought would collapse once forced to strike. There was no collapse. While the strike vote was 66 percent, only 10 percent of the union membership scabbed. In fact, while I was assigned to help coordinate CAW strike support to OPSEU in the Toronto area, I saw the strikers' militancy and resolve harden as the strike wore on. On March 18, 1996 the para-military Ontario police riot squad assaulted OPSEU picketers without warning at the legislative buildings, sending four people, including a Metro police officer, to hospital. Far from breaking the strike, this assault was answered by more determined mass picketing of downtown Toronto OPSEU strike locations. The OPP were conspicuous by their absence at a 3000 strong solidarity march of OPSEU and other unions the following week in which OFL President Gord Wilson demanded Solicitor General Runciman resign over the OPP's unprovoked attack. Harris had to agree to set up an all-party special investigation of the OPP actions on March 18.

OPSEU, a union on strike for the first time and more familiar with an environment of arbitration than mobilization, learned fast how to set up picket lines in hundreds of locations, many of them at multi-use buildings. OPSEU flying squads often defied property managers and trespass laws in setting up mass pickets inside multi-use sites, taking back in action a right gained under Bill 40 and then lost under Bill 7. Harris succeeded in turning OPSEU into a militant organization.

OPSEU's militancy has been buttressed and echoed by a total of almost 200,000 people who have participated in the days of action organized by the OFL and community groups in London, Hamilton, Kitchener-Waterloo-Cambridge, and Peterborough (See Turk Chapter 14).

The key to fighting Harris is the corporations. If you are going to put feet to fire, better the ventriloquist's than the dummy's. Rarely has a government so slavishly followed the dictates of big business as has Harris's. Former Canadian UAW Director, Dennis McDermott was fond of saying that the bosses have a nerve that runs from their heart to their pocket book. Pinch that nerve, and you have their undivided attention—and Harris's.

Julie White, a union committeeperson at the 3M plant in London, Ontario, was on the phone at the CAW Local 27 office from the early hours of December 11, 1995. She was taking calls from one picket captain after another. They were calling in to tell her that the lines were solid at the London CAW organized plants. Like the Ford plant in St. Thomas and the Cami plant in Ingersoll and dozens of other union workplaces private and public in the London area, they were all down. It was the satisfying culmination of weeks of tireless effort by thousands of union activists in bringing about the first OFL day of protest against the Harris policies.

At 8:00 am, Julie White got a call she was not expecting. It was from a woman in Toronto, who said: "I called you because I just wanted to thank the unions." This woman saw the day of protest as the unions standing up for *all* people who were suffering at the hands of the Harris government. The caller was a single parent woman who had had to drop out of school because she could no longer afford the child care (White 1996).

Sam Gindin, assistant to CAW President Buzz Hargrove, echoed her sentiments:

"The London protest was the first time during any of our lives [in Ontario] that workers in mass walked off the job over social issues.... London showed workers at their best: discussing the issues, generating a wider debate, organizing for action, and stubbornly carrying out that action in spite of employer intimidation and a steady barrage of 'there's-no-alterative-so-why-fight-back.' London was about turning our back on cynicism, and finding some hope in solidarity. London was about putting the movement back in labour, and putting labour at the head of the movement."

"It wasn't just that we were able to empty so many workplaces, though anyone who roamed the city in those magic hours will never forget the thrill of passing one group of pickets only to come to another one at a different worksite.

And it wasn't...that we followed the picketing with the largest political march and demonstration the city had ever seen. Something beyond militancy and numbers was happening. Something that had to do with political consciousness. Workers were saying that they were no longer content to leave politics to the politicians. Workers gave up a day's pay and risked employer retaliation because they understood the danger of the Harris direction to themselves, their families, and their communities. London was the beginning of a new politics in which workers, as individuals and through their organizations, would take dramatic action to focus attention on the kind of society we were becoming." (Gindin 1995)

Notes

1. The most recent setback was the defeat of the United Autoworkers' four-year struggle with Caterpillar in Illinois. The terms Caterpillar imposed on the UAW are a sobering reminder of what can happen to the most powerful of unions when unions find themselves isolated, and when wages and benefits union members enjoy become the exception rather than the rule. Caterpillar broke pattern bargaining, the union strategy of making companies in the same industry sign substantially the same agreements. In addition, the heavy equipment manufacturer also made major inroads against the union's ability to defend the workers on a day-to-day basis in the workplace. Now Caterpillar can unilaterally reject grievances it considers repetitive or frivolous. In-plant competition between workers will be intensified by work reorganization along the lines of "business units." Every form of workers' concerted activity, otherwise protected by law, will be banned. The 150 activists terminated during the strike will not even see their cases go to arbitration. A permanent two-tiered wage and benefit structure ensures new hires will never catch up to the higher rates over the term of the contract. The company can have a new part-time or temporary workforce. Over six years, Caterpillar will take $1.50 off the cost-of-living allowance (Moody 1996: 13–14).

Part Three

Strategies of Resistance

Chapter 12

Community Strategies for Surviving and Resisting the Cuts

Michèle Kérisit and Nérée St-Amand

"This is not a context of cutbacks, this is a context of rape and pillage. What our governments are doing is bleeding more and more wealth from our communities, out of these communities and into the pockets of people who are controlling most of the wealth in the world."[1] Joan Kuyek, community organizer, interview, July 1995.

Under the Harris's government deprived families and people living in poverty are often presented as the cause of our social and economic ills. Politicians and the media describe them as dependent, unstable and unmotivated, and accuse them of bleeding the financial resources of the province. This manipulation directs popular discontent onto the poor and the disadvantaged, who often do not have the means to defend themselves or voice their side of the story (De Gaulejac and Léonetti 1994; Berrick 1995).

From the study described in this chapter, we discovered that, on the contrary, poor families strive to improve their situation. Local projects and community initiatives counter the political agenda of the Conservative government (Warren 1986; Harrison and Laxer 1995). Poor families involved in alternative networks try to create local economies and local solidarities to resist the downgrading which global strategies have imposed on them (Plant and Plant 1992). In Ontario as well as in all Canadian provinces and territories, organizations are fighting the ideological bulldozing of the Right's agenda, despite the numerous difficulties they face. Moreover, the resistance that we observed is not based exclusively on political action that we will call "acts of resistance," but also includes everyday acts of solidarity which create, as one of the community leaders called them, "nodes of protection" on which a "culture of resistance" can be built (Kuyek 1996).

Our purpose is to show that people's initiatives are creative, democratic, empowering and based on actual needs and resources (Perry and Lewis 1994); they should be encouraged and supported by governments. Harris's policies function to destroy these initiatives and everything they stand for, not only to the detriment of low-income groups but to the detriment of Ontario society as a whole.

We will illustrate our argument with examples of alternative organizations that constitute self-help and help networks for low-income families; in doing so, we will describe some of the facets that community-based empowerment can take. These illustrations are taken from data collected during a Canada-wide study on what we called "alternative resources" (Kérisit and St-Amand 1995).

During this study, we conducted a survey of community support systems and collective survival strategies designed to create models of development different from institutional models. We found that the groups we met invent ways of doing things that depart from the conventional practices of the public bodies in charge of child protection, welfare, housing, employment, and other services. These alternative resources force us to rethink professional and institutional policies, as well as the attitudes and practices of many professionals working with so-called deprived families and communities.[2]

Local communities, especially very poor and socially isolated ones, have dignity and a sense of survival. Their dynamism disproves the prevailing discourse depicting them as being dependent, unmotivated, dysfunctional and prone to multiple problems (Liffman 1978; Kérisit and St-Amand 1995). Here is what some of the women we interviewed said: "We're an asset, not a burden on society. We refuse to be considered simply as bundles of problems," said one mother. "We want to counter the current economic situation that systematically results in exclusion. We want another model of development," added another participant involved in a community kitchen.

To be part of our project, resources had to meet three criteria: they had to have a poverty mandate, to work with families, and to comply with a definition of alternative resources we proposed to them (St-Amand et al. 1996). This definition, largely inspired by work previously conducted in the mental health field, emphasizes the following components: the involvement of disadvantaged families in the organization's decision making process; an approach based on a social rather than an individual analysis of families' problems; advocacy work for and with the families; and respect for the history and culture of the participants.

Among the thousands of community-based organizations that exist in Canada, we identified 350 alternative resources that fit our definition. To locate them, we started with municipal, provincial or territorial directories; we subsequently used a snowball approach, making numerous telephone calls and visits to various community groups interested in participating in our project. An advisory committee also helped us to identify several networks.

In the rest of this chapter, we will focus primarily on community strategies created by local communities, with particular reference to alternative resources developed in Ontario. In describing these projects, we recognize that poverty is not a choice (another myth perpetuated by a Conservative agenda) and that deprived community groups and families do not have access to goods, services and resources that would enable them to counter poverty. In suggesting that people are resources, our purpose is not to glorify poverty, but to recognize the ability of low-income families to cope, and the many "nodes of solidarity" they create, even in extremely difficult conditions. In a province where poverty means spending up to 60 percent and even 80 percent of one's social assistance cheque on housing, and where many essential services have been reduced or cut completely, there is no advantage to being poor. Furthermore, poverty is by no means only manifested and defined by a lack of material goods, but also by solitude, isolation, insecurity and low self-esteem. Therefore, a major thrust of our search was to find groups that attempted not only to alleviate economic hardship, but also to create or re-create a sense of community, to reweave the strands of lives disrupted by isolation. And we found them; as one mother we interviewed said, "This is one big family. I feel at home here."

This sense of belonging to a place and this sense of family warmth seem to constitute the basis upon which alternative community networks develop strategies for survival and resistance. This is achieved by a twofold movement: on the one hand, by challenging conventional or institutional ways of "assisting" low-income families, and on the other hand by building new forms of solidarity and emphasizing empowerment and control by the families not only over their individual lives, but also over their local communities and over the "help" available or offered to them (Godbout 1992).

We will illustrate our discussion of empowering practices with the words of community organizers and low-income mothers interviewed during the research. We will present a few of the seventy alternative resources working with poor families in Ontario that participated in our project and focus particularly on one case study that clearly demonstrates the many nuances of local empowerment and democratic process.

The delicate issue of local leadership versus government intervention is omnipresent in this chapter and can be formulated in the following manner:

- How can governments recognize and encourage local leadership projects and initiatives without directing their mandate or controlling their activities through funding policies and practices? Alternative resources are quite wary of government intrusion in their affairs. As one community leader stated our principle: we do not want to prostitute the kids' suffering and it's very important. We can fall so easily into that trap, because of our need for money. Yes, we need money; if you want to give us money, fine, but you can't set your own agenda for us.
- By developing and insisting on their autonomy, do the groups we are about to describe play into the new Conservative agenda of state dismemberment?

Our central point is to show that, ingrained in the everyday practices of low-income families working together, there exist ways of "doing things" that are incompatible with the individualistic and alienating life that is presented to us by the Conservative government of Ontario as *the* exclusive model of human development. Alternative resources are mapping a new course of action that might be extremely valid for reformulating social services in this province.

The "Nodes of Protection"

During this project, we were forced to alter our initial definition of the family: it quickly became synonymous with the social or constructed family rather than the biological or legal one. One participant said it well: "What we do in this program is primarily try to create an alternative family for people." When we refer to "family" in this chapter, we therefore recognize that the majority of the people involved (i.e. women) come from families "broken by suffering," to quote one mother. Alternative resources try to create a different type of family based on common needs, proximity and shared resources.

Our study confirms that single, female-headed households are the most likely to find themselves in situations of extreme poverty (Ross 1994; Robichaud et al. 1994)—reflecting structural and patriarchal social constraints which are at the very basis of poverty.

"What it reminds me of, it's a blanket. It's like security and everything is knitted together...." These are the words of a mother describing the organization she comes to for her childrens' daycare. The organization itself is one of the many groups that offers daily refuge for low-income single mothers and that attend to the development of their children. Many of the organizations we visited when compiling *This is Our Place* (St-Amand et al. 1996) are of a similar nature. This is not surprising, since the most vulnerable groups of people targeted by provincial welfare cuts in Ontario are included in this project.

The metaphor of a tightly woven social fabric echoes the words of numerous others and expresses the most difficult issues facing people living in poverty. Immersed in the whirlwind of daily survival, and faced with the ongoing difficulty of finding secure accommodation and ensuring adequate food and clothing, the people we interviewed have all expressed the need for a place where they can feel secure, where they can be themselves, a place that contrasts with either their own or the government offices and other public places where they have to go to secure a daily living. The other metaphor used to describe the feeling of security and warmth is that of the "family." "I dropped in here with my kids and it was just like a real family. We were very, very close and we didn't know each other," says another mother. "This is our place," says another. This emphasis on a secure environment is not to be taken lightly since it constitutes the basis on which community development can occur by creating or weaving social interactions. This is what Joan Kuyek, a community organizer said:

> What we are faced with is really having to work at creating that kind of base in the communities where people really do support each other, understand each other and know each other and have some opportunity to work together with some joy. Because they won't come together in protest if they don't understand and know each other as partners and friends. The big thing is to create the opportunity for people to take care of one another. (Kuyek 1995)

The challenges facing organizations that attempt to create alternative ways of empowering those who are the most disempowered in our society are twofold: to create a place where interpersonal links are built and strengthened—which is no small feat in a world where the ideology of survival of the fittest dominates—and to make sure that this basis is secure enough to launch projects capable of making a difference in the lives of people participating in the organization. The first part of the challenge is met by rethinking and reorganizing the space people move in and the time that is devoted to projects. It is also met by reworking the position of permanent staff within the organizations and "democratizing" them. We will touch upon these three aspects in the following pages.

The Use of Time and Space

Because time and place are deeply anchored in cultural values and fashioned by customs and behaviours, we could ultimately summarize this aspect of the creativity of alternative resources as part of a general respect for the culture of the community in which the organization is rooted. In the organizations we visited, space is indeed organized very differently from that of institutionally-based services, both with regard to the inner space of the organization and its spatial relationship with the world outside.

Most groups we visited, for instance, were organized around a common room, whether a kitchen or a meeting room. Very often, meetings are held in the kitchen, conversation flows among people engaged in different activities; children are often present while other activities take place. Informality is the key to such arrangements and a sense of open space is paramount. Priorities are not necessarily set according to an instrumental view of space: some organizations prefer to start with a make-over of the place through a paint job or posters, rather than structural work on the building, which would tie up the energy and the few resources that are available. In other instances, the organization itself is located in an area that is immediately accessible to people passing by on the street, or it promotes a sense of community by surrounding itself by plants and community gardens. "One of the things that's happened is that we have been able to get gardeners and naturalists throughout our funding. So we have plants everywhere all over the building, outside. We've got little community gardens starting. It is very informal and very non-threatening to people" (Kuyek 1996).

Other organizations are attempting to create different forms of public space for low-income people. For instance, *Field to Table* in Toronto buys fresh food products from farmers and suppliers and delivers them the same day to community groups. Their goal is to foster nutritional security and health. It is also designed to give communities the opportunity to develop social interaction mechanisms and a sense of community belonging. As an alternative to food banks, it solves the problem of accessibility to low-price supermarkets, which are usually located far from low-income neighbourhoods and public housing projects. But in doing so, it also attempts to recreate a market atmosphere in underprivileged neighbourhoods as a means of promoting sociability and self-help.

In all these instances groups attempt to change the way people relate to each other and redefine relations of power. As Kuyek says:

> [Institutions] construct physical space to intimidate people and to reinforce the power of those who have power over others. In our resource, a lot of creativity happens just because people have the freedom to arrange the space the way they want and courage not to replicate business relationships (interview, July 1995).

Despite the constraints often imposed by architecture, people are finding ways to organize the space available to them to express supportive relationships, rather than market-driven hierarchical patterns of power. In doing so, they not only create for themselves a "node of protection," they also resist dominant ideological forces.

Alternative organizations also find ways to pattern time which resist the fragmented, measured time structurally imposed by the dominant capitalist culture. One of the most common recurrent remarks we encountered concerns the amount of time it takes to build an alternative resource. Many participating members in the organizations we visited said that they appreciated the fact that the resource was not exclusively "program-driven" and that there was time for "living together." Describing her program, one community worker said:

> Our program is not really structured, so people can come in when they want during the day and they're never late for anything. Therefore, there is no program to worry about since the program is ongoing. The Centre builds friendships, networks and contacts.

In fact, one of the scarcest commodities for people living in poverty is time. Life is often spent haggling over obligations and multiple social roles performed with difficulty, dealing with the numerous agencies and bodies that still permit survival—not to mention the everyday grind caused by the lack of transportation in a province that has modeled its urban development on suburbia. Alternative agencies recognize the current split between two ways of experiencing time. One of these is what Melucci (1989: 104) calls "inner time" (the subjective periods of inner experiences, affections, emotions and natural cycles). The other is "social time," characterized by the objective division marked by the clock, the fragmented time of the market, work and social roles. By letting the experience of social time be affected by the inner workings of personal timeframes, alternative resources encourage a reconciliation which, in many respects, is one of the great difficulties of living in poverty and unemployment (Burman 1988: 139).

Enmeshed in the redesigning of time and space patterns, we found two key aspects of alternative resources: first, in order to simply exist, these organizations have to be extremely attentive to the local culture of the participants; second, they are built to minimize, as much as possible, patterns of power. We now turn to this second aspect in order to demonstrate that the organizations we visited provide a space where a "culture of resistance" can be developed.

Acts of Resistance: Democratizing Organizations

In the preceding section we attempted to show how alternative resources create links between people whose lives are marked by isolation and the absence of secure, long term relationships. This in itself constitutes an achievement since structural constraints in our society tend to prevent people from forming and getting the most out of everyday trusting relationships. Distrust is increasingly built into the system: the "snitch line" put in place by the Harris government has seriously jeopardized the already fragile, informal networks developing in housing projects or other sites where low-income Ontarians are often ghettoized.

In the following pages, we will address one of the most challenging and pressing issues facing people working collectively in alternative resources, namely their attempt to invent for themselves new relationships which are, as much as possible, exempt from the inequalities that they encounter on a daily basis—be it with the "helping profession" or the grocer at the street corner. To do this, we will focus on the experience of one of the organizations we included in our study, the Better Beginnings, Better Futures (BBBF) program in Sudbury. In our opinion, it constitutes a sort of blueprint for all the other organizations in Ontario and the rest of Canada.

According to our original criteria, organizations had to include low-income families in all levels of decision making in order to be "alternative." We did not specify the ways in which such participation should take place. Our research findings clearly indicate that we were both right and wrong to take this approach. We were right to include democratic functioning as a defining criteria; we were also right to refrain from specifying which forms this participation could take. Where we went wrong was to take for granted that as long as the rules were democratic, participation would just happen once the organization got on its feet. In fact, it appears that participation could best be described as a process that reaches a certain degree of equilibrium at one point in time, to be changed and reconfigured at others. In other words, what counts is not only the formal structure of the organization but the process it undergoes to make democracy work and become useful to the participants.

Many things contribute to this complex process. As community workers have mentioned, it is not easy to create a structure that allows the voice of low-income people to be effectively heard and transformed into action and concrete projects. First, the constraints of poverty are numerous, preventing many poor people from following through on long term projects.

A lot of people, even if they are not formally working or going to school are very busy surviving. Those people who are not doing that are generally depressed and it's very hard to get out and do things if you are depressed. A lot of people are unemployed and on welfare because they are unwell. They have been disabled by bad backs or they are sick. This combination of things means it is hard to get people involved and participating on a regular basis (Kuyek 1996).

Second, despite good intentions on the part of the social service sector, at least among the front-line workers, it takes time to re-invent ways of making decisions; it's hard to break the habit of "taking charge" of people. As another community organizer said to us: "You have to disempower yourself in order to empower others... and many people can't deal with disempowering themselves."

Third, many of the people involved in organizing, running and participating in alternative resources are women. The burden of care for their own families competes constantly with their other responsibilities.

However, instead of focusing on the many difficulties that can be encountered, let us now turn to the way the Better Beginnings, Better Futures of Sudbury successfully managed its democratizing process, and the strategies it adopted to circumvent these difficulties.

1989: The Early Beginnings
Two social workers and community leaders (one from a First Nations organization, one from a mental health organization) come together while attending community development workshops.

1990: Securing Funding and Stabilizing the Organization
The Ontario government announces funding for Better Beginnings, Better Futures projects in different areas of the province. A group of front-line social workers come together from seven different agencies and submit a proposal. The current coordinator is contacted to get involved in the project. The group meets every week and develops a very tight relationship.

1991: Project Funded
The original group brings in poor people's leaders. Job descriptions are written for the first hirings. A pattern of weekly meetings with hired staff and any person from the community is established.

1994: Democratizing Process
The association is formalized, extending membership to all participants in the program and all staff living in the neighbourhood. No more than 25 percent of membership is extended to individuals not living in the neighbourhood. An attempt to establish an agency working group fails during the process. A community advisory council is established with a representative of local government. A council is elected consisting of two representatives of the five caucuses

that constitute the association (Native, French-speaking, Black, English-speaking, staff) and three members at large.

Many points arise from this example. In addition to the obvious democratic practice of electing members to its governing body, it departs from the general practice of having a community board in three ways:

- a whole process is created whereby professionals, staff and community members interact in order to build consensus. Staff have representation on the council. The professionals who were instrumental in launching the organization "were all committed to consensual decision making and respect for diversity;"
- the organization is anchored in the immediate neighbourhood: only 25 percent of the membership originates from the community "at large," i.e. members of the public who are particularly interested in supporting the project. The impact of such a measure is important, since it prevents people from other more privileged areas of town becoming "interpreters" of the voices of the disadvantaged, as often happens; and
- diversity and culture are included within the organizational grid.

How do groups like these establish a relationship between staff and participants that would be as egalitarian as possible?

- First of all, participation is encouraged by taking into account people's real needs. For example, the systematic organization of transportation, child care and dinners/lunch during meetings and activities;
- secondly, organizations adopt a careful hiring policy to ensure that permanent staff have a thorough knowledge of the neighbourhood, either because they live in it or because they have lived in a similar environment. As one community worker said, "They not only talk the talk but they have walked the walk." In many of the Ontario alternative resources we visited, the staff in fact mainly consisted of women who had started as "clients," then went on to take charge of one aspect of the organization's activities as volunteers, then were hired and went on to college to formalize the hands-on training they had acquired in the organization.

Leaders suggest that generating projects, sometimes of short duration in which people not only receive training and acquire new skills but also are paid for the work they do, promotes participation and develops community leadership. Community development can only occur if recognition is given to people who put time and effort into creating a new community, and if the people living in poor neighbourhoods are themselves hired to develop their community—not outside "experts" who do not understand the culture, dynamics and history of the community. In some organizations, for instance, activities such as neighbourhood watch are developed and are considered real work (as opposed to volunteer work); the women are paid accordingly. In fact, the organization becomes a place for a "practicum" that could lead to other income. It should be noted, however, that this is done on a volunteer basis, as a social utility, not as disguised workfare which is based on budget cuts and poor-bashing instead of real community development.

In many ways, alternative resources are already playing an important part in the social economy (Quarter 1992; Ninacs 1995) or community-based economy (Rosanvallon 1995; Yakabuski 1996), meaning the development of employment for people who will perform the many tasks that need to be done to maintain and sustain a community. There are many arguments in favour of the emerging "social economy," which are currently the buzz words in many governmental circles. One doubts, however, that the Harris government is ready to think of the social economy as it was promoted by the more progressive thinkers who created it (Nozick 1992; Shragge 1993).

The last section of this chapter will be devoted to the Ontario government's assault on alternative resources. It will attempt to demonstrate that, despite the current discourse that promotes "community leadership," everything is being done to undermine the communities of which every person is a member, irrespective of his or her level of income. The consequences of such destruction is not a matter of concern for just the low-income people in Ontario. Our project shows that "doing things differently"—by developing other ways to relate to space and time, and to develop egalitarian relationships—could not only be a matter of survival for the less advantaged but could also create a model for the whole society.

The middle class will gradually feel the brunt of the Ontario government cutbacks. Many already experience the fragmented, instrumental, "social time" that we described earlier. The numerous roles imposed by an ever-growing reliance on services from family members (read women) already take their toll on harassed lives. No time is left for "inner time" or for reinventing one's physical environment. The manner in which alternative resources design programs and activities may map the escape route for many people who do not yet feel trapped by poverty.

The Effects of Cutbacks on Alternative Resources: What Should be Done?

There are many ways in which the current Ontario government affects alternative resources. There are also many ways in which its discursive practices mask its real agenda. The official discourse promoting local leadership and volunteer work as a source of community ownership could be taken as recognition of the work already being done in communities in Ontario. Similarly, by denouncing in the name of freedom, the domineering role of government in community affairs or private affairs, neo-liberals seem to echo some of the complaints of the past: many community-based, grassroots organizations were suspicious of the kind of help offered by an array of professionals, somewhat disconnected from the lives of the people they were "helping" and sometimes quite intrusive in people's lives, especially poor people's lives.

Furthermore, the government and its rigid or maladapted system of evaluation and funding-by-project could not realistically generate the type of holistic practices adopted by alternative organizations. On the surface, therefore, there appears to be a meeting of interests between a discourse that promotes the disappearance of government regulation and a community-based criticism of techno-bureaucratic culture "which taylorizes [sic] the social, with its professionalization and its emphasis on specialized or expert knowledge" (Lamoureux 1994: 122).

We should point out, however, that the rationale behind the current government's reluctance to interfere with community affairs and the progressive critics' analysis of social services are not at all similar. Here is how the Harris government sees "community work" according to its September 1995 throne speech:

> Neighbours helping shut-in seniors, corporations sponsoring nutrition programs for children, service clubs funding community projects, private sector employees and executives volunteering for public service, this is the spirit of Ontario. Your government will support and nurture this spirit (Throne Speech 1995).

In fact, what is really envisioned by this rosy picture of volunteer work and top-down charity is the use of cheap labour to replace existing service providers. One can wonder how "private sector employees and executives" could find the time, in their busy schedules, to volunteer. One could imagine how seniors would feel if they were cared for by their neighbours, when one knows how much pride seniors have in being self-sufficient. In fact this agenda, which will be put into practice through the appointment of a parliamentary assistant to oversee the promotion of volunteer work, signals one of the major contradictions of the Harris revolution: on the one hand, it reproduces an imaginary past in which the rich and wealthy "took care" of the poor and the "community" had a tight social fabric. On the other hand, it is dismembering the actual capability of real communities to take care of themselves. The Harris government is withdrawing support from the emergent social movements of the 1990s, which are based on the creation of a social economy following community economic development principles.

Many of the alternative resources we visited were gradually introducing micro-enterprises and small-scale income-generating projects (from catering co-ops to community gardens). Loan Circle co-ops were also being established by many groups. Crafts and arts are being developed and provide many First Nations people with an opportunity to develop a skill and raise some money in the context of traditional or inter-community powwows. All this activity created not only expertise and money but also social relationships: isolated people got to know each other and meet people from other communities. This community development model takes considerable time to establish and is geared toward social interaction and interdependence (McKnight 1995). It is not a money saving device, but a different kind of investment. The current government's "community model" is not at all of the same nature. "They tell us to set up businesses to support our [community] work," says Kuyek. "What they fail to tell us is that 80 percent of all small businesses fail within five years, and it is a 16-hour a day job for everyone who is involved in it, and that it rarely pays any salary" (Kuyek 1996: 7). In other words, starting such an enterprise without capital and bank loans, equity and leverage is virtually an impossible task. The illusion that this is the only way to get out of poverty is a lie, as is the illusion of the paradisiac Ontarian village of the premier's childhood.

In fact, developing communities on a model that would be different from the privatization/volunteer model takes time, money and dedication, at a time when low-income people are already seeing their own resources diminish dramatically. The obsessive focus on deficit reduction and cutbacks to institutional services creates a vacuum in communities, and very often it is the alternative resources that see the increasing wave of desperate people laid at their door, without being able to respond to them.

It seems that the increasing demands on alternative resources could force them to abandon exactly what makes them worthwhile and effective, namely their ability to sustain dignity, and to continue asserting that our lives are not only driven by profit but also by meaning.

Conclusion

In this chapter, we chose to illustrate how doing things differently in terms of the daily use of space, time and relationships can constitute creative acts of resistance to the current so-called models of social intervention. No wonder the Harris government wants to slash them, from a lack of understanding of the uniqueness of human communities, maybe, but no doubt also from a sense that these local "nodes of resistance" are a threat to a government that just wants to do business, without pressures from communities defending local interests, cultural diversity, and the lives of the poorest.

Harris's short term political view goes against any local development initiative; it threatens the survival of local, regional, cultural identities. Families and communities need time, space, recognition. One community worker involved with families for many years reminds us of the importance of the process of empowerment:

> There is no short cut to empowerment. It takes time and practice to develop skills and learn about the issues, so that everyone can participate effectively

in democratic structures. Individuals learn at different paces; confidence grows slowly. To cut short the process is to stifle the participation of women and other community members who are not customarily involved in decision making.

Notes

1. We sincerely thank Joan Kuyek for her valuable suggestions and comments, after reading a preliminary version of this chapter.
2. Our thanks to Fran McIninch, Évariste Thériault and David Thornton, Human Resources Development Canada, for supporting this project. The views expressed in this chapter do not necessarily represent those of Human Resources Development Canada.

Chapter 13

Fighting to Win
John Clarke

The confidence of the resistance movement against the Harris government is growing. Nonetheless, there is still a great deal of confusion around the question of how to have a political impact on the Tories. People are far from clear on how a social movement can deal with a government that is as single-minded in its pursuit of social retrogression as is the Harris regime.

Unless we develop a clear perspective of mobilizing to prevent this government's attacks and unless we have confidence in the possibility of victory, we are in the untenable position of calling on people to join us in an exercise in futility. If it is true that Mike Harris is a block of political granite, impervious to all forms of extra parliamentary activity, then we can only offer up mobilization strategies as some kind of mass therapy session. That may have some appeal to the thin layer of the population that goes to demonstrations routinely but it will never inspire the mass of previously politically dormant people to embark on a course of social struggle. If Harris is to be seriously challenged, it is imperative that we know that we can win this fight, and that we are conducting ourselves in such a way as to build that victory.

Since the Tories were elected, the Ontario Coalition Against Poverty (OCAP) has taken up the fight against them with great vigour. Through OCAP and the Toronto Direct Action Committee (TDAC) we have mobilized in many communities and around a range of poverty-related issues. The vicious 21.6 percent cut to social assistance rates has sparked the greatest level of resistance, and it has been our organization in Toronto that has achieved the best level of mobilization. TDAC had started to pull around it a new grouping of unemployed and poor activists in the months leading up to the Harris victory. This had been achieved mainly by a shift in the committee's tactics. In addition to mobilizing around the broad political grievances that affected those it spoke for, TDAC began to use direct action mobilizing to defend the individual victims of abusive landlords, employers, welfare offices and the like. In dozens of cases, people saw the benefits of collective action in the most tangible fashion. This had produced for TDAC a number of committed activists who were ready to provide resistance leadership when Harris came to power and announced his cuts.

Faced, in the summer of 1995, with the most important struggle our coalition has ever been up against, and with over a hundred people turning out for bimonthly business meetings, TDAC sought to take stock of the situation. A number of things were apparent. First of all, it was clear that the 21.6 percent cut to social assistance vastly intensified the attack on the poor and unemployed. We anticipated the likely impact of such a reduction on income for people already in poverty. Five months after this cut, food bank use in Toronto was up by 50 percent. The population in the emergency shelters had mushroomed and the sheriff's office acknowledged a 38 percent increase in eviction applications. These, of course, were only the initial effects. We expected the situation to worsen with the passage of months. The upsurge of resistance is being fuelled by an unprecedented attack. In this, as in other policies Harris has adopted, we are seeing a qualitative increase in the dismantling of the social safety net.

Secondly, we realized that this was a regime that could rapidly pass from confident intransigence to political crisis. It was not a government of tried and trusted representatives of Bay Street, but a crowd of largely small town petty exploiters. The big-monied interests had given them a temporary vote of confidence, in the hope that they could humble the unions and take back the social wage by their sheer audacity; but this was by no means a blank cheque. If the scale of resistance were to reach crisis levels, Big Capital would soon dump Harris and his rednecks in favour of a kinder, gentler political option. Based on this, TDAC calculated that the task facing it was to dramatically raise the level of resistance to the welfare cut and, more generally, to contribute to the building of an overall movement of opposition to Harris that could pose a fundamental challenge to their ability to proceed with their attacks and to function as a government. For this to become a reality, a huge number of people who had no history of mobilizing would have to move into struggle. Moreover, we would have to find ways to disrupt the government and cause it political pain. On this basis, we adopted a five point plan of action to fight the welfare cut. Its elements were as follows:

1. Continue to Build Large-Scale Actions

Mike Harris has been very vocal on the issue of professional protesters. In the time-honoured tradition of reactionary governments trying to ride out social mobilizations, he has gone out of his way to label those moving into struggle against his government as a collection of the "usual suspects," people who always protest because it's what they like to do. Of course, the impact of the welfare cut will be felt by hundreds of thousands. TDAC sees its greatest challenge as the task of bringing out a mass of people who, until recently, would have no more attended a political protest than attempted to fly through the air. This is precisely the layer of people we have begun to tap into.

Shortly before one of our first major actions, a woman who was planning to attend called the OCAP office. She was a single mother on welfare, sitting around her kitchen table with a group of her neighbours, and they had just gone out and bought some material to make picket signs. She had two problems, however. First of all, none of the women present had ever actually made a picket sign and they wanted some guidance on the kinds of slogans they should write. Even more importantly, she had before her one of our leaflets telling people to assemble at the Ontario legislature at Queens Park. She and her friends had no idea what that was or how to get there. When people who have no idea what the "seat of government" is—or where it is located—start to move into political struggle, you can be sure that something very fundamental is stirring in society. An over-confident government that sloughs off such considerations is heading for serious trouble.

The event this woman called us about was a March Against Poverty that brought in marchers from the suburbs for a rally that took place at the legislature on July 29, 1995, and attracted some 2000 people. When we saw our tiny organization with negligible resources able to turn out such numbers, we realized that we were seeing the beginnings of a serious upsurge in the struggle.

In August 1995, we decided to organize an action that would have a more defiant tone to it than the traditional march on the legislature. A Queens Park rally may be the best way to get out large numbers, but we considered it important to inspire people with something that would make those backing Harris much more ill at ease. We assembled roughly 600 people in the large public housing project of Regent Park and marched them into the ultra-wealthy neighbourhood of Rosedale. Specifically, we went to the home of Hal Jackman, Ontario's lieuten-ant governor, who would actually be signing the order-in-council to authorize the 21.6 percent welfare cut. Our research had shown us that the scale of the income reduction and the tax break that Harris was preparing to give to Rosedale residents meant that, in effect, $1 million a month would be leaving Regent Park and the surrounding area bound for the moneybags in Rosedale. Our march, then, was not a formless condemnation of the free ride of the rich but a very concrete demand for our money back!

I don't believe I've ever participated in an action that was as spirited and defiant as this one. One woman in a wheelchair told us that she had lived eight years in Regent Park and had never been anywhere close to Rosedale before. I'll never forget the look on her face of shock and anger when she saw the mansions of the people who were taking a slice out of her neighbours' basic income in the form of a tax break. The lights in the plush homes were out when we entered Rosedale and the roar coming from our march reverberated through the streets. The police, at the last minute, had decided to withdraw a ban they had tried to impose on our marching in the streets and, although present in full force, they stood by while we held a rally few will forget, on Jackman's doorstep.

In September 1995, a major rally was called at Queens Park by the Metro Labour Council and the Embarrass Harris Coalition. We contributed to this by putting a march on the road at Social Services Minister David Tsubouchi's constituency office in Markham. Beginning at midnight, we marched through the night the twenty miles to the legislature. Close to a thousand people were behind our banner by the time we arrived. This event was particularly inspiring because it enabled us to mobilize as part of an emerging common front of unions and social movements.

Since September 1995, the colder weather and the need to respond to a wider range of issues have made it impossible to go for large-scale mobilizing in

Toronto. We have, however, continued to hold an ongoing series of smaller actions, involving 70–300 people and have been able to bus large contingents to the Days of Protest in four Ontario cities that have been called by the Ontario Federation of Labour (see Turk, Chapter 14).

2. Organize Bold and Disruptive Actions Against the Tories

I cannot stress enough that TDAC's main method of resisting Harris has been based on mobilizing new layers of people. We are not going to challenge the Tories if we confine ourselves to ultra-audacious behaviour that brings into action only a few dozen activists who are happy to mix it up with the authorities. We have tried to tailor our events to people who are nervous about collective action and the risk of confrontation. Still, we see a role for freeing up our more militant activists to take actions that can disrupt the political life of the Tories. In this regard, we have held a number of very defiant and bold actions.

For example, we learned from a source that Labour Minister Elizabeth Witmer would be holding a private breakfast with business leaders in the plush Royal York Hotel. This had been pulled together by an organization that arranged such "intimate" meetings with government leaders for a fat fee. Our response was to organize a fifty-strong invasion of the hotel to expose the meeting. While the Tories had got wind of our coming and abandoned the meeting room, we were entirely successful in bringing this cosy little gathering to public attention.

Even solitary members of TDAC have been able to find the means to disrupt the Harris regime and its work. One of our members, who is active in the Catholic Worker Movement, learned to his disgust that Toronto's Catholic hierarchy would be putting on a dinner—with Mike Harris as the guest of honour. He rented a tuxedo and slipped into the function. Making his way to the microphones without drawing attention, he launched into a spirited denunciation of the premier. He demanded to know why the Church was not leading the fight against him, rather than giving him a forum for his twisted views. He created a media sensation and got out several minutes of excellent comments before they came and dragged him out. We have had similar success with getting members into the public gallery at Queens Park to disrupt the proceedings and deliver our message. As the struggle escalates, we will be paying more and more attention to finding opportunities to crash functions and close down meetings organized by the Tories. With a classic "no justice–no peace" outlook, we aim to grind their normal round of baby-kissing and ribbon-cutting to a halt.

3. Taking the Struggle to the Doorsteps of Harris's Wealthy Backers

Following the success of our march into Rosedale, we realized that a key aspect of our strategy must be disrupting the lives of those who designed the Tory agenda and who are benefiting from it. The personally wealthy and the corporations will do very nicely out of the Harris tax cut and profit no end from the general cheap labour bonanza that social cutbacks and union busting are calculated to generate. Going after the organ grinder instead of the monkey is a prime tactic of TDAC. We have arranged a whole series of actions that fall under this heading. We supplemented our big march on Rosedale by taking a score of our members back into the neighbourhood for Trick or Treat Night in October 1995 to ask them to give us back their tax break. We have also found several opportunities to take on the corporate backers of the Tories. When the 1995 Toronto Santa Claus Parade got underway, a contingent of TDAC members took up a position in the middle of it with signs denouncing the Scrooge-like conduct of Mike Harris. Unwilling to suffer the acute embarrassment of having the cops haul us away, the organizers of this major corporate advertising event were compelled to allow us to join the parade, between two lavish business entries. Over a million people watched us march past them and, even in December 1995, we realized the mood against Harris was rising fast. We were cheered loudly from many sections of the parade.

Again in December 1995, after Harris responded to questions about the severity of his welfare cut by holding up the want ads in the legislature, we organized seventy of our members to hold a collective job search in downtown Toronto. Entering the Bay and the Eatons Centre with our banner and signs, we demanded to be given the right to fill in applications for some of Mike Harris's jobs. Faced with a major disruption of their Christmas rush, both the Bay and Eatons (the latter with much more persuasion) agreed to provide our job seekers with applications and a room in which to sit and fill them in. One of the members of TDAC's executive committee tells me that she is still waiting to hear back on her application for CEO of the Bay!

In February 1996, we decided to intervene at one of the major shareholders' meetings of the Big Banks. We took sixty people into the hotel where the Toronto Dominion Bank was meeting and attempted to get to their buffet. Locked out of the meeting hall, we took up the chant of "Cuts no thanks. It's time to tax the banks!" At the end of the annual general meeting, the shareholders were forced to walk the gauntlet of TDAC members. Our linking of the TD's bloated profits to the policies of the Tories was featured in the business pages of all the Toronto papers the next day.

Probably our most successful action against the corporate backers of Harris, was held back in November 1995. After Social Services Minister David Tsubouchi made headlines with his suggestion that the victims of his cuts could negotiate cheaper groceries with store owners, we decided to put his theory to the test. We decided to do this, moreover, in a way that would bring some economic pain and public discomfort into the life of a major corporation. We mobilized about seventy people to hold an unorthodox "shopping spree" at a Loblaws grocery store outlet in an upscale neighbourhood.[1] The cops expected that we would try to enter the store as a group, but we had marshalls positioned up and down the street from a dummy assembly point and discreetly told our people to enter the store singly, fill up their carts and wait for a signal. This done, we lined up at the checkouts and had our thousands of items rung through. As each person was asked for payment, they handed in a 21.6 percent "Dave's Discount" card with Tsubouchi's face on it. The whole operation ground to a halt and the police were called. After a lengthy stand-off, five of us were arrested on trespass charges. When we went to court, we subpoenaed Tsubouchi as the star witness for the defence because, afterall, the minister himself had told us to look for discounts. To avoid appearing, Tsubouchi was forced to concede the truth of our claim and, as a result, the charges against us were dropped. Both the government and one of its corporate friends have experienced some well deserved political pain by way of this action and, in the case of the latter, suffered a little at the cash register for good measure.

4. Showing That We Can Defend Individual Victims of the Tory Agenda

Even before Harris came to power, TDAC had realized that mobilization on broad issues, vital as it may be, is not enough. You have to show that collective action can make a practical difference. We have, therefore, continued to intervene to challenge situations where the general climate of rule-tightening for people on welfare is producing harassment or denial of benefits. We have also taken up the cases of people facing eviction and, in some cases, have been able to convince landlords to shelve plans to evict tenants. To date, however, the victories we have won on this front have been confined to small landlords or social housing agencies. We realize that we have to find the means to resist the wave of legal economic evictions by the big, corporate landlords. As this is written, we are meeting with some tenants in the Parkdale area of Toronto and developing a plan to organize in high-rise buildings. The idea is to get a big chunk of tenants in a given building to agree to sign up to a system whereby, if one family faces eviction, all the others will withhold a portion of their rent until a promise is secured not to evict. Even if the landlord tries to put the family out, in such a situation we would be well enough organized that we could actually turn out neighbours to block any attempt by the sheriff to execute the writ of possession. In this way, we could be looking at the kind of struggles that would start to pass on the cost of the welfare cuts to the big landlords and unleash their fury on Harris and his friends.

We recently invaded a major men's hostel in Toronto to defend homeless victims of a heartless system of barring alleged "troublemakers" from staying there. The superintendent of the place boasted to a film crew that he had been phoned by Mike Harris, personally, to urge him to stand up to us. With this gesture the premier rather tended to confirm our notion that direct action can't be confined to general themes but, in order to be effective, must become a weapon of self-defence in the day-to-day lives of those you are organizing. The two elements of broad issues and individual situations constantly complement each other. For example, the other day our Scarborough committee organized a picket outside the constituency office of a local Tory MPP. The intention had been to raise only a general opposition to the government's cutbacks. In the course of the action, however, I got talking to a single mother on welfare who told me that she had been trying to get a meeting with the MPP for weeks on a problem she had. However, they had refused to give her an appointment. She was convinced (and I don't doubt it) that the office staff had no interest in assisting her with a welfare problem. Since her right to see her MPP was important to her, we had a couple of people secure the door and then announced that we would be going in as a group to make sure an appointment was granted to this woman. It worked like a charm and, as small a victory as it may have been, demonstrated very practically that collective action works a great deal better than individual supplication.

5. Contributing to a Common Front to Drive the Tories Out

The final part of our plan of action has been to unite with unions and other social movements and to press for a common front that mobilizes socially and industrially to force Harris from office. In this, we are pleased with the progress but always concerned to go further and faster. There is, already, a great deal of anti-Tory mobilization. London has been close to shut-down by a day of protest as was Hamilton, Windsor, Kitchener-Waterloo, and Peterborough (see Turk, Chapter 14). The Hamilton day of action culminated in one of the largest demonstrations in Canadian history. The OPSEU strike held powerful and garnered wide-ranging support from other organizations (see Watson, Chapter 11).

Our coalition's work is getting more and more help from trade unions. Jointly with the Ontario Council of Hospital Unions, we organized a series of six community forums in Metro Toronto to unite hospital workers and working-class neighbourhoods to defend health care services and fight hospital closures. The Canadian Auto Workers (CAW) supplied buses to us and enabled us to participate in the London and Hamilton Days of Protest. Concrete cooperation with the CAW's social action committees and OCAP is developing. There is a great deal of action and increasing coordination.

In the overall struggle however, there is not yet a sufficient degree of explicit determination to defeat the Harris government. If our resistance is only about making some noise and letting off some steam while the Tories dismantle the gains of a lifetime, then we are mobilizing people under false pretences. This has to be about winning and driving the Tories from office and, in the immediate term, politically hurting them to the point where they pull back from particular policies they are attempting to implement. The mobilization against Harris continues to grow and that is marvellous to see. The challenge, however, is to give that mobilization a winning orientation. We see the work we have done in Toronto as an important contributing factor in this regard.

The Harris government is, very clearly, an outstandingly determined and dangerous expression of the international corporate agenda. It would be a mistake, however, to be so totally focused on the Ontario Tories that we fail to see that this agenda will live on once they have been removed from the scene. As our movement develops and grows, basing ourselves on the needs of working people and not the ledger books of corporations and governments, we have to extend our struggles into national politics. We must also guard against the tendency to demobilize once a less severe regime has taken power. The dumping of Harris by Bay Street, in favour of a more incremental and less immediately provocative attack on our social gains is a danger we should be ready to face in the period ahead of us.

What then can we say of the impact of the work of OCAP's Toronto organization to date? We know that the Tories, themselves, have developed a distinct dislike for us. So, too, have the cops. Members of Metro's Intelligence Division have come to my home to harass my family and have visited our office in a failed attempt to intimidate us. Undercover police officers now routinely attend our meetings and actions (at the last one we counted eight of them). In an editorial on October 3, 1995, no less a paper than the *Wall Street Journal* condemned our coalition, urged Harris to stand up to the broad mobilization against his government and called on "U.S. conservatives" to "notice the political courage of their neighbour to the north."

As heart-warming as these well-placed detractors are, the real success to date lies in the unemployed and poor that we have brought out and the example we have set for others fighting Harris. We have not yet, of course, reversed the 21.6 percent cut to welfare, although we would not doubt that our work and potential for growth is a factor in calculations of just how far the Tories are prepared to go in gutting social assistance in the period ahead. Generally speaking, however, the Tories will make only the most limited tactical retreats until they face mobilization on a scale that generates political crisis.

Still, this is a government whose whole function is to attack working people and the poor. If the work we are doing with the Toronto Direct Action Committee helps to create a resistance movement that is ready to defend social gains with the same determination that the Tories show in attacking them, then we will have made a real contribution to the defeat of this government.

Note

1. Loblaws ranks 64th among profitable corporations in Canada. In 1995, it made $147 million in profit, a 12 percent increase over 1994. See "Ranking by profits", *The Globe and Mail Report on Business Magazine*, July 1996, 102–140.

Chapter 14

Days of Action: Challenging the Harris Corporate Agenda

James L. Turk

Introduction

The election of the proudly right-wing Mike Harris government has sparked an unprecedented response. Groups have rallied, marched, protested as never before. Rather than lapsing into cynicism and despair—an all-too-common reaction to right-wing victories in the United States and Canada—large sections of the Ontario population have decided to stand up and speak out. In this article, we will look at the nature of that response and its likely effect.

Opposition began quickly. A hastily assembled group of activists dubbed themselves "Embarrass Harris," and, with the help of the Labour Council of Metropolitan Toronto and York Region, organized a large and angry rally in front of the legislature at Queens Park in Toronto. On the September day of the Tories' first throne speech, tens of thousands of people turned out—determined to let the Harris government and the people of Ontario know that the Tory plans were not going to go unopposed. Skirmishes took place at the doors to the legislature as angry Ontarians were confronted by heavily armed police who started lashing out, clubbing a number of women at the front of the doors.

This initial major protest sent a signal that many in Ontario were not going to go along quietly with the destruction of policies and programs built up over the past fifty years. The anger of many in the crowd and the violent response of the security forces guarding the legislature were a foretaste of the new Ontario under the Harris government.

In every corner of the province, progressive groups discussed and debated what should be done. For many, what was emerging as a response to the Harris government had disturbing similarities to the nature of the fight against Brian Mulroney's federal government. In the face of the Mulroney government's harsh economic policies, cuts to social programs and embrace of free trade with the United States and then the North American Free Trade Agreement (NAFTA), opposition had focused on Mulroney himself. Pilloried as a sleaze, a sell-out, and an insecure American toady, Mulroney dropped so low in popularity that he was persuaded to retire by his own party so they would have a chance in the next election. The federal Conservatives, unable to wash away the Mulroney taint, suffered the worst defeat of a major party in Canadian history—eliminating substantial parliamentary majority and winning only two seats in the House of Commons.

Progressive groups and individuals cheered. Few expected that the Chrétien government would seize the Conservative agenda and carry on the policies of their predecessors with a determination and scope unmatched in the Mulroney cabinet.

The federal Conservative government had been defeated largely as a result of personality politics. Mulroney, the individual, was vilified, and through this vilification the whole of the Conservative government was brought down. A new personality and a new party, however, were able to carry on the same agenda. The antagonism created for Mulroney did extend to his colleagues in the House of Commons and to his party, but did not extend to his party's political agenda. Personality politics, in short, won Progressive Conservatives a battle but lost the war.

In Ontario the same pattern began to shape up around Mike Harris. He proved to be such an easy target for ridicule. A not-too-bright former golf pro, Harris had spent virtually his whole working life on public payroll and now proudly announced that public payrolls were a terrible way to provide jobs. As his government cut social assistance by 21.6 percent, Harris talked about making do with bologna in his boyhood—only to be corrected by his own father who pointed out their family's rather privileged circumstances had never forced Mike to eat bologna.

Harris's choices for cabinet ministers added to his comical stature: a car salesman as minister of transport; a high school dropout as minister of education; a minister of housing and municipal affairs who bragged that what he knew about his portfolio "you could put on the head of a pin alongside the Lord's Prayer."

But there has been nothing comical about the policies brought forward by this group. Fundamental changes were made to social assistance, health care, labour law, transportation, environmental standards, housing and education before the Tories had been in office for a year. In every case, the changes involved drastic financial cuts and a greater role for the private (corporate) sector. In every case, the changes hurt the poorest and most vulnerable. In every case, the ideological framework was one that denied collective rights in favour of a nineteenth century version of primitive capitalism in which individualism overrode any notion of community or collective responsibility.

It is little wonder that delighted praise emanated from leading centres of corporate power—the Business Council on National Issues, the Fraser Institute, the Canadian Federation of Independent Business and the C.D. Howe Institute. The robber barons of the past were being redefined as the kind of people that Ontario needed, wanted and was prepared to nourish.

Labour Responds

Leaders of the labour movement in Ontario decided their organizations had to act. In meetings during the fall of 1995, they debated tactics and strategy. Petitions, protests, lobbying, workplace actions, even a general strike were on the table, reflecting the political and ideological diversity of the labour movement. At its

November convention, the Ontario Federation of Labour agreed to organize a series of community shutdowns, starting with London on December 11. A team of organizers from various unions went to London and began work.

A host of questions remained to be answered. What was meant by "community shutdown"? Was this a "labour" event? What was its objective? What would follow?

Serious attempts to answer these questions were put off. Divisions within labour were sufficiently serious that most were happy to have found consensus on a time and location for a protest and did not want to jeopardize their agreement by being too precise. Answers had to be crafted, however, as organizers began putting together plans for December 11. It was in the context of practical consideration that the nature of the event came to be defined.

Day 1: London
The first protest was a resounding success. Ten to fifteen thousand people turned out on a bitterly cold day in London. The temperature with the wind chill was minus 35°C. People came on buses from across Ontario—not wanting to miss the first massive day of protest. Some people had travelled as long as eighteen hours to get to London. They rallied in two sites in opposite parts of the city and then marched over two kilometres to a huge pavilion in the Western Fairgrounds for speeches, music and warmth.

The size of the turnout amazed everyone. People were jubilant. In the bitter cold of Tory Ontario, people felt a real sense of hope that somehow the evil of the Ontario government could be stopped. Workers all over the city had stayed away from work to protest both the government's policies and their employers' actions in supporting the government. Picket lines had shut the General Motors' diesel plant, 3M, the post office, the municipal transit system, and many more in both the public and private sectors.

In the fairgrounds, people were singing along with the Rank-and-File Band, eating warm bowls of chili produced in huge quantities by a local coalition of church and social activists. The Rev. Susan Eagle brought down the house when she countered the oft-heard comment that "God must not be on our side because of the bitter weather" with the retort that, "Quite the contrary, the Almighty is trying to shut down the whole province."

What remained unclear after London was whether the objective was a "shutdown" or simply a "day of action." The communications part of the organizing team had cautioned everyone not to use the term "shut down" because it promised something we could not deliver—the shutdown of the whole city. Workers in non-union workplaces risked their jobs if they walked out for the day. And, in the new Canada and Ontario, a fired worker was no longer eligible for unemployment insurance and had to wait three months to qualify for welfare—harsh inducements to forego anything that could result in discharge.

In unionized workplaces, the protections were greater. Some employers, like Canada Post, played hard ball with their employees but the postal workers shut their facilities down anyway. Ford somehow found a judge willing to issue an injunction in the middle of the night and tried to stop picketing at their large plant in nearby Talbotville. They failed, and subsequently sued the Canadian Auto Workers for millions in damages. While the Canadian Auto Workers and Canadian Union of Postal Workers and their members stood firm, other unions were more ambivalent. For some, battered by four years of a tough economy, the prospect of another avoidable battle with the employer was too much. For other unions, there was a reluctance to threaten the accommodation they had made with their employers. But these cases were the minority and, even when such a position was taken by the head office of the union, it was sometimes overruled by the local rank-and-file who did not want to be left out of the action.

The role of the broader community in the day of action did not get clearly resolved. Community speakers were invited to address the crowd. Money was made available so that a representative of the Ontario Coalition for Social Justice[1] could work full-time on getting greater community group involvement in the day's activities. Local religious and social activists put considerable energy into helping arrange entertainment, providing food and setting up community information tables. But the day remained largely a labour event in the eyes of the media and most participants. Both co-chairs of the London day were from labour. And since the co-chairs were the public spokespeople,this gave the event a labour image. The bulk of the speakers who addressed the rally were from labour. The highest profile entertainment was associated with labour and labour songs were predominant. The major actions on the 11th, apart from the march and rally, were the picketing of workplaces.

Despite these difficulties, almost everyone felt London had been a success. It had shown that opposition to the Harris government was alive and well. It held out the prospect, reiterated by the president of the Ontario Federation of Labour at the rally, that this was the first of many such events. It showed the determination of many people not to let distance or weather deter them. It had put forth a face of unity as the heads of almost all major unions joined together on stage. It acknowledged, in rhetoric more than reality, the importance of community involvement and that this was far more than just a labour event.

Four days after London, the Ontario Coalition for Social Justice (OCSJ) held a special meeting for provincial and national groups to discuss and evaluate what happened in London. There was a large turnout and a spirited discussion. Pleased with the day, most representatives felt that the days had to continue and that there had to be a more significant role for the broader community. The OCSJ was beginning to understand that days of protest were valuable as long as they were part of a strategy of grassroots mobilization at the community level. In this regard, it was essential that the community (non-labour) groups have at least as large a role as the unions in planning the days. Out of this OCSJ meeting came a series of recommendations: that the days continue in other centres, that in every case there be a community co-chair and a labour co-chair; that there be as many community speakers as labour speakers; that representatives of the OCSJ join labour leaders in choosing sites and dates; and that the days of protest be on weekdays to put pressure on employers.

This last point was especially important to the OCSJ because its work had focused on the exposure of the role of corporate interests in shaping government policy—nationally and provincially. It had increasingly come to describe the Harris government's policies as "bad medicine" since they worsened the condition of the majority of people. The "bad medicine" analogy also allowed the OCSJ to point out that Harris and his ministers were *administering* bad medicine but that the medicine had been *prescribed* by business interests—through their lobby groups like the Business Council on National Issues, the Canadian Chamber of Commerce, the Canadian Manufacturers' Association and the Canadian Federation of Independent Business; by corporate-sponsored think tanks like the Fraser Institute, the C.D. Howe Institute and the Atlantic Institute for Market Studies; and by corporate-supported front groups like the National Citizens' Coalition and the Canadian Taxpayers' Federation. Protests, the OCSJ felt, must put pressure on employers if such protests are to have any success in changing government policy.

In January, the Ontario Federation of Labour called a meeting of heads of unions to have an evaluation of London and plan what should follow. The meeting proved difficult as different perspectives on fighting the Tories surfaced. While all viewed London as a success, some questioned whether this was an appropriate use of money and whether such days would have any influence on the Tories. Such critics felt that governments can only be changed at the ballot box, and that labour would be better served by concentrating its efforts on running educational seminars for members on the impact of the Tory government and the necessity to build for an NDP victory in the next provincial election coming near the turn of the century .

To others, this suggestion was unacceptable. Some were still smarting from the previous NDP government's Social Contract that overrode collective agreements, and, from their perspective, the view that Bob Rae helped open the door to the election of the Tories. This group also felt that we simply could not wait until 1999 to stop what the Harris government was doing. Cuts to social assistance were plunging many people into destitution and homelessness. Cuts to health care had the potential of decimating our health care system. Everything possible, they felt, must be done to stop such initiatives now.

Many also felt that the distinction between education and action was false. London, they argued, resulted in more discussion and real education among workers than all labour's seminars and educationals in that community in the past decade. As soon as labour leaders indicated their desire to shut every unionized workplace, a discussion began in every lunch room about whether this was desirable. Questions abounded: will taking a day off without pay do any good?

Is it democratic to try to stop an elected government from acting? Are the Tory policies wrong?" These questions provided an opportunity to debate and discuss, and to put a lot of information into workplaces. Still others felt that London had been important because it featured work stoppages—a tactic that penalized employers.

The differences among the heads of unions ran deep. Finally agreement was reached on the basis of compromise: there would be another protest site—the city of Hamilton, a major industrial centre southwest of Toronto on Lake Ontario. The protest would coincide with the provincial Conservative's policy conference scheduled for Friday, February 23 and Saturday, February 24.

The continuation of the protests and the choice of a weekday pleased one side in the debate. The choice of a Saturday mollified the other, since they could spend their energy on that day and avoid confrontation with employers. Part of the compromise also entailed a commitment for the OFL also to run a series of educational seminars for members that would highlight the importance of the NDP. Following the meeting, the president of the OFL indicated that this compromise meant all of the money the OFL raised from affiliates for its fightback would be split evenly between these two different approaches. Whereas the OFL fightback money had funded all of the costs [about $110,000] for London, the president indicated that the OFL would cap its contribution to Hamilton at $45,000 (later raised to a total of $54,000).

Days 2 and 3: Hamilton

The success of London was magnified many times in Hamilton. The Friday march and rally attracted the largest crowd ever organized by the OFL since it was founded in 1957. More than 30,000 people attended—many of them stopping work to take part.

Then, on the next day, between 100,000 and 120,000 people turned out for the largest social justice protest rally in Canadian history.

There was nothing magical about the organization that resulted in these numbers. The organizers simply helped create a vehicle for protest against an abusive and reactionary government and a lot of people wanted to get on that vehicle to express their opposition to what was happening under the Harris government.

As soon as Hamilton was announced as the site of the protest, the president of the Hamilton and District Labour Council, Wayne Marston, phoned the chair of the Hamilton-Wentworth Coalition for Social Justice, Andrea Horwath, to suggest that they co-chair the event. This was an initial signal of an approach more inclusive of non-labour groups.

A planning committee was established consisting of the executive of the labour council and an equal number of representatives selected by the Hamilton-Wentworth Coalition for Social Justice. The committee was expanded to include some major organizations that were not part of either group. The recommendation of the OCSJ, that there be an equal number of labour and non-labour speakers, was accepted.

The Friday workplace closures slowed the economic life of the city. Most major unionized workplaces were shut, as were most non-emergency public services and workplaces. Some had argued that picket lines should be set up around non-union workplaces, but this was rejected. The purpose of the day, it became increasingly clear in practice, was to target only those unionized workplaces where the union wanted work stopped.

What was emerging was a day of protest, not a general strike. The goal was becoming defined as less of a general "shutdown" and more of an economic protest. In part, this grew out of a recognition that not all unions agreed with shutting down workplaces. Therefore it seemed premature to press for a complete shutdown when that could not be delivered consistently across the unionized sector. Likewise it seemed hypocritical to try to force non-unionized workers into shutting down when this could not be achieved universally among unionized workers. A strong shutdown component coupled with a large march and rally had the dual advantages of making the point about the corporate role in supporting the Tories while also providing a more inclusive opportunity for others to participate.

Many local unions that had not planned to participate, or whose head office had not been supportive of workplace actions, chose to join anyway. The sense of solidarity and the excitement of the protest reached beyond divisions and prompted many to act. The turnout Saturday exceeded everyone's expectations.

The presence of the full Harris cabinet and the Tory party faithful served as a magnet. But equally important was the growing unease about what Tory policies were going to mean. This was especially true in education. In January, the Ontario English Catholic Teachers' Association (OECTA) had organized an education rally at the Ontario legislature. Planning for 10,000–15,000, OECTA attracted more than 37,000. Hamilton provided an opportunity for the other teacher federations to turn out their numbers. A serious concern about cuts to education, coupled with some organizational rivalry, brought out tens of thousands of teachers—pushing attendance at the Hamilton days to record levels.

The post-event evaluation was a replay of discussions after London. Groups in the OCSJ, while praising the significantly greater role afforded community groups, felt more needed to be done to prevent these events from being viewed as only "labour" events. Recommendations ranged from having more community people on staff to provide a greater spotlight on community events and a greater community participation in cross-picketing. The coalition groups argued that future events should be on weekdays in order to put pressure on employers and that a schedule of days of protest should be set—stepping up their frequency and intensity.

Heads of unions, at their post-Hamilton meeting, remained divided. Opponents of days of protest argued that they were costly, that they were not building electoral support for the NDP, that they soured good working relationships with employers. Supporters saw the days of protest as the most successful labour initiatives in years and pointed to the turnout in Hamilton as proof. They saw the protests as strengthening their local unions and putting them in a stronger position when it came to collective bargaining. They saw the strengthening links with community groups as essential to eventual social change. Unable to reach consensus, the majority of major unions pressed for a continuation of protests and recommended going to the neighbouring cities of Kitchener, Waterloo and Cambridge in April. Opponents tried to prevent this being done under the OFL umbrella, but eventually backed down. They did extract a commitment that, apart from freeing up some staff, the OFL would make no financial contribution to the April 19 day of action in the Waterloo Region.

Day 4: Waterloo Region
Plans for the three-city protest were the most complex challenge yet. A staff of thirty five was assembled from supportive unions and teachers' federations. The OCSJ again donated the time of its coordinator, and campaign money was allocated to put additional local coalition activists on staff. Once again the event was co-chaired by the local labour council president and the chair of the community coalition for social justice.

Building on experiences in the previous cities, there was a more concerted effort to match the emphasis on shutting workplaces with an emphasis on a number of community events that would highlight a variety of issues. The Cooperative Housing Federation of Canada freed up two staff who, with the Ontario Coalition Against Poverty, planned and set up a tent city—dubbed "Harrisville"—on the downtown Kitchener site of a co-op housing project cancelled by the Harris government. A dozen other community events rounded out a full day of action that featured the closing of about 100 workplaces, rallies and marches in 3 cities, and a large main rally in front of Kitchener City Hall that drew about 30,000 people. This was the largest demonstration in the region's history.

Divisions within labour intruded into the planning of the day. Leaders of unions less keen on the "days of action" approach pressed for the inclusion of the interim leader of the Ontario NDP as a speaker at the main rally. But the local organizing committee, made up largely of New Democrats, unanimously vetoed this idea. As the head of the Kitchener-Waterloo Inter-faith Coalition for Social Justice, the Rev. Oscar Cole-Arnal, put it, this was to be a day for politicians to listen, not to speak.

An important division was laid bare in this debate. On one side were community groups and unions that felt social change would occur only through the building of a broadly-based social movement that would hold any party or government accountable. While many in this camp were staunch New Democrats, their experience with the Rae government reinforced their conviction that an electoral victory without a social movement always proves hollow.

On the other side were leaders primarily of private sector unions, other than the CAW, that felt social change only comes through the ballot box. Most were suspicious of community groups that refused to swear allegiance to the NDP, fearing that they were simply closet Liberals. There seemed to be a fear that broadly-based social movements would not be sufficiently loyal to the NDP and the compromises it would need to make to come to power and stay in power.

The post-event evaluations once again repeated themselves. For the groups in the OCSJ, there was joy at the obvious success of the Waterloo Region day of action and at the significant growth in community involvement and outreach. But there was a nagging frustration at the media's persistence in labelling it a labour event. Having shed the London practice of two labour co-chairs; having had a much more significant community presence on the coordinating committee and on the staff; having had significant and visible community events; having had a large number of well-known and articulate community speakers, the day seemed mired in a media view that this was still just unions. To the OCSJ, a major contributing factor was the fact that the decisions about whether, when and where to have days of action were still being made by closed meetings of heads of unions. Previous recommendations to include leaders of other groups had not been acted upon.

Accordingly, the OCSJ pointedly recommended that the next heads of unions meeting be expanded to include the leaders of all provincial and national organizations in the Ontario Coalition for Social Justice. This recommendation was forwarded to the OFL and distributed to all unions with a request for an immediate response. Union leaders split along the same fault line that had run through all other discussions of days of action. Because of the division, the non-labour group leaders were again not allowed to participate in the post-Waterloo heads of unions meeting.

That meeting proved a replay of the previous three. There remained no consensus about days of protest being a useful approach despite the fact that each had exceeded anyone's expectations in terms of turnout, breadth and depth of local discussion of issues, strengthening of local unions and community coalitions and local enthusiasm. Since the Waterloo Region day had been entirely financed by supportive unions and community groups and the OFL had put in no money, the opponents were not able to use financial arguments. There was discussion of the refusal to allow an NDP speaker (actually a refusal to allow any politicians to speak).Some attempted to rally opposition to future days of action on that basis. But unions that supported days of action, even those that preferred allowing the NDP leader to speak, felt such decisions were the business of the local community coordinating committee.

With a sense of resignation, the opponents to days of action were over-whelmed by supporting unions who put forward a proposal for a June 24 day in the eastern Ontario community of Peterborough. While still an OFL-sponsored event, all financial support was to be raised by the supporting organizations, with no contribution from the OFL other than the release of two staff who would serve as coordinators.

Day 5: Peterborough

The trend toward broader involvement continued in Peterborough. The co-chairs came from the Peterborough Labour Council and the Peterborough Coalition for Social Justice. The coordinating committee was a joint venture as well—following the pattern of Hamilton and Waterloo. The staff had its significant labour component augmented not only by a local coalition person and the coordinator of the OCSJ, but also by four additional community group activists who donated their time to work on the day's staff team. The Peterborough day of action provided an opportunity to learn how this way of organizing would work in a smaller community.

The results were excellent. Virtually every industrial workplace was closed, as were municipal services, libraries, the transit system, provincial government offices and federal services including the Trent-Severn Waterway. There were many community events and wonderfully creative local street theatre. More than 10,000 people attended the rally. Given the size of the community, this was proportionately a much larger turnout than in London, the Friday in Hamilton and Waterloo Region. While the day got substantial local media coverage, the national print media paid almost no attention. For them, the only item of interest is absolute numbers at the rally, not the breadth of workplace closures and community events nor the extent and success of community organizing and base-building.

So, What's the Strategy?

The key question is what is the real strategy behind these days of action. Where are they leading?

The evolving pattern of days of action form a strategy based on a recognition that we must simultaneously do four things: actively resist right-wing corporate and government policies and actions; build our long term capabilities and infra-structure at a grassroots level; give ourselves and the public hope in the face of adversity; and provide an alternative vision of the future.

All four are interrelated and must be pursued simultaneously. Ignoring any one undermines our ability to achieve the others. Active resistance engages people, but in planning and executing that resistance, we must always keep in mind not only what would be successful in the short term, but what will build our collective capabilities in the long term.

Despair and cynicism are our most dangerous enemies. Drawing on the long experience of the American civil rights movement, Jesse Jackson repeatedly exhorts crowds to keep hope alive. Actively resisting builds hope, and hope provides the fuel for resistance.

While resistance can be organized without an alternative vision, such resistance cannot be sustained. On the other hand, an academic exercise in dreaming up alternatives, cut off from ongoing struggle and active movement building, proves hollow and alienating. We live with the contradiction that we must know where we want to go in order to chart a path, but we make our path by walking on it.

Days of protest have helped us articulate these four necessities and our increasing recognition of them have shaped the days themselves. From London to Peterborough, the strength has been the bringing of people together in large numbers in an exhilarating display of solidarity. By participating, we come to realize we are not alone. We are given, at least in the short term, a sense of hope and of being partners in struggle.

Also in all four communities, there has been active resistance—primarily in the willingness of tens of thousands of workers to confront their employers by walking out of work and shutting their workplaces. This has not been without risk and worry—from loss of a day's pay to possible discipline and discharge. Every person has had to confront his or her own fears and dangers. Tens of thousands have done that and taken a personal and collective stand.

To date, the non-labour events generally have not required the same risk and therefore have not been examples of serious resistance. But community groups and the OCSJ have begun recognizing the need to up the ante. In Waterloo Region, the public authority that owned the land on which Harrisville was to be set up refused permission to use the site. The organizers went ahead anyway—feeling that this abandoned site for a cancelled co-op housing project should be used even if there could be legal fallout. Increasingly, there is a recognition that the very nature of our common law serves to inhibit or prevent change in the balance of power in society. Almost every progressive change that labour and community point to with pride involved challenges to existing law and practice. A foretaste of the future lies in the program of training begun by the OCSJ and several major OCSJ unions in direct action and non-violent civil disobedience. The OCSJ has also begun distributing a new book by the Law Union of Ontario on what activists need to know about the law.[2] If the success of days of action is to continue, the level of resistance must also grow and broaden.

A major change as we have moved from London to Peterborough has been the increasing clarity about the importance of long term movement building, not just short term crowd assembly. In each successive city, planning for the rallies, the workplace closures and the community actions has been guided more specifically by what will leave organizations stronger and better able to work together after the day, not just what will have the biggest impact on that day. The measure of success of days of action is less what happens on the day than on what happens within that community afterwards in terms of working relationships among groups and group organizations and mobilizational capabilities and commitments.

Days of action have stirred the pot. They have mobilized individuals and organizations. They have brought people together in unprecedented numbers. They have inspired and given hope. They have been the occasion for tens of thousands to confront their employers. They have *begun* to set the stage for successfully ending the oppressive actions of a hateful, right-wing government that is acting in the narrow interests of the corporate sector.

They will prove to be a useful strategy if they evolve so that they lead to the kind of active resistance that changes or brings down governments, as in the anti-Vietnam war and civil rights movements in the United States, the anti-apartheid movement in South Africa, and the liberation struggles in many countries of the world.

The issue is not primarily the number of people at a rally. The days of protest must grow in militance of resistance, breadth of involvement, and determination to stop the government and its corporate backers. Unless this happens,the days of protest will prove not a strategy for change but only a diversion: one-day shows of force that lead nowhere but to despair. They can either roll forward or backward. There is no standing still.

Notes

1. The Ontario Coalition for Social Justice is a coalition of 50 provincial and national organizations as well as of local coalitions in more than 30 Ontario communities.
2. Law Union of Ontario, *Offence/Defence: Law for Activists*. Toronto: Ontario Coalition for Social Justice, 1996.

Chapter 15

Strategies for the Post-Harris Era
Diana Ralph

What can we do to win against the Harris government and the multinational powers he serves? Earlier chapters laid out the corporate agenda underlying Harris's Common Sense Revolution and described the disastrous toll it is exacting on most Ontarians. They also described initial forms of resistance. In this chapter, I will suggest some strategies to build for long term victory.

What Is the Opposition's Strategy?

Harris's policies and tactics have all been developed through many trials around the world (Dobbin 1994; Marsden and Warnock 1995). Common tactics include generating an artificial economic crisis, blaming the poorest for the resulting deficit, and then bringing in a flood of "reforms" so quickly that the opposition is unable to respond effectively (Laxer 1995: 5). New Zealand is one of the most recent "success" stories of this method (in spite of its disastrous impact on the New Zealand economy, standard of living, and democratic rights) (Kelsey 1996: 1,6). As Murray Dobbin points out:

> The New Right and its corporate benefactors have decided to promote the New Zealand experiment as the model for all other Western nations. Sir Roger Douglas was knighted by Margaret Thatcher for the revolution that bears his name. He now travels around the world promoting his free-market solutions and advises the Alberta government. NDP premiers in Saskatchewan and Ontario, and now the federal Liberal government refer increasingly to New Zealand and its lessons. (Dobbin 1994: 25)

Billing himself as "champion of the business community" (Campbell, Mittelstaedt and Rusk 1995: A3), Harris is following Douglas's tactics to the letter. As quickly as possible, the provincial government is setting up everything needed to make Ontario "open for business." It is gutting environmental regulations, rent control, and minimum wage. It has eliminated mechanisms for corporate and governmental accountability. Human rights, labour rights, welfare rights, Aboriginal rights, women's rights and advocacy group funding are all on the chopping block. Harris's government is privatizing social housing and medical care, cutting corporate taxes, restructuring workers' compensation and occupational safety legislation, bringing in workfare, slashing social programs, education and health care, and restructuring universities to fit corporate priorities (see Clarke, Chapter 1; Mittelstaedt 1996: B1).

At the same time, the Harris government (with support from corporate media) is engaged in a public relations war to transform the hearts and minds of Ontarians to fit the mean-spirited, selfish vision of the free market (see Weinroth, Chapter 6).

The Current State of Resistance

Resistance is growing against the Harris government. From the day he took office, Harris has been dogged by demonstrations and legal challenges. Everywhere he goes, he faces angry crowds, protesting his inhumane policies. The Ontario Coalition for Social Justice is spawning new branches across the province. The threat of Harris's policies has begun to re-unite the factions of organized labour which had become badly divided under Bob Rae's NDP government (see Watson, Chapter 11; Turk, Chapter 14). The days of action have pulled out record numbers and began the task of on-the-ground mobilization. Groups are organizing alternative budget workshops, economic literacy classes, schools on how to organize, and many other creative events (see Clarke, Kérisit and St-Amand, Watson, Welch in Chapters 13, 12, 11, and 10 respectively). Resistance in Ontario has grown relatively quickly, in part because activists have learned from the successes and mistakes of those who opposed previous Tory and Social Credit governments in Alberta, Saskatchewan, and British Columbia.

These initiatives are all heartening contradictions to the shocked dismay and fear that gripped popular sector groups in the months after Harris was elected in June 1995. However, most of them suffer from three serious limitations.

First of all, they are reactive protests against policies already implemented. They do not proactively promote a unified people's agenda.[1] Activist Jason Ziedenberg recently quipped: "We proved in Hamilton [at the Day of Action which brought out over 100,000 protesters] that we have the numbers to get the message out, but what do we want to say?" (Ziedenberg 1996, 20).

Secondly, most protests are targeted at Harris personally, rather than effectively challenging the corporate powers behind him (Turk, Chapter 14). We may turf out Harris, but the corporations which have bought and coerced support from all political parties will continue to impose their agenda regardless of who governs at the Ontario legislature in Queens Park.

Thirdly, and most seriously, these protests do not define a strategy to win power (as opposed to concessions) from the corporations and the governments and political parties they control.

Protests certainly are better than silence. They build popular morale and to some extent help to counteract the ideological hegemony the Right holds. But they also play into Harris's strategy. The media portrays us as unreasonable, selfish, and violent. A comment by *Financial Post* columnist and real estate baron David Frum is typical:

Ontario's public-sector unions and *militant activists* are readying themselves for *confrontation*. And the local left has already made it abundantly clear that it will not hesitate to turn *violent*.... As the *agitators punch cops and smash glass, reasonable Ontarians* should remember: the Harris government is working for them. And they should urge that government to do its damnedest. (Frum 1995: 22: emphasis added).

In the face of screaming picketers, Harris sells himself to his corporate constituency as a resolute, embattled soldier. For example, while protesters rallied outside an Ottawa-Carleton Board of Trade meeting, businessmen inside applauded Harris for saying: "Believe me, there are easier and less controversial ways to govern, previous governments proved that.... But we were elected to take the harder road, the one that leads to greater rewards" (Harris quoted in Winsor 1995: A3).

So even as we protest, we have followed the script assigned to us in the "common sense" morality play. Basically, Harris's handlers have managed to turn our ethical commitment to the rights of women, labour, and oppressed groups into a liability. No wonder Harris persists in scheduling events which provide news clips of his courageous resolve in the face of rabid "special interest groups." Even in the rare instances where Harris has been forced to back down— e.g. reinstating some legal aid funding cuts, slowing the passage of the Omnibus Bill (Bill 26), and retreating from threats to slash children's winter clothing allowances—these victories are only minor detours along Harris's fast track route to a globalized Ontario. Being reactive leaves the New Right agenda on track and entrenches Harris's corporate base of support.

Most protests so far have the desperate, urgent tone of those without power who do not expect to be heard, much less to win. The most ambitious of these, the rotating days of action have demonstrated the ability of labour and community groups to pull out huge numbers and to shut down business (at least for a day). They have the potential to build momentum to take the offensive against capital with a real general strike and mobilized resistance (see Turk, Chapter 14). However, at this point the OFL leadership aims far lower: "What we're doing is providing people with a vehicle by which they can at least get into the street and at least protest" (OFL President, Gord Wilson on the Kitchner Waterloo day of action, quoted in Rusk 1996: A4A).

We need to set our sights much higher than protesting specific policies or even than ousting Harris altogether.

Eventually, popular resistance will succeed in ousting Harris, just as it turfed out William Bennett in B.C., Grant Devine in Saskatchewan, Maggie Thatcher in England, Ronald Reagan in the United States, and Sir Roger Douglas in New Zealand. However, like Harris, all of them were only pawns of a much larger transnational corporate agenda. Even though they left office, the corporate power brokers did not.

While this reality is daunting, we can win if we start now to plan strategically. It took twenty years for big business to achieve this hegemony in Canada. And it may take us at least as long to regain the initiative. Mobilized people's movements around the world (for example in South Africa, Vietnam, and China) have turned around situations far more one-sided than ours is now, but in each case it took many years of dedicated struggle. We too need to plan for the long haul.

If we focus our anger only on Harris and on piecemeal reactions to his policies, we'll win a few battles, but lose the war. By the time we oust Harris, the infrastructure and the social contract of the Keynesian welfare state will be gone. Unless we begin to plan differently, our future will look much like the aftermath of the New Zealand New Right experiment:

> Once you start setting the market mechanisms in place in all areas—you start moving into the universities and transform the universities on the market model and the schools on the market model and the health system on the market model, and state-owned industries become a market model and they're privatized and local government and so on—once you've done this people have to work within that framework. So people who mightn't even agree with it have to adjust their feelings to that framework, because that's the framework they're working within. So it becomes self-fulfilling. (Dobbin 1995a: 23–24).

Even with the best of intentions, the next premier will take office in a government stripped of the regulatory powers, the civil service, the tax base, and the social service infrastructure needed to curb corporate greed. And it is not likely that the next premier *will* have the best of intentions. Canadian politics is following the American model of issueless campaigns led by individuals heavily financed by big business (Browne, Chapter 2 and Régimbald, Chapter 3; Marsden and Warnock 1995: 12).

We already know that neither the Liberal Party nor the NDP is likely to take a strong stand in reversing the Harris debacle. At the federal level, the Liberals, like the Tories, are prioritizing deficit reduction, destroying national standards, slashing social programs, supporting the North American Free Trade Agreement (NAFTA), refusing to raise corporate taxes, and ending corporate regulation. Even if the NDP won the next election in Ontario, it likely would behave as Bob Rae did (or worse). NDP governments in Ontario, Saskatchewan and British Columbia have all prostrated themselves to the demands of the credit bond raters: promoting deficit hysteria, slashing social programs and labour rights, and recruiting foreign investment. Guy Marsden and John Warnock conclude:

> the NDP's promotion of debt reduction, privatization, globalization, deregulation, cutbacks and workfare have rendered the party irrelevant as a vehicle for social change, as it has social democratic parties world-wide. (1995: 13)

Strategic Suggestions

We need to strategize to win this class war. "Winning" means more than a few temporary concessions from whatever party is in power. It means winning political power. Good strategy depends on a clear assessment of the strengths and vulnerabilities both of ourselves and our opponents. It also requires thinking several moves ahead so that we can anticipate the reactions of our opponents and position our side's resources effectively. Especially when the power of the two sides is dramatically unequal, strategy has been the key factor in winning victories of national and revolutionary people's movements worldwide.

We are not far away from being able to force the Tories out of office. But we are still a very long way from achieving the unity, political analysis, and skills necessary to build a mass movement than could put in place a real people's agenda. We are just beginning to step out of the politics of competing "identity" groups and to start building the trust and organization (e.g. our own media, political party, and training centres) necessary to develop a common strategy.

So, rather than aiming simply toward the next election, we need to start planning for twenty years from now. Of course, while we do that, we will continue to resist—and win victories. But our work will have the initiative and direction which is missing now. Here are a few strategic suggestions to guide us in that path.

1. Dismantling Corporate Rule

We need to refocus our goals from reactively attacking Harris's policies to dismantling the corporate juggernaut behind him. Tony Clarke (1995a: 8) suggests five steps to defeat the corporate agenda:

- Defining the Corporate Agenda (analyzing the corporate power structures and how groups like the BCNI control key policy decisions);
- Dissecting Corporate Rule (researching the links between specific policies and the corporations and banks who promote them);
- Denouncing Corporate Rule (publicly exposing and protesting those links);
- Disrupting Corporate Rule (direct action campaigns to disrupt functioning of the BCNI and specific corporations);
- Dismantling Corporate Rule (promoting a platform of policy alternatives which will dismantle corporate power over the economy and public policies).

Most resistance groups have barely begun step one. Instead of researching and developing strategy related to corporate powerbrokers, we leap to knee-jerk lobbies of or protests against "the government." Where actions have been taken against corporations—such as the Clayoquat Sound protest against Macmillan Bloedel in British Columbia, they have mobilized massive public support and won substantial victories.

2. Building the Movement

Each of these steps requires the cooperative work of thousands of Ontarians (linked with other Canadians and people around the world). In order to carry them out, we have to build and mobilize an informed, broad, popular base of resistance.

Since the 1970s, identity groups—women, Aboriginal people, students, labour, people of colour, poor people, gays and lesbians, Franco-Ontarians, and people with disabilities—have all organized separate movements (generally reliant on state funding). These have each won important concessions from the government, including funding, protective legislation, and popular recognition of the rights of each group. However, while they have cooperated (for example through the Action Canada Network), overall these movements have lost the sense of a unified working class position which the previous generation used to win our current social programs. We need to step outside of the model of duelling oppressions and forge a unified resistance. As Gordon Laxer points out:

> The new right has wide appeal because it appears to speak for the whole of the community, or at least for the great majority. The left and centre, on the other hand, are often mired in the politics of identity and difference. That means they can end up talking about the rights and the authentic voices of one or another disadvantaged group, but they seldom talk much about what unites us all. (Laxer 1995: 1)

The Canadian Left, divided by sectarian disputes and preoccupied with political correctness, generally has failed to attract or excite large numbers of people. John Clarke (Chapter 13) demonstrates the effectiveness of prioritizing actions which expand beyond the small group of committed "Lefties," to build a unified popular resistance movement. That movement needs to emphasize mutual respect, practical and emotional support, culture, friendship and love. We need to take the time to develop broad agreement on long-range strategies and the mutual trust to carry them out. Some solidarity is beginning to emerge through the diverse resistance initiatives that have begun. We need to diversify the leadership and membership of the movement, putting people of colour, Aboriginal people, women, and people with disabilities in central positions of leadership.

We also need to restructure our organizations to empower those outside of the central leadership. Over the past twenty years, many of our national and provincial umbrella groups have become more accountable to government funders than to the membership. The members need to be actively involved in decisions, and not just be used as passive demonstration fodder.

3. Planning Tactics Strategically

The powers-that-be have perfected the art of keeping us leaping to react to their initiatives. Too often, we have set our tactics to fit their events, "participating" in their consultations, budget statements, and elections. While these official events can offer opportunities for popular mobilization, more often they co-opt and diffuse resistance. Instead, we need to organize in terms of our own priorities and pace and create our own creative initiatives outside of "official" channels of complaint which draw the links between who is winning and who is losing from the cuts (Clarke, Chapter 1). We need to develop escalating tactics which actually build our strength (skills, numbers, resources, legitimacy) and weaken the power of the business opposition (embarrassing them, dividing them, costing them profits, and blocking them).

4. Building Structures Both to Support Each Other and to Carry On the Fight

We need to prioritize building strong fight back organizations and coalitions, which draw in, train, and actively involve those who have not previously been well integrated into the "Left"; youths, unemployed people, non-unionized workers (many of them women), parents, immigrants, people with disabilities, Franco-Ontarians, and Aboriginal people.

To support them, we need to create viable alternatives to corporate employment and consumption such as worker and consumer cooperatives (see Kérisit and St-Amand, Chapter 12).

We also need to create our own structures, both to support our mobilizing and to presage the kind of society we are trying to create. High priorities include:

- *encouraging* workplace education and resistance;
- *building our own media*—newspapers, alternative television and radio, and internet websites;
- *creating people's social justice organizing centres* similar to the High-lander Centre in Kentucky which, since the 1930s, has been key in supporting union, civil rights, peace, and environmental struggles throughout the Southern United States (Horton and Kohl 1990). Such centres in cities and rural areas can train organizers, conduct corporate research, strategize, and publish and distribute resistance information;
- *training the next generation*, starting camps and clubs for young people and youth;
- *encouraging popular theatre troupes, protest singers and artists* to build spirit and a culture of resistance;
- *building international and interprovincial alliances and coalitions*: in this era of global production and consumption, we have to build our connections with workers and people's groups around the world. We can, for example, support twinning between schools, workers in similar industries, and between farm and factory workers in the developing world and consumer cooperatives here.

5. Creating a New Kind of Political Party

At this point, all Canadian political parties, including the NDP, prioritize the needs of capital over those of Canadian people. None reliably represents our interests. We are stuck at election time choosing the least bad alternative while we should still work from within to push the NDP to a more class-struggle orientation. We can aim also to build a new people's party, one which is accountable to and grows out of the unified popular movement (Barlow and Campbell 1995: 239). At this point, few Canadians have any idea of what a revolutionary political party is and how it can be held accountable to the popular movements which create it. The corruption and collapse of Soviet Bloc governments has lent credibility to heavy anti-Communist propaganda, and made many justifiably wary of socialist party options. As an early step, study groups might analyze the problems with social democratic and socialist parties in Canada and worldwide, and develop new models of "party" which are really democratic. Rather than trying to win elections, our party's emphasis should be on promoting a people's agenda, on exposing the corporate agenda underlying the mainstream parties, and on supporting a strong popular base which can force the government of whatever political stripe to comply. Class warfare is real. Even when socialist governments are elected (as in Republican Spain, Allende's Chile, and Granada) they have faced a massive array of military and financial attack.

From this perspective, Harris's overtly mean-spirited assault has a silver lining for building a people's movement. Harris creates the conditions for unity among groups targeted by his axe, unlike the confusion and splits we experienced under Bob Rae's NDP government. Rather than rushing to get rid of Harris, we should focus on building the mass base and political organization which will force any government (including the NDP, Reform, and Liberal Parties) to recognize our power and our demands for a more just society.

6. Financing the Movement

Dependence on government grants has been a major barrier to building a unified, independent people's movement. The Harris cuts can spur us to develop autonomous funding sources. Our pension plans, savings accounts, and consumer dollars potentially give us significant sources of capital. Ed Finn estimates that Canadian occupational pension plans amount to $360 billion (1996: 4). Our collective savings accounts and mortgage payments are what helped Canadian charter banks in 1995 to make a record $5.2 billion profit (Rubin 1996: B8) and our purchases allowed Canadian corporations to earn the highest profits on record (Fortune 500 1996: B14). We have been giving control of this money to the corporations which oppose our interests. We need to repatriate our pension funds, savings, and consumer dollars to serve our movement. We can demand investment control over our pension funds. We can encourage people to transfer funds and loans from charter banks to local, community or union controlled credit unions, and direct their investments to funding workers and consumer coopera-

184

tives and social justice efforts. We can also mobilize consumer power both positively (through supporting producers' cooperatives) and negatively (through boycotting products of key corporations). A more immediate tactic is to organize wide-sector, fundraising events which raise consciousness and solidarity, which ridicule the opposition, and which involve many people. As part of the campaign to involve the uninvolved (especially the middle class), groups can develop fundraising teams to do door-to-door canvassing in ways that educate and involve people, as well as raising funds. We also need to consider charging dues on a sliding scale from our members. This will increase their ownership of the movement as well as fuelling our independence.

Conclusion

We have a long way to go to build this kind of movement. But if we want a better future, there is no short-cut. Paul Browne (Chapter 2) spelled out the dangers of relying on simply electing a social democratic government. To win in the long run, we will have to break out of our rigid, bureaucratic or doctrinaire organizational structures. We have to abandon the urge to separate our issues into isolated identity group compartments. We have to let go of the urgency which fuels unimaginative, reactive tactics. And we will have to give up any vestiges of faith in the ability of existing political parties to save us. We have to dare to take on the task of dismantling corporate rule and building the kind of society we all deserve. As Brian Palmer says: "All eyes are on Ontario. A great deal is at stake. This is one of those moments when the working class can make history, or go down in it" (1996: 25).

The Tories were able to capitalize on a backlash against the NDP to win a mandate to completely dismantle the rights and services won under all previous administrations (including the Conservatives). If we think and act strategically, we also can mobilize a backlash of outrage against the Tories to create a movement to win—not just an election—but a humane and just Ontario.

Note

1.   The alternative budgets developed by CHO!CES and CCPA, and now being taken to provincial and municipal levels, are a refreshing exception to this trend. They lay out clear alternatives, and expose the vested corporate interests behind the TINA (There Is No Alternative) deficitist stance of the federal and provincial finance ministers (*Alternative Budget* 1996; Weinroth, Chapter 4). But the alternative budget process has, so far, remained a largely academic exercise, relatively isolated from a process of mass mobilization.

References

Advisory Group on New Social Assistance Legislation. 1991. *Back on Track*. Toronto: Ministry of Community and Social Services, March.

Agreement on Trade Related Investment Measures. 1995. Geneva: World Trade Organization, Article 9, January.

Alternative Budget. 1996. Ottawa: CCPA, *Choices*.

Apple, M.W. 1993. "Constructing the 'Other': Rightist Reconstructions of Common Sense." In C. McCarthy and W. Crichlow (eds.), *Race, Identity, and Representation in Education*, New York: Routledge, 24–39.

Arnopoulos-McLeod, Sheila. 1982. *Hors du Québec point de salut?* Montréal: Libre Expression, 287 "A year at a glance." 1996. *Toronto Star*, Saturday June 8: C4.

Banting, K. 1986. *The Welfare State and Canadian Federalism*. 2nd edition. Montreal/Kingston: McGill-Queens University Press.

Barlow, M. and B. Campbell. 1995. *Straight through the Heart: How the Liberals Abandoned the Just Society*. Toronto: Harper Collins.

_____. 1993. *Take Back the Nation*. Toronto: Key Porter Books.

_____. 1991. *Taking Back the Nation: Meeting the Threat of NAFTA*. Toronto: Key Porter Books.

Barlow, M. and H. J. Robertson. 1994. *Class Warfare: The Assault on Canada's Schools*. Toronto: Key Porter Books.

Barnet, R. and J. Cavanagh. 1994. *Global Dreams: Imperial Corporations and the New World Order*. New York: Simon and Schuster.

Beaud, M. and G. Dostaler. 1993. *La pensée économique depuis Keynes*. Paris: Éditions du Seuil.

Bellemare, D. and L. Poulin-Simon. 1994. *What is the Real Cost of Unemployment in Canada*. Ottawa: Canadian Centre for Policy Alternatives.

Berrick, J.D. 1995. *Portraits of Women and Children on Welfare. Faces of Poverty*. New York: Oxford University Press.

Blatchford, C. 1996. "Father has one question from his son." *Toronto Sun*, February 15: 5.

"Blood spilled at Ontario provincial park Anthony George killed at Ipperwash." 1995. *Windspeaker* 13(6) October: 3.

Blumstein, P. and P. Schwartz. 1983. *American Couples: Money, Work, Sex*. New York: William Morrow.

Boback, L. 1996. "U.S. bank eyes public housing." *Ottawa Sun*, April 2: B4.

Brittain, L. 1992. *European Competition Policy: Keeping the Playing Field Level*. McLean, Va.: Brasseys.

Brodie, J. 1996. "Canadian Women, Changing State Forms, and Public Policy." In J. Brodie (ed.), *Women and Canadian Public Policy*. Toronto: Harcourt, Brace.

_____. 1995. *Politics on the Margins: Restructuring and the Canadian Women's Movement*. Halifax: Fernwood Publishing.

Brown, L. 1987. *When Freedom was Lost: the Unemployed, the Agitator, and the State*. Montreal: Black Rose Books.

Browne, Paul Leduc and Pierrette Landry. 1995. *The "Third Sector" and Employment*. Un-published. Canadian Centre for Policy Alternatives. Ottawa.

Building a Better Ontario: A Progress Report on the First Six Months of the Mike Harris

Government. 1996. Toronto: Queens Park, January.

Burman, P. 1988. *Killing Time, Losing Ground: Experiences of Unemployment*. Toronto: Thompson Educational Publishing.

Business Council on National Issues. 1995. *Business Leadership in Canada and Abroad*. Ottawa: BCNI.

Campaign 2000. 1995. Report Card. Ottawa: Child Poverty Action Group.

Campbell, B. 1996. "Liberals Get $6 Million from Corporations in 1994." *CCPA Monitor* 2(10): 1,7.

_____, with A. Jackson. 1993. *"Free Trade": Destroyer of Jobs*. Ottawa: Canadian Centre for Policy Alternatives.

Campbell, M., M. Mittelstaedt and J. Rusk. 1995. "Harris Woos Business with Tax Cuts." *Globe and Mail* May 3: A3.

Canadian Centre for Policy Alternatives/CHO!CES. 1996. *Alternative Federal Budget*. Ottawa/Winnipeg.

Cardinal, Linda. 1992a. "La recherche sur les femmes francophones vivant en milieu minoritaire: un questionnement sur le féminisme." *Recherches féministes* 5 (1): 5–29.

_____. 1992b. *Théoriser la double spécificité des Franco- Ontariennes, dans Actes du Colloque Relevons le défi! Actes du colloque sur l'intervention féministe dans le Nord-Est de l'Ontario*. Sudbury, Ontario: Les Presses de l'Université d'Ottawa, 177–188.

_____ and Cécile Coderre. 1991. "Éducation et identité: l'expérience des femmes francophones vivant en milieu minoritaire." *Éducation et francophonie: femmes et éducation* 19 (3) 23–26.

_____. 1990. "Les francophones telles qu'elles sont: les Ontaroises et l'économie." *La Revue du Nouvel-Ontario* 12. 151–181.

Carrière, Fernand. 1993. "La mètamorphose de la communautè franco-ontarienne 1960-1985," in Cornelius J. Jaenan (èd) Les Franco-Ontariens, Ottawa, Les presses de l'Université d'Ottawa.

Carrière, Richard. 1995. "La loi 8 et les services sociaux destinés aux familles francophones." Dans Christiane Bernier, Sylvie Larocque et Maurice Aumond (éds.) *Familles francophones: multiples réalités. Actes du colloque*. Sudbury, Ontario: Institut franco-ontarien, 279–291.

Cashmore, E.E. 1987. *The Logic of Racism*. London: Allen and Unwin.

Centre for International Statistics. 1995. Based on Statistics Canada's Survey of Consumer Finances microdata tapes. Ottawa: Statistics Canada.

Centre on Social Welfare Policy and Law. 1995. *Welfare News*, August.

Chamberlain, A. 1995. "Go Slow on Tax Cut, Harris told: Soaring Deficit Would Hurt Credit Rating, Firm Says." *Toronto Star*, June 16: A1.

Chorney, H. 1992. "Deficits—Fact or Fiction? Ontario's Public Finances and the Challenge of Full Employment." In D. Drache (ed.), *Getting on Track*. Montreal and Kingston: McGill-Queen's University Press, 186–201.

_____. 1989. *The Deficit and Debt Management: An Alternative to Monetarism*. Ottawa: Canadian Centre for Policy Alternatives.

_____ and P. Hansen. 1992. *Toward A Humanist Political Economy*. Montreal: Black Rose Books.

_____, P. Hansen and M. Mendell. 1987. "Les sources de la Nouvelle Droite américaine." In L. Jalbert and L. Beaudry (eds.), *Les métamorphoses de la pensée libérale, sur le néo-libéralisme actuel*. Montreal: Presses de l'université du Québec, 87-118.

Clarke, T. 1996. *The Emergence of Corporate Rule—And What to Do About It*. San Francisco: International Forum on Globalization.

_____. 1995. *Challenging Corporate Rule in Canada*. Ottawa: Council of Canadians.

_____. 1995a. *Dismantling Corporate Rule: Towards a New Form of Politics in an Age of Globalization*. Unpublished. Ottawa: International Forum on Globalization.

Claridge, T. 1996. "Judges accept welfare cuts by Tories." *Globe and Mail* (Metro edition), February 9: A1, A7.

Cloward, R. and F. Piven 1993. *Regulating the Poor: The Functions of Public Welfare*. 2nd edition. New York: Vintage Books.

Coderre, Cécile. 1995. "Femmes et santé, en français s'il- vous-plaît." *Reflets: Revue ontaroise d'intervention sociale et communautaire* 1 (2) automne: 38–71.

Cohen, M.G. 1995. "Debt and Deficit. A Problem or *the* Problem?" Ottawa: NDP Renewal Conference.

Collier, K. 1995. "Social Policy versus Regional Trading Blocs in the Global System: NAFTA, the EEC and 'Asia.'" *Canadian Review of Social Policy* 35: 50–59.

Cook, P. 1994. "That same, old Ottawa shell game." *Globe and Mail*, February 10: A12.

Commission on Systemic Racism in the Ontario Criminal Justice System. 1995. *Report of the Commission on Systemic Racism in the Ontario Criminal Justice System*. Toronto: Queens Printer.

Compton, F. 1995. "Why have people become so desperate." *Toronto Star,* July 29: B3.

Constante, K. 1996. Affidavit, Ontario Court (General Division) Divisional Court. Court File No. 810/95 in the Matter of Judicial Review Procedure Act, R.S.O. 1990, c.J.1 and Ontario Regulation 409/95 and 410/95 and the Canadian Charter of Rights and Freedoms, s.24, Constitution Act, 1982, R.S.C. 1985, Appendix II, No.44, as amended. April 16.

Coyle, J. 1996. "Tories display siege mentality." *Ottawa Citizen* February 25: A8.

Crone, G. 1996. "Ontario has '2 solitudes' with Harris government." *Vancouver Sun*, January 4: A3.

Cross, Phillip. 1993. "The Labour Market: Year-end Review." *Perspectives on Labour and Income*. Spring: 1-2.

Currie, C. and Sheedy, G. 1987. "Organizing Eatons." In R. Argue, C. Gannage and D.W. Livingston (eds.), *Working People and Hard Times*. Toronto: Garamond Press.

Daly, S. 1995. "Haves against have-nots." *Toronto Star*, Letters, July 29: B3.

Davis, L.V. 1994. *Building on Women's Strengths. A Social Work Agenda for the Twenty-First Century*. New York: The Haworth Press.

De' Ath, E. 1983. "Support and Intervention: Help or Hindrance?" *The Family in a Political Context*. Proceedings of a one-day conference in London. Aberdeen: Aberdeen University.

De Gaulejac, V. and I.T. Léonetti. 1994. *La lutte des places*. Paris: Épi.

Delacourt, S. 1995. "Harris, Manning show signs of forging alliance." *Globe and Mail* (metro edition), August 30: A5.

Di Matteo, E. 1996. "Tories intimidate democracy." *Now* March 28–April 3: 18.

Dobbin, M. 1995. "The Manning-Harris Axis." *Reform Watch* 2(3), September 1: 1.

_____. 1995a. "The Making of New Zealand." *Ideas* CBC Radio, October 26.

_____. 1994. "The Remaking of New Zealand." *Ideas* CBC Radio, October 12, 19.

Doherty, A. and O. Hoedeman. 1994. "Misshaping Europe: The European Round Table of Industrialists." *The Ecologist* 24(4), 135–141.

REFERENCES

Dominelli, L. 1988. *Anti-Racist Social Work*. London: Macmillan.

Drache, D. and A. Ranachan. 1995. *Warm Heart, Cold Country*. Ottawa: Caledon Institute of Social Policy.

Dranoff, L. 1996. "Myopic cutters pose grave threat to Family Support." *Toronto Star,* March 1: A21.

Drohan, M. 1996. "Economic Forum a Clamour for Cash." *Globe and Mail*, February 5: A10.

Eber, N. 1996, "Bill 7 quickly becomes law," *McCarthy Tetrauly Legal Update*, 6, 1–6, http:\\www.Mccarthy.ca\mt-7up.html.

Eko Research Associates. 1993. *Privacy Revealed: The Canadian Privacy Survey.* Ottawa: Eko Research Associates.

Élie, B. 1982. "La gestion de la crise et les fondements monétaristes." In G. Dostaler (ed.), *La crise économique et sa gestion*. Montreal: Boréal Express, 165-182.

Esping-Andersen, G. 1989. "The Three Political Economies of the Welfare State" *Canadian Review of Sociology and Anthropology* 26(1) February: 10–36.

Essed, P. 1991. *Understanding Everyday Racism: An Interdisciplinary Theory*. London: Sage.

Estable, A. and M. Meyer. 1992. *A Discussion Paper on Settlement Needs of Immigrant Women in Ontario*. Ottawa: Immigrant Settlement and Adaptation Program.

Eves, The Honourable Ernie, Q.C. 1996. *1996 Ontario Budget: Budget Speech*. Toronto: Queen's Printer. May 7.

_____. 1995. "Fiscal and Economic Statement." Toronto: Queen's Printer.

"Executive Compensation." 1995. *Globe and Mail*, April 10: B5.

Feldberg, R. 1986. "Comparable Worth: Towards Theory and Practice in the United States." In B. Gelpi, N. Hartsock, C. Novak and M. Strober (eds.)*Women and Poverty*. Chicago: University of Chicago Press.

Fennell, T. 1995."Deadly confrontation on an Ontario reserve." *Maclean's*, September. 18: 22.

Ferrand-Bachmann, D. 1992. *Bénévolat et solidarité*. Paris: Syros-Alternatives.

Finn, E. 1996. "Why Don't Our Unions Flex Their Pension Muscles?" *CCPA Monitor* 2(8), February: 4.

_____. 1995. "Comes the Revolution? Waiting for the Pendulum to Swing Back." *Canadian Forum*, July, August: 7–8.

_____. 1995a. "Machiavelli's advice to the princes of industry." *CCPA Monitor* June: 12.

Flood, A. 1994. "Call the debt by its real name: a national emergency." *Globe and Mail,* September 22: A21.

"Fortune 500 Club Enjoys 13% Profit Gain." 1996. *Globe and Mail*, April 9: B14.

Fraser, N. and L. Gordon. 1994. "A Geneology of Dependency: Tracing a Key Word of the U.S. Welfare State." *Sings* Winter: 309.

_____. 1992. "Contract Versus Charity: Why is There No Social Citizenship in the United States?" *Socialist Review*, 22: 3, 45-67.

Frideres, J.S. 1993. *Native Peoples in Canada: Contemporary Conflicts*. Scarborough: Prentice Hall.

Frum, D. 1995. "What's Right: Harris Cuts Designed to Bolster Economy, Halt Bad Programs." *Financial Post,* 89(46) November 18–20: 22.

Furguson, J. 1995. "Who Has Bay Street's Backing for Premier? Ralph Klein's Clone: Tory Mike Harris Promises the Big Spending Cuts Business Wants." *Toronto Star*, March 27: D1, D2.

Gabriel, C. 1996. "One or the Other? 'Race' Gender and the Limits of Official Multiculturalism." In J. Brodie (ed.), *Women and Canadian Public Policy*. Toronto: Harcourt, Brace.

Gamble, A. 1983. "Thatcherism and Conservative Politics." In S. Hall and M. Jacques (eds.), *The Politics of Thatcherism*. London: Lawrence and Wishart in association with *Marxism Today*.

Gee, E. 1993. "Adult Outcomes Associated with Childhood Family Structure: An Appraisal of Research and an Examination of Canadian Data." In J. Hudson and B. Galaway (eds.), *Single Parent Families: Perspectives on Research and Policy*. Toronto: Thompson Educational Publishing, 291-308.

Gilder, G. 1981. *Wealth and Poverty*. New York: Basic Books.

Gimpel, D. 1995. "Welfare: It all boils down to responsibility for one's own." *Toronto Star,* July 29: B3.

Gindin, S. 1995. "The London Protest." *Contact* December: 1–2.

Gingrich, N. 1995. *To Renew America*. New York: Harper Collins.

Godbout, J.T. 1992. *L'esprit du don*. Paris: Éditions la découverte.

Gombu, P. "Welfare diet depressed testers, left some of them lacking energy." *Toronto Star,* November 11: 9.

Gordon, L. 1990. "The New Feminist Scholarship on the Welfare State." In L. Gordon (ed.), *Women, the State and Welfare*. Wisconsin: University of Wisconsin Press.

Gough, I. 1983. "Thatcherism and the Welfare State." In S. Hall and M. Jacques (eds.), *The Politics of Thatcherism*. London: Lawrence and Wishart in association with *Marxism Today*.

Government of Canada. 1996. *Budget in Brief*. Minister of Finance. March 6. Ottawa: Supply and Services Canada.

Government of Canada, House of Commons. 1995. *Bill C-76*. An act to implement certain provisions of the budget tabled in Parliament on February 27–June 6. Ottawa: Supply and Services Canada.

Government of Canada, Minister of Finance. 1994. *Agenda: Jobs and Growth, Improving Social Security in Canada*. October. Ottawa: Supply and Services Canada.

Government of Ontario. 1995. *Fiscal and Economic Statement*, November. Toronto: Queen's Printer.

Grange, M. 1995. "Anti-Harris forces come together." *Globe and Mail* (Metro edition), December 9: A10.

Grenier, Gilles. 1996. "Analyse de la performance économique de la population franco-ontarienne." Au colloque *l'Ontario français, valeur ajoutée?* Université d'Ottawa, 26 avril.

Groupe C'est le temps. 1981. "C'est l'temps." *Revue du Nouvel Ontario* 3: 110–114.

Guest, D. 1993. *Histoire de la sécurité sociale au Canada*. Trans. by Hervé Juste with Patricia Juste. Montréal: Éditions du Boréal.

Haliechuk, R. 1995. "Bond Raters Shrug at Harris' Alarm." *Toronto Star,* August 23: E1.

Hall, S. 1983. "The Great Moving Right Show?" In S. Hall and M. Jacques (eds.), *The Politics of Thatcherism*. London: Lawrence and Wishart in association with *Marxism Today*.

Hall, T. 1996. "Who killed Dudley George." *Canadian Dimension*, December, January: 8–12.

Hanlon, M. 1995. "The Man Who Led Ontario's Tories out of the Wilderness." *Toronto Star,* June 9: B1, B8.

REFERENCES

Harris, The Right Honourable Michael D. 1995. Statement. July 21.

_____. 1995a. Address to the Association of Municipalities of Ontario." Toronto: August 22.

Harrison, T. and G. Laxer. 1995. *The Trojan Horse. Alberta and the Future of Canada.* Montreal: Black Rose Books.

Harriswatch. 1995/96. Ottawa, Ontario.

Henry, F., W. Mattis, T. Rees and C. Tator. 1995. *The Colour of Democracy: Racism in Canadian Society.* Toronto: Harcourt, Brace.

Hirschman, A.O. 1991. *The Rhetoric of Reaction. Perversity, Futility, Jeopardy.* Cambridge, Mass.: The President and Fellows of Harvard College.

Hobsbawm, E. 1995. *Age of Extremes. The Short Twentieth Century, 1914–1991.* New York: Pantheon.

Horton, M. and H. Kohl. 1990. *The Long Haul: An Autobiography.* New York: Doubleday.

Hotson, J.H. 1993. "Dette fédérale et culpabilité nationale." In P. Paquette, P. and M. Seccarecchia (eds.), *Les pièges de l'austérité.* Montreal: Presses de l'Université de Montréal.

Human Resources Development Canada, Cost-Shared Programs. 1995. *Social Security Statistics.* Hull, P.Q.: Supply and Services Canada.

Ingram, R. 1988. "Empower." *Social Policy* 19(2): 11–16.

Ip, G. 1996. "Jobs cut despite hefty profits." *Globe and Mail,* February 6: A1.

_____. 1996. "Shareholders vs. job holders." *Globe and Mail,* March 23: B1.

Jackman, M. 1994. "Constitutional Contact with the Disparities in the World: Poverty as a Prohibited Ground of Discrimination Under the Canadian Charter and Human Rights Law." *Review of Constitutional Studies.* 11 (1): 77.

_____. 1988. "The Protection of Welfare Rights Under the Charter." *Ottawa Law Review,* 20: 257.

Jackson, A. 1990. *Against John Crow: A Critique of Current Monetary Policy and Proposals for an Alternative.* Ottawa: Canadian Centre for Policy Alternatives.

_____.1990a. *Deficit, Debt and the Contradictions of Tory Economics.* Ottawa: Canadian Centre for Policy Alternatives.

Jaenen, Cornelius J. (éd). 1993. *Les Franco-Ontariens.* Ottawa: Les Presses de l'Université d'Ottawa.

Jefferson, T. 1988. "Race, Crime and Policing: Empirical, Theoretical and Methodological Issues." *International Journal of the Sociology of Law* 16 (4) November 521–39.

Jessop, B. 1993. "Toward a Schumpeterian Workfare State? Preliminary Remarks on a Post-Fordist Political Economy." *Studies in Political Economy* 40 (Spring): 7-39

_____, K. Bonnett and S. Bromley. 1990. "Farewell to Thatcherism? Neo-Liberalism and 'New Times.'" *New Left Review* 179, January/February: 81-102.

Johnson, A., S. McBride and P. Smith. 1994. *Continuities and Discontinuities: The Political Economy of Social Welfare and Labour Market Policy in Canada.* Toronto: University of Toronto Press.

Juteau, Danielle and Lise Séguin-Kimpton. 1993. "La collectivité franco-ontarienne: structuration d'un espace symbolique et politique." Dans Cornelius J. Jaenan, (éd.), *Les Franco-Ontariens,* . Ottawa: Les Presses de l'Université d'Ottawa, 265–304.

Juteau-Lee, Danielle. 1983. "Ontarois et Québécois : Relations hors- frontières?" Dans Dean R. Louder et Eric Waddel, (éds.), *Du continent perdu à l'archipel retrouvé : Le Québec et l'Amérique française.* Laval, Québec: Les Presses de l'Université, 42–53.

Juteau-Lee, Danielle and Barbara Roberts. 1981. "Ethnicity and Femininity: (d')après nos expériences." *Études ethniques du Canada* 8 (1): 1–23.

Kelsey, J. 1996. "New Zealand 'Experiment' A Colossal Failure." *CCPA Monitor* 2(9), March: 1, 6.

Kérisit, M. and N. St-Amand. 1995. "Taking Risks with Families at Risk: Some Alternative Approaches with Poor Families in Canada." In J. Hudson, and B. Galaway, *Child Welfare in Canada. Research and Policy Implications.* Toronto: Thompson Educational Publishing.

Kitchen, B. 1992. "Framing the Issues: The Political Economy of Poor Mothers." *Canadian Woman Studies* 12 (4), Summer: 10–15.

———. 1984. "Women's Dependence." *Atkinson Review of Canadian Studies*, 1 (2), Spring: 13.

Korten, D. 1995. *When Corporations Rule the World.* San Francisco: Kumarian Press Inc. and Berrett-Koehler Publishers Inc.

Kristol, I. 1995. *Neoconservatism. The Autobiography of an Idea.* New York: The Free Press.

Kuyek, J. 1990. *Fighting for Hope: Organizing to Realize our Dreams.* Montreal: Black Rose Books.

———. 1996. *Sustaining Our Work in Challenging Times.* Unpublished. March 26, 1996.

Lamoureux, J. 1994. *Le partenariat à l'épreuve.* Montréal: Éditions Saint-Martin.

Langille, D. 1987. "The BCNI and the Canadian State." *Studies in Political Economy* 24, 41–85.

Law Union of Ontario. 1996. *Offence/Defence: Law for Activists.* Toronto: Ontario Coalition for Social Justice.

Laxer, James. 1996. "Only bond holders win the 'debt game.'" *CCPA Monitor* 2 (10) April: 8.

———. 1995. "Countering the New Right Agenda: Lessons from Ralph Klein's Alberta." *Taking on the Right: The New Context of Politics.* Ottawa: Council of Canadians 106th Anniversary Annual General Meeting, September 29–October 1.

Le Devoir. 1996. "L'ancien gouverneur de la banque centrale serait responsable de la crise." 11 juin: B2.

Lesemann, F. 1988. *La politique sociale américaine: les années Reagan.* Montréal: Les Éditions Saint-Martin.

Liffman, M. 1978. *Power for the Poor. The Family Centre Project: an experiment in self-help.* Australia: George Allen and Unwin.

Livingstone, K. 1983. "Monetarism in London." *New Left Review* 137, January/February: 69.

Macfarlane, D. 1996. "The King of Common Sense." *Toronto Life*, June: 55–60

Macfarlane, E. 1995. "No Lock on the Door: Privacy and Social Assistance Administration." *Review of Current Law and Law Reform* 1:1.

Mackenzie, H. 1996. "Gains wiped out by lost jobs, user fees." *Toronto Star,* May 1: A23. Opinion.

MacLeod, L. and M. Shin. 1994. "Like a Wingless Bird: The Experience of Immigrant and Visible Minority Women." Ottawa: Minister of Supply and Services Canada.

Major, J. 1996. "Tee Time." Photo. *Ottawa Citizen,* July 19: A4.

Marsden, G. and J. W. Warnock. 1995. "The Americanization of Canadian Politics." *Briarpatch* 24(7): September 11–13.

Marshall, T.H. 1949. "Citizenship and Social Class." Reprinted in D. Held et. al., *States and Societies*. 1983. London: Open University.

Martin, P. and P. Savidan. 1994. *La culture de la dette*. Montreal: Boréal.

Martin, The Honourable Paul. 1995. *Budget Speech*. Ottawa: Department of Finance, February 27.

Massé, J. 1995. "Feu sur la protection sociale!" *Le Monde diplomatique* 42 (491), February: 20.

McCracken, M.C. 1993. *The Consequences of Deficit Shifting for Ontario*. A paper prepared for the Ontario Ministry of Intergovernmental Affairs. Ottawa: Infometrica Limited, November.

McDowell, R.M. 1995. "Time to make welfare less attractive option." *Toronto Star*, July 29: B3.

McKnight, J. 1995. *The Careless Society. Community and Its Counterfeits*. New York: Basic Books.

McQuaig, L. 1996. *Shooting the Hippo*. Toronto: Penguin Books.

Melucci, A. 1989. *Nomads of the Present. Social Movements and Individual Needs in Contemporary Society*. London: Brookmount House.

Menzies, Heather. 1996. *Whose Brave New World?* Ontario: Between the Lines.

Merrett, C. D. 1996. *Free Trade: Neither Free nor about Trade*. Montreal: Black Rose Books.

Michaud, C. 1996. *An Evaluation of the Ottawa–Carleton Opportunity Planning Pilot Project*. Ottawa: Regional Municipality of Ottawa–Carleton.

"Mike Harris: Winner Gathers Wisdom at Backyard Fence." 1995. *Globe and Mail*, June 10: A6.

Minc, A. 1987. *La machine égalitaire*. Paris: Grasset.

Mittlestaedt, M. 1996. "Ontario to Overhaul Labour Legislation." *Globe and Mail*, April 16: B1.

_____. 1995. "Tories Get a Boost from Bay Street: 'Neck and Neck' with Liberals as More than 100 Executives Endorse Harris Platform." *Globe and Mail* May 27: A5.

_____. 1995a. "Leach unable to explain Ontario Omnibus bill to MPPs." *Globe and Mail* December 1: A6.

_____. 1995b. "Harris confirms workfare to rely on community clubs," *Globe and Mail* (Metro edition), November 18: A10.

Moody, K. 1996. *Labor Notes*, January: 13-14.

Mosher, J. and I. Morrison. 1995. "Access to Justice for Disadvantaged Groups." Forthcoming: Ontario Law Reform Commission.

Myles, J. 1988. "Decline or Impasse? The Current State of the Welfare State." *Studies in Political Economy* 26, Summer: 73-107.

Narrulla, A. and S. Bournette. 1995. "Business Wants Tories to Move Fast on Agenda." *Globe and Mail*, June 10: B1, B5.

National Council of Welfare. 1996. *Poverty Profile 1994*. Ottawa: Supply and Services Canada.

Neu, D. 1996. "Dissent and Discipline in Alberta." *Canadian Dimension* April: 35-37.

Ninacs, W. 1995. "Entraide économique, création d'entreprises, politiques sociales." *Nouvelles pratiques sociales* 8(1): 97-119.

Nisbet, R. 1986. *Conservatism: Dream and Reality*. Minneapolis: University of Minnesota Press.

Nozick, M. 1992. *No Place Like Home. Building Sustainable Communities*. Ottawa:

Canadian Council on Social Development.

Offe, C. 1984. *Contradictions of the Welfare State.* Cambridge, Mass.: MIT Press.

Ontario Federation of Labour. 1996. *Alternative Ontario Budget.* Toronto: Ontario Federation of Labour.

Ontario Federation of Labour. 1996a. *The Common Sense Revolution: 11 Months of Destruction.* Fact sheet, May 2. Toronto: Ontario Federation of Labour.

Ontario. Legislative Assembly. 1996. *Official Report of Debates (Hansard).* Standing Committee on Government Agencies, February 7: A-135 ff.

Ontario. Legislative Assembly. 1995. *Official Report of Debates (Hansard),* 36th Parliament, First Session, Vol. 1: 258.

Ontario. Legislative Assembly. 1994. *Official Report of Debates (Hansard).* Standing Committee on Government Agencies, January 19. M-204.

Ontario. Minister of Community and Social Services. 1996. *Statement to the Legislature,* June 13. Toronto: Queen's Printer.

Ontario. Ministry of Community and Social Services. 1996a. News Release, *People Will Work for Their Welfare Cheques Starting This September.* June 12. Toronto: Queen's Printer.

Ontario. Ministry of Community and Social Services. 1996b. *Ontario Works Backgrounder.* June 12. Toronto: Queen's Printer.

Ontario. Ministry of Community and Social Services. 1996c. *Ministry Announces Supports to Get Welfare Recipients Back to Work.* June 18. Toronto: Queen's Printer.

Ontario. Ministry of Community and Social Services. 1995. *Eligibility and Entitlement Initiatives.* October. Toronto: Queen's Printer.

Ontario. Ministry of Community and Social Services. 1994. *Enhanced Verification and Case File Investigation for General Welfare Assistance.* Toronto: Queen's Printer.

Ontario. Ministry of Community and Social Services. 1994a. *News Release, 94-66.* June 21. Toronto: Queen's Printer.

Ontario. Ministry of Community and Social Services. 1993. *Turning Point.* Toronto: Queen's Printer.

Ontario. Minister of Finance. 1996. *Budget Speech* (Text version). May 7. Toronto: Queen's Printer.

Ontario. Minister of Finance. 1995. *Ontario Fiscal Overview and Spending Cuts.* July 21. Toronto: Queen's Printer.

Ontario. Ministry of Finance. 1995a. *Fiscal and Economic Statement,* Toronto: Queen's Printer, November.

Ontario. Ministry of Finance. 1995b. *Fiscal and Economic Statement.* November 29. Toronto: Queen's Printer.

Ontario New Democratic Party Caucus (news release). 1996. "Tory hit list from Year One." June 4.

Ontario Progressive Conservative Party, Corporate Campaign List. 1995. Toronto: Ontario Elections Commissioner. November 16.

Ontario Progressive Conservative Party. 1995. *The Common Sense Revolution.* Toronto.

Ontario Social Safety NetWork. 1995. *Welfare Rate Cuts: The Real Issues, Backgrounder #2: Welfare Rates.*

Ontario Social Safety NetWork. 1995a. *Social Assistance Cuts.* Net Backgrounder #1: 3.

"Ontario Tories' Welfare Menu Substandard: Poverty Groups." 1995. *Montreal Gazette,* October 21: A11.

Orloff, A.S. 1993. "Gender and the Social Rights of Citizenship: The Comparative

Analysis of Gender Relations and Welfare States." *American Sociological Review* 58: 303.

Palmer, B. 1996. "Showdown in Ontario: Build the General Strike!" *Canadian Dimension* 30(3): 21-25.

Pascal, C. 1996. "Time to act for the sake of our children's children." *Toronto Star*, April 25: A4.

Pateman, C. 1987. "Feminist Critiques of the Public/Private Dichotomy." In A. Phillips (ed.), *Feminism and Equality*. London: Basil Blackwell.

Pelletier, Jacqueline. 1987. *Discours d'ouverture*. Sudbury, Ontario: Rencontre des féministes franco- ontariennes.

_____. 1980. "Les Franco-Ontariennes." *Les cahiers de la femme*. 2(2): 60--63.

Pelletier, Jean-Yves. 1987. *Le conflit minier*. Toronto: TVOntario.

Perry, S. and M. Lewis. 1994. *Reinventing the Local Economy*. Vernon: Center for Community Enterprise.

Philp, M. 1996. "Social-services restructuring set out." *Globe and Mail*, February 28: A5.

Pierson, C. 1991. *Beyond the Welfare State? The New Political Economy of Welfare*. University Park, Penn.: Pennsylvania University Press.

Pilon, France. 1994. "360 logements pour les francphones." *Le Droit*, 26 août: 13.

Plant, J. and C. Plant. 1992. *Putting Power in Its Place. Create Community Control!* Babriola Island, B.C.: New Society Publishers.

Pollack, A. 1996. "Japanese Business Is Breaking Out of Its Old Orbit." *Globe and Mail*, April 6: D4.

Proulx, Pauline. 1981. *Femmes et francophonie: double infériorité*. Ottawa: Fédération des femmes canadiennes-françaises.

Quarter, J. 1995. *Canada's Social Economy*. Toronto: James Lorimer.

Racine, Jean-Luc. 1995. "Des coûts considérables et une injustice flagrante aux francophones." *Le Droit,* 1 août: 3.

Robichaud, J.-B., L. Guay, C. Colin and M. Pothier. 1994. *Les liens entre la pauvreté et la santé mentale*. Montréal: Gaëtan Morin éditeur.

Rosanvallon, P. 1995. *La nouvelle question sociale: repenser l'État-Providence*. Paris: Seuil.

Ross, P., E. R. Shillington and C. Lockhead. 1994. *The Canadian Fact Book on Poverty*. Ottawa: The Canadian Council on Social Development.

Rubin, S. 1996. "Banks Punished for Profit: Lobbyist." *Globe and Mail*, April 10: B8.

Rusk, J. 1996. "Labour Targets More Ontario Cities." *Globe and Mail*, April 19: A4A.

Safire, W. 1995. "Welfare As A Euphemism." *Globe and Mail*, July 12: A9.

Saul, J.R. 1995. *The Unconscious Civilization*. Concord, Ontario: Anansi.

Saunders, L. 1988. "Une analyse des postulats philosophiques du conservatisme libéral." *Les cahiers de la recherche sur le travail social*. Université de CAEN. No. 14, 73-88.

Seabrook, J. 1990. *Myth of the Market. Promises and Illusions*. Bideford, Devon: Green Books.

Seldon, A. 1995. "Appendix III." In R. Crockett, *Thinking the Unthinkable. Think Tanks and the Economic Counter-Revolution, 1931-1983*. London: Fontana Press.

Sheppard, R. 1995. "The bill that ate Ontario." *Globe and Mail*, December 18: A21.

_____. 1996. "Democracy and billy clubs." *Globe and Mail*, March 20: A25.

Shragge, E. 1993. *Community Economic Development: In Search of Empowerment*. Montreal: Black Rose Books.

Siddiqui, H. 1993. "Media and Race: Failing to Mix the Message." *Toronto Star*, April 24:

D1.

Skelton, E. 1995. "You could be next." *Toronto Star,* July 29: B3.

Smith, D. E. 1990. *The Conceptual Practices of Power: A Feminist Sociology of Knowledge.* Toronto: University of Toronto Press.

Smith, J. 1995. "Class War Conservatism': Housing Policy, Homelessness and the 'Underclass'." In L. Panitch (ed.), *Socialist Register 1995: Why Not Capitalism.* London: Merlin Press, 188-206.

Social Assistance Review Committee. 1988. *Transitions: Report of the Social Assistance Review Committee.* Prepared for Ontario Ministry of Community and Social Services, Toronto.

Social Planning Council of Metropolitan Toronto. 1996. "Workfare yesterday and today." *Workfare Watch* 1(1), February. Toronto.

Spouse-in-The-House Interveners and Interested Others Meeting. 1996. Minutes, January 18. Toronto: Clinic Resource Office, Ontario Legal Aid Plan.

St-Amand, N., M. Kérisit, L. Martineau, G. Cloutier and B. Malenfant. 1996. *This is Our Place.* Ottawa: University of Ottawa.

St-Amand, N., M. Kérisit and D. Vuong. 1994. *Alternative Resources: An Investment in Human Dignity.* Ottawa: University of Ottawa.

Stafford, J. 1992. "The Impact of the New Immigration Policy on Racism in Canada." In V. Satzewich (ed.), *Deconstructing a Nation: Immigration, Multiculturalism and Racism in '90s Canada.* Fernwood: Halifax.

Stanford, J. 1996. "Budget Highlights." Toronto: Canadian Auto Workers: May 7.

_____. 1995. "Saving the Social Safety Net", CAW *Council Resolution.* CAW National Office, North York, Ontario: September.

_____. 1994. Internal CAW Memorandum calculation based on *The National Finances.* Toronto: Canadian Tax Foundation, Tables 7.18 and 7.21.

Stasiulis, Daiva. 1980. "The Political Structuring of Ethnic Community Action: A Reformulation?" *La revue canadienne des études ethniques* 12(3): 19-43.

Statistics Canada, Housing, Family and Social Statistics Division. 1991. *Lone Families in Canada.* Target Groups Project. Cat. No. 89-522E (Table 1.8). Statistics Canada. 1991.

Steering Committee on Social Assistance (Ontario Legal Clinics). 1994. *Presentation to the Standing Committee on the Legislative Assembly: Re Municipal Freedom of Information and Protection of Privacy Act.* January 20. Toronto: Ontario Legal Clinics.

St. George, D. 1996. "Children of downsizing grow up fast." *Toronto Star,* February 24: B3.

Struthers, J. 1995. *The Limits of Affluence: Welfare in Ontario 1920-1970.* Toronto: University of Toronto Press.

Teeple, G. 1995. *Globalization and the Decline of Social Reform.* Toronto: Garamond Press.

Tester, F. 1992. "Local Power Versus Global Profits: The Odds Against." In J. Plant and C. Plant (eds.), *Putting Power in its Place: Create Community Control!* Gabriola Island, B.C.: New Society Publishers.

Throne Speech. 1995. *Speech from the Throne.* Address of the Honourable Henry N. R. Jackman, Lieutenant Governor of the Province of Ontario, on the opening of The First Session of the Thirty-Sixth Parliament of the Province of Ontario, September 27th.

Tissot, Georges. 1981. "L'auto-détermination." *Revue du Nouvel Ontario*, vol. 3, p. 91-96.

Titmus, R. 1974. *Essays on the Welfare State*. 2nd edition, Fifth impression.

Toronto Coalition Against Racism. 1996. *Factsheet*. Toronto: Coalition Against Racism.

Toronto Injured Workers' Advocacy Group. 1996. *Critical Times*. #2. February. Toronto: Union of Injured Workers and Community Legal Education Ontario.

Toronto Star. 1995. "Harris cuts supported by thousands." July 24: A7.

Toughill, K. 1996. "Police unions balk at aiding replacment civil servants." *Toronto Star*, February 16: 2.

_____. 1996. "Day-care review takes the Tories off the map." *Toronto Star*, Febrary 4: F1.

_____. 1995. "Foes Say Tories Threatened Them." *Toronto Star*, November 2: A1, A16.

Turk, J. 1996. *Unfair Shares*. Toronto: Ontario Federation of Labour, February.

United Nations. 1995. *World Investment Report*. New York and Geneva.

Valpy, M. 1995. "Why the Cheers?" *Globe and Mail*, July 25: A11.

Vallières, P. 1980. *L'Ontario francais par les documents*. Montréal: Etudes vivantes.

Vanier Institute of the Family 1994. *Profiling Canadian Families*. Ottawa: 71.

Vipond, R. 1995. "Mike Harris, Imperial Premier." *Globe and Mail*, December 11: A15. Commentary.

Walker, J. 1995. "The Man Who Sharpens the Harris Hatchet." *Financial Post*, November 28: 8.

Walker, W. 1995. "From X-rays to Abortions, Ontario Opens the Door Wide for American For-profit Medical Clinics." *Toronto Star*, December 2: A3.

_____. 1995. "Where $772 million cuts will hit hardest." *Toronto Star*, October 6: A1.

Walkom, T. 1994. *Rae Days*. Toronto: Key Porter Books.

_____. 1995. "Harris Cabinet Gains New Clout with Secret Bill." *Toronto Star*, December 2: C1.

_____. 1995. "Tories savaging the poor today to reward the rich tomorrow." *Toronto Star*, July 22: A9.

_____. 1996. "The Tory revolution has 'people like us' on a roll." *Toronto Star*, June 8: C1.

Wallach, L. 1994. *Talking Points: The World Trade Organization's Threat*. Washington: Public Citizen.

Wamsley, A. 1996. "Decline of the Company Man." *Report on Business Magazine*, March: 19-20.

Warren, C.E. 1986. *Vignettes of Life. Experiences and Self Perceptions of New Canadian Women*. Calgary: Detselig Enterprises Limited.

Warnock. J.W. 1995. "The Poor Must Wait." *Briarpatch*, May: 33-35.

Welch, David. 1993. "Early Franco-Ontarian Schooling as a Reflection and Creator of Community Identity." *Ontario History* 85(4), December: 321--347.

_____. 1991. "Les luttes pour les écoles secondaires franco-ontariennes." *Revue du Nouvel Ontario*. 13--14: 109--131.

Welsh, M. 1996. "Tories hit on Ipperwash delay." *Toronto Star*, March 22: A8.

"What's in the deal." 1996. *Toronto Star*, March 30: A10.

White, J. 1996. *Report to CAW Education Conference*. Family Education Centre, Port Elgin, Ontario: February 2.

Wiggins, C. 1995. "Dismantling Unemployment Insurance: The March Toward a Lower

Wage Economy," *Canadian Review of Social Policy* (36): 93-94.

Wills, G. 1987. *Reagan's America: Innocents at Home*. New York: Doubleday.

Winsor, H. 1995. "Harris Vows not to Cave in to Unions, Other Groups." *Globe and Mail*, November 28: A3.

Wright, L. 1995. "Door Opens for U.S. Health Firms." *Toronto Star*, December 2: A3. Workfare Today and Tomorrow. 1996. *Workfare Watch* 1(1). Toronto: Social Planning Council of Metropolitan Toronto, February: 4.

Yakabuski, K. 1996. "Entre Gingrich et Rocard: l'économie sociale constitue un point de convergence entre la France et les États-Unis." *Le Devoir*, April 2: A1.

Ziedenberg, J. 1996. "A Great Day in Hamilton: A Personal Notebook." *Canadian Dimension* 30(3): 17-20.

About the Contributors

Paul Leduc Browne
Before joining the Canadian Centre for Policy Alternatives as a researcher in 1994, Paul Leduc Browne worked as a translator and taught at the Universities of Ottawa and Regina, as well as the Collège de l'Outaouais. He holds a D.Phil. degree from the University of Sussex. He is the author of *Love in a Cold World? The Voluntary Sector in an Age of Cuts* (CCPA, 1996). He and Michelle Weinroth were finalists for the 1995 Governor General's Award for their translation into English of Guy Laforest's *Trudeau et la fin d'un rêve canadien*.

John Clarke
John Clarke came to Canada in 1976 after some early activity in trade unions in Britain. He worked at the Westinghouse Plant in London, Ontario until 1982 and was a shop steward in United Electrical Workers, Local 546. After being laid-off, he helped to found the London Union of Unemployed Workers and stayed with them until 1990 when he moved to Toronto to take up the job of provincial organizer of the newly formed Ontario Coalition Against Poverty.

Tony Clarke
Tony Clarke is the director of the Polaris Institute in Canada which is designed to enable citizen movements to develop new tools for democratic social change in an age of economic globalization. In the past, he has served as the national chair of the Action Canada Network (1987–1993), the nationwide coalition of labour, coal and environmental organizations which mobilized in opposition to the free trade deals (FTA and NAFTA). He also worked as social policy director for the Canadian Conference of Catholic Bishops (1975–1994) where he was instrumental in the formation of a variety of interchurch coalitions on economic and social justice issues. His most recent publications include: *The Emergence of Corporate Rule—And What We Can Do About It* (a workbook for social movements soon to be published by the International Forum on Globalization) and *Behind the Mitre: the Moral Leadership Crisis in the Canadian Catholic Church* (Toronto: Harper Collins, 1995).

Bill Dare
Bill Dare is a social worker and researcher living in Ottawa.

Michèle Kérisit
Michèle Kérisit has obtained a doctorate in sociolinguistics from l'Université de Rennes, France. A professor at the University of Ottawa School of Social Work, she is involved and has published in the fields of gerontology, qualitative methodologies and minorities. Some of her areas of interest include women in a

minority context; cultural and social dimensions of intervention and visual representations of violence. Prior to her actual position as professor, she was the coordinator of a national project on Poor Families: Alternatives to Professional Practices, and has co-signed numerous publications written about this project. She is also on the Editorial Board of *Reflets, revue ontaroise d'intervention sociale et communautaire.*

Brigitte Kitchen

Brigitte Kitchen has a doctorate in social administration from the London School of Economics. She teaches at the School of Social Work, Atkinson College, York University. She is also a co-chair of the Child Poverty Action Group, an advocacy group committed to the elimination of child poverty in Canada. She has written extensively on the issues and social policies affecting the living standards of families raising children.

Linda Lalonde

Linda Lalonde is a social policy consultant working on social assistance and poverty issues with clients like the Social Assistance Recipients Council, National Anti-Poverty Oganization (NAPO) and Ottawa-Carleton's social services department. Her most important qualification is years of post-graduate level studies in the School of Life, some as a single parent on social assistance. She chaired the Ontario government's Social Assistance Advisory Committee until it was disbanded by the Tories in July 1995.

Ian Morrison

Ian Morrison is a lawyer specializing in social welfare law and policy. He is executive director of the Clinic Resource Office of the Ontario Legal Aid Plan, co-chair of the Ontario Social Safety NetWork and is on the editorial board of the *Journal of Law and Social Policy*, which publishes an annual review of developments in poverty law in Ontario.

Allan Moscovitch

Allan Moscovitch is a professor of social work and director of the School of Social Work at Carleton University, Ottawa, where his has been a member of faculty for 20 years. He is the author/editor of three books and many articles on social welfare policy. During 1988–89 he was on a secondment with the Regional Municipality of Ottawa-Carleton as director of planning for the social services department. Between May 1990 and June 1992 he was the chair of the Ontario Minister of Community and Social Services' Advisory Group on New Social Assistance. The advisory group completed a review of Ontario's social assistance legislation entitled *Time for Action.*

Diana Ralph

Diana Ralph is an associate professor of social work, specializing in community organizing at Carleton University. She has been active in social justice movements for over 35 years. She now works with a wide range of local, provincial and national social justice groups. She is the author of *Work and Madness: The Rise of Community Psychiatry* (Montreal: Black Rose Books, 1993).

André Régimbald

For the last six years, André Régimbald has taught political science at the University of Ottawa. He has also lectured on social policy at the Université du Québec à Hull. Between 1993 and 1996 he was a research officer with the Social Planning Council of Ottawa-Carleton. He is a member of the Editorial Working Group (Editor, Refereed Articles) of the *Canadian Review of Social Policy* (Carleton University). He has published articles on social policy (e.g. the federal social security review, workfare).

Nérée St-Amand

Nérée St-Amand has a doctorate in sociology from the Université de Nice, France. For the past six years, he has been professor at the School of Social Work, University of Ottawa. He is terminating a four-year national project on Poor Families: Alternatives to Professional Practices. Inspired by the teachings of the Medicine Wheel, he draws upon his experiences as a teacher, a protection worker and a councellor to propose a holistic approach to social intervention. His publications include *Self-Help and Mental Health: Beyond Psychiatry* and many articles deriving from the Poor Families–Alternatives Project.

Jean Trickey

Jean Trickey is actively involved in peace; environmental issues; women of colour concerns; developing leadership among minority youth; anti-racist education; violence against women; cultural interpretation; police minority relations; anti-racist feminism; civil rights/resistance. She works with communities on these issues in such venues as training workshops, conferences, articles and the popular media. She is currently researching models of leadership which reflect the everyday reality of diversity in Canadian society. As a teenager, Jean was part of a collective resistance with eight other teenagers (Little Rock Nine) in the desegregation of Little Rock Central High School, Arkansas, U.S.A. Jean currently lives in Ottawa and is the mother of three daughters and three sons.

James Turk

James L. Turk is a senior trade union staff member who helped coordinate the Hamilton, Waterloo and Peterborough days of action for the Ontario Federation of Labour. He also serves as co-chair of the Ontario Coalition for Social Justice.

Steve Watson

Steven Watson is a national representative in the Canadian Auto Workers education department. He was the education director for the Canadian Brotherhood of Railway Transport and General Workers which merged with the CAW in 1994. Steve coordinates the work of Canadian Auto Workers Social Action groups, among other activities. He was the chairperson for the Transport Route Canada Workers in British Columbia before going on staff with his union in 1986.

Michelle Weinroth

Michelle Weinroth is an independent researcher and translator whose main areas of expertise are nationalism and propaganda. She has a doctorate degree from the Centre for Contemporary Cultural Studies at the University of Birmingham, England. She is the author of *Reclaiming William Morris: Englishness, Sublimity and the Rhetoric of Dissent* (McGill-Queen's University Press, 1996). She and Paul Leduc Browne were finalists for the 1995 Governor General's Award for their translation into English of Guy Laforest's *Trudeau et la fin d'un rêve canadien.*

David Welch

David Welch is a professor at the School of Social Work, University of Ottawa. Author of numerous articles and papers on the social and historical development of the Franco-Ontarian community, professor Welch has been more recently turning his research towards the social economy as a possible means for social and economic development. Besides his research, he is active in various social action and Franco-Ontarian community groups.

Index